THE OTHER SIDE OF DECEPTION

THE OTHER SIDE OF DECEPTION

A Rogue Agent Exposes the Mossad's Secret Agenda

Victor Ostrovsky

HarperCollinsPublishers

HarperCollins books may be purchased for educational, business, or sales promotional use. For information, please write: Special Markets Department, Harper-Collins Publishers, Inc., 10 East 53rd Street, New York, NY 10022.

FIRST EDITION

Designed by George J. McKeon
Insert design by Barbara Dupree Knowles

Library of Congress Cataloging-in-Publication Data

Ostrovsky, Victor.
    The other side of deception : a rogue agent exposes the Mossad's secret agenda /
by Victor Ostrovsky.
        p.   cm.
    ISBN: 0-06-017635-0
    1. Ostrovsky, Victor. 2. Intelligence officers—Israel—Biography. 3. Israel. Mosad
le-modi' in ve-tafkidim meyuhadim—Biography. 4. Espionage, Israeli. I. Title.
UB271.I820846   1994
327.125694'092—dc20
[B]   94-30942

94 95 96 97 98 ❖/HC 10 9 8 7 6 5 4 3 2 1

To Bella with love

ACKNOWLEDGMENTS

There are many friends and ex-colleagues I'd like to thank, but owing to the nature of the intelligence world, they must remain anonymous.

I would, however, like to thank my agent, Tim Hays, whose belief in this project helped bring it to publication against so many protests, and my editor, Rick Horgan, an open-minded, diligent fellow whose sharp eye was a blessing. A final word of thanks goes to Harper-Collins publisher Jack McKeown and his staff, Judy Tashbook, Kathy Saypole, Chris McLaughlin, and Mary O'Shaughnessy.

Victor Ostrovsky

Author's Note

wrote this book to make known the truth about my journey. I have
no doubt that there are those who would prefer that their account
of the events be the record and who will do all in their power to
make it so.

Because of the complexity of the subject matter, I decided that a
book was the most appropriate medium through which to convey the
facts. I also decided to present the material in more or less chronologi-
cal order.

Although it's not usual for members of the intelligence services
to keep written notes or records, I had kept some in order to carry
out operational assignments I'd been given. Although they weren't
originally intended as such, these notes did provide a useful additional resource in writing the book. Aside from these notes, I've
relied largely on my memory to reconstruct the events described
here and have made every effort to ensure that inaccuracies are minimal. Given that my capacity for recall was one of the main reasons
I was originally sought by the Mossad, I feel confident in saying
that the book is accurate in all but the most minor of details. All
names in the book are real, with the exception of Dina, Rachel,
Albert, David, Sarah, Rami, Edward, and Fadllal, which are aliases.
Other names, such as those of active field operatives, are given by
first name only to prevent those individuals from being exposed.
Additionally, I've arranged for the Mossad to receive a copy of the
book just prior to publication to allow them to take whatever pre-
cautions they deem necessary. The intention of this book is not personal vendetta.

Most major events in this book have been covered extensively by the media, and articles on them are in the public record. I've provided a partial list of such articles at the end of the book to enable those interested to pursue further research on particular subjects.

That being said, this book is a factual account of events as they happened to me.

Victor Ostrovsky

PROLOGUE

My paternal grandparents immigrated to Canada from Russia at the turn of the century. They settled with other immigrants in the small Saskatchewan town of Wakaw, where my grandfather, Aaron Ostrovsky, built up a successful retail business, only to lose it during the Great Depression. Subsequently, he moved the family to Edmonton, Alberta.

At about the same time that the Ostrovskys arrived in Canada, the Margolin family—Esther, Hayyim, and their baby, Rafa—escaped the Russian pogroms and made their way to Palestine. They settled in Jerusalem and had two more children, Mira and Maza.

Sid Ostrovsky, the fifth of Aaron's seven children, served a full tour of duty as an airman in a Canadian bomber squadron over Europe during World War II. After the war, he joined the fledgling military of the newly formed state of Israel.

There he met Mira Margolin, who'd recently completed her tour of duty in the British army, fighting the Germans in North Africa.

The newlywed couple made their home in Edmonton, where, on November 28, 1949, I was born. My mother, who wasn't a typical housewife in any regard, found a job as a teacher in the Jewish school in Edmonton and left the chore of raising her child to my paternal grandmother, Bessie Ostrovsky.

I was fortunate in the grandparents fate had selected for me. My mother was what might be called a free spirit, a bohemian type. A graduate of the Israeli Haganah underground and the British military, she'd dreamed of becoming an actress. Theatrical parts were few and far between, though, which left her an extremely frustrated person. My father, on the other hand, knew that he would one day reach his goal: the American dream of financial security and a quiet life. But the road was long and hard. The unbridgeable difference in character between my parents finally led them to separate. I was five at the time.

My mother took me back to Israel, where her parents, Hayyim and Esther Margolin, took on the job of looking after me. I remember fondly the small house on Ha-yod-daleth Street as a warm, loving home, full of books and long talks about the fulfillment of the Zionist dream and how it could be translated into everyday life.

Since I'd shown an inclination for the arts, my grandparents introduced me to a painter by the name of Gilady, who was living in our neighborhood. He gave me a box of oil paints and some of his time, instructing me in the basics of perspective and the use of color. Gilady's lessons were ones I'd apply ever after—even as my childhood hobby ripened into a midlife passion.

My early years were quiet. My mother would reappear from time to time like a swirling tornado, disappearing back into the blue sky just as fast. On one of her touchdowns, she decided that I would be better off in boarding school. All my grandmother's pleading was to no avail, and I wound up spending a year in a dreadful place called Hadasim, a boarding school in the center of Israel funded and supervised by Hadassah Wizo, a Jewish women's organization in Canada. I liked to think that, had the organization been fully aware of the school's strict, spartan quality and its penchant for putting the kids to work, they would have closed it.

They weren't aware, though—as far as I knew—and by year's end, I'd taken the initiative and returned to my grandparents' home. Shortly after, my self-confidence was lifted when I joined the Gadna youth brigades and attained second place in a countrywide shooting competition as a member of the Abu Kabir target shooting club headed by an old army major named Dan David.

During my high school years, I met Bella, and it was love at first sight. We spent every moment we could together; we enjoyed reading the same books, hiking, and talking about politics, and especially being with each other. At about the age of eighteen, we were recruited to the Israeli military. Bella was assigned to the ministry of defense, and I was sent to the military police.

After basic training, I completed a noncommissioned officers' course, and then went on to an officers' course, graduating as the youngest officer at the time in the Israeli Defense Force. I then graduated from the military police officers' course and the special military law course, and followed that up with demolition and sniper training.

Once I'd completed my military education, Bella and I got married. We were not yet twenty. We were told we were too young, but I never regarded our union as burdensome; it was something we were building together. A year later, Sharon was born, and things were looking up.

After I completed my three-year term, I left the military, having attained the rank of lieutenant. We went to visit my family in Edmonton and wound up staying there for five years. Our second daughter, Leeorah, was born in Edmonton when Sharon was four.

We returned to Israel in 1977. The day after our arrival, I enlisted in the navy and was given the rank of captain. I served for the next five years, rising to the rank of lieutenant commander. For most of that period, I was in command of the department coordinating and testing new weapons systems before they were incorporated into the navy's arsenal. During that time, I was also sent to and graduated from staff and command college, where I was a guest lecturer for the duration of my service.

Bella and I had a great time in those days. We had a wide circle of friends with whom we enjoyed weekend trips, family outings, and parties. Then I got my first call from the guys in the security services. I guessed it was Mossad or something similar, and I went through a long and strenuous series of tests before more information about the job was forthcoming. Ultimately, I learned that I was being considered for a "combatant" position, which would mean that I'd be separated from Bella and the kids for long periods of time. I declined, and after numerous attempts to persuade me, some of which bordered on harassment, they finally accepted my refusal.

In 1982, I left the navy and started a video magazine that was the first of its kind in Israel. Like many firsts, it was a flop (the country's being embroiled right then in what was later known as the Lebanese quagmire didn't help). After that, I started a small stained-glass business (it also folded fairly quickly, owing to a lack of demand). I was also taking classes in computer programming, since I believed that was the wave of the future.

At that point, the Mossad came calling again. This time they made it clear that long separations from my family were not what they had in mind. I entered a second round of testing that was to last nearly a year.

While I was still working in my stained-glass shop in Herzelia, I was approached by two men I'd gotten to know in my dealings with the video magazine. They were the manufacturers of the plastic casings in which videocassettes were sold, and I'd done some graphic work for them. As it turned out, one of them, Itsik Zarug, was well connected in the Israeli underworld. He approached me on behalf of some of his friends, asking me to take part in a scam to forge large numbers of credit cards—Visa, MasterCard, and the like. He handed me several stolen cards, telling me they wanted similar ones made.

I called a friend of mine, an attorney in Tel Aviv who was a former soldier of mine in the military police. I asked him to make contact with the police for me. I didn't want to put a stop to this affair without proper legal protection. My lawyer set up a meeting for me with a police officer named Eitan Golan, the head of the fraud department in Tel Aviv. I gave him all the information. He asked me if I'd be willing to work for the police undercover on a volunteer basis, and I agreed as long as my name was kept out of it.

Several months later, the entire ring was captured and sent to jail. The papers reported that the police had obtained the help of a graphic designer, but my name was not mentioned. The Mossad security department managed to squelch any police efforts to get me to testify. I was now under the aegis of the Mossad, a member of the elite team, a protector of the state. My life would never be the same again.

CHAPTER 1

THURSDAY, JULY 17, 1986

The tiny cell was hot and musty. In a dim corner by the barred window, an old dingy-looking fan rattled, barely moving the foul-smelling air. I was trapped.

Three days earlier, I had arrived in Cairo on an Aer Lingus flight from New York. I was whisked away from the airport terminal by two burly men in short-sleeve gray safari suits. One of my seemingly friendly gorilla escorts spoke English. He explained that he and his friend were taking me to a safe place. They held my arms firmly and ushered me to a small white car parked at the curb outside the main doors.

"Welcome to Egypt," said the English speaker, who shared the back seat with me as the car took off. That was all he said until we cleared the airport complex. Then he handed me a blindfold and asked me to put it on.

Those who spend any time in the espionage world come to expect these things. For the next thirty minutes, I sat in the dark. I assumed we were on our way to meet the Egyptian intelligence and security brass, since the sole purpose of my visit was to sell out my former employer, the Mossad, Israel's famous intelligence agency.

It wasn't every day that a Mossad case officer appeared on Egyptian intelligence's doorstep, ready to deal. I'd expected the proverbial red carpet treatment, but this was not it. Since my hearing was unimpaired by the blindfold, I could hear the hustle-bustle of a large Middle Eastern city loud and clear. The noisy blend of honking cars and merchants announcing their wares sounded familiar to me. Soon the sounds commingled with the smell of charcoal stoves and camel dung, and I was reminded of Jaffa or East Jerusalem.

After a while, the sounds faded, and there was only the sensation of the scorching air rushing by the open window. At one point, I thought I heard the revving sounds of a diesel engine and the squeaking of tank tracks. I'd spent enough time in the military to know we'd entered a military base.

When my blindfold was finally removed, I saw we were parked in the inner yard of an old British-style compound. The large square yard was surrounded by a dilapidated five-story building.

I was taken up a dark staircase to the third floor. Two uniformed guards armed with submachine guns greeted us and led the way through a long dim corridor to a green metal door. I expected to be taken to an office of some sort. Instead, I found myself in a ten-by-twelve cell. The heavy metal door slammed behind me. Then came the hollow sound of the key turning in the lock and the footsteps of my escorts as they walked away.

I assumed at first that this was a temporary holding room. But my confidence shrank as I looked around. There was a stench in the air of old urine and human excrement. The window, which gave a view of the inner yard, was secured with heavy metal bars. And the big iron bed that filled most of the cell hinted at a lengthy stay. Panic started to set in. At that instant, I realized I was a captive, and no one on the outside knew where I was.

I walked through an uneven opening knocked through the thick wall into what seemed like a crypt. I found a shower stall closed off by a stained plastic curtain. Facing the shower was a sloping floor with a hole in the center, known in the army as a shit hole, a primitive toilet. I backed away once I realized that the hole, which was the source of the stench, was swarming with cockroaches.

A minute later, I heard the key turning in the lock. That's it, I thought, they are here to get me out and apologize. I decided to accept their apology and brush it off as just one of those things.

An old man wearing a white galabia walked in, carrying a tray with fruit, a large glass pitcher of cold lemonade, and a single glass. He smiled and put the tray on the end table by the bed while a uniformed guard stood at the door watching. The old man entered the tiny, crypt-like shower and hung up the towel he had slung over his hand. I tried to speak to him, but he would only smile and nod his head.

Several hours later, the old man returned with more food and a fresh pitcher of lemonade. By nightfall, I'd begun to accept that I would be there a while, and the implications worried me. There was no logical reason for the way I was being treated—unless the Egyptians knew something they shouldn't have and were now playing some sort of game. What were they up to? Nothing made any sense.

From the window, I could see a uniformed guard seated on a wooden chair by the large gate. Occasionally, he'd open a small side door in the gate and talk to someone.

The big gate opened noisily every morning at nine, permitting a white car, similar to the one that had brought me there, to enter the compound. Each morning, I would get dressed and wait for someone to come and talk to me. But no one ever did. My watch slowly ticked off the hours until, finally, at six P.M., I would look out the window and see the white car leaving. I shouted and banged on the bars with the metal tray, but no one seemed to care.

The heat didn't let up, even after dark. I put the rattling little fan on the end table and directed it toward me. I then lay on my back in my underwear, wetting my face and chest with a damp towel. My head rested on a hard pillow as I tried to sleep.

After the first day, the stench didn't bother me. The swarming cockroaches didn't bother me either, as long as they stayed in the shit hole and away from my food. At night, a multitude of thoughts would run through my head, keeping me awake.

One question kept torturing me. How the hell did I end up in this ten-by-twelve hell somewhere outside Cairo? I couldn't shake the terrifying thought that this was where I'd spend the rest of my life, that my wife and children back in Canada would never know I hadn't run away, that I was trapped.

I couldn't tell where or when this was going to end, but I could almost pinpoint the time, if not the precise moment, it had all started . . .

Six months before, on Monday, February 3, 1986, I'd been at the Sun Hull Hotel in Larnaka, Cyprus. I was there to meet a Belgian terrorist, and in my pocket I had a false British passport under the name of Jason Burton. The Belgian was a member of a left-wing terrorist organization called the Communist Combatant Cells (CCC).

According to my passport, I'd arrived at the Larnaka airport the day before, and I had the Olympic Air ticket and boarding pass to prove it. The Belgian was expecting to receive from me a key to a car parked in Brussels, loaded with untraceable plastic explosives and several thousand top-of-the-line detonators. In exchange, I was to receive proof that over two million dollars had been transferred to a Swiss bank account.

It was a sting operation, and I was a full-fledged Mossad case officer at the time. It was on this assignment that things started to go haywire. I'd actually arrived in Larnaka by boat and not by plane. The first leg of the journey, from the Ashdod harbor in Israel to a point fifty miles south of Cyprus, was made aboard a patrol boat, called a Dabur. I then transferred from the Dabur to a yacht. The yacht had a Greek registry and regularly anchored in the Larnaka harbor. It was a floating safe house for Mossad operatives.

I was only a pawn in this game planned by the Belgian desk in Melucha.[1] Once the ultra left-wing CCC members approached the car in Brussels, their entire ring would be nabbed by the Belgian police and security services. Another group would be arrested simultaneously by the Dutch police. The two police forces were already on the terrorists' trail, thanks to a series of tips the Belgium desk in the Mossad was feeding them.

There was more than one reason behind the sting. The CCC was involved in selling and buying arms from the Palestine Liberation Organization and other Palestinian groups. Putting them out of business would be a major victory for the Mossad in combating terrorism.

Another reason for the operation was more sinister, and I learned about it much later. Itsik Efrat, head of the Israel desk, handled that part. It involved a veteran case officer named Barda, who in 1984 had tracked down and contacted a band of Belgian renegade lawmen who were originally formed by NATO (North Atlantic Treaty Organization) as an anti-Communist body to be activated in case of a Communist invasion. This plan, which was called Operation Gladiator, was never put into action, but NATO neglected to dismantle the special cells it had created, and so the Mossad stepped in to make use of one of them.

The dormant cell was activated with the consent of the Belgian state secret service and the Mossad's antiterrorist advisory section.

Barda made it clear to the Belgians that to create a public outcry for a strengthening of the security services, extreme measures were needed—that is, terrorist atrocities that could be blamed on the Communists. "Hesitation should be left to environmentalists and bleeding-heart democrats," he told them.

In addition to the NATO cell of right-wing lawmen, the Belgian secret service could draw from a deep well of right-wing fanatics—including a fascist party called Westland New Post (WNP), or so it was reported by sources within the Mossad. Under the auspices of the

---

1. Melucha: Code name for the recruitment branch of the Mossad; the branch is divided into geographical departments that have desks assigned to support stations.

Belgian secret service, this new combined right-wing element, which included several active policemen, carried out a series of robberies with extreme violence, eventually earning the nickname "the Murderers of Brabant." In September and November 1985, they hit several supermarkets and carried out the political assassination of a Belgian minister. They also engaged in several truck hijackings that were later attributed to crooks who were "killed in the chase." The attacks were not financially motivated. Their purpose was terror and the destabilization of the Belgian government, which was leaning left. Three members of the group had to leave the country in 1985. They escaped to Israel and were given new identities by the Mossad, as part of the initial agreement made with the Belgian extreme right wing.

The Belgians' request that the Mossad find a way to pass arms to the right-wingers, while keeping the Belgian authorities out of the picture, led to my being in Cyprus in February 1986 to help with the sting.

Barda gave the right-wing terrorists the location of the CCC stashes of arms the Mossad had sold them. He told them they could help themselves to the goods while the Communists were getting stung.

The day before I was to transfer the key to the CCC man, after a ten-minute struggle to transfer from one rocking boat to another on a choppy sea, I had met Ze'ev Alon. He was in charge of special technical operations, and on his way off the island. His presence on the boat was highly unusual. I was in the recruitment department and not part of special operations. He, on the other hand, provided services from his Proudot subdivision, mainly to combatants[2] from the highly secretive Metsada[3] department. They would normally employ combatants in Arab countries on special Kidon[4] operations.

Ze'ev briefed me on a new secondary assignment. I was now going to

---

2. Combatant: An Israeli who is recruited to carry out dangerous operations behind enemy lines. A combatant is trained separately from the rest of the Mossad and doesn't possess any information about the organization, so that if captured he will have no information to disclose.

3. Metsada: Code name for the Mossad section that employs combatants and the hit team called Kidon.

4. Kidon: Loosely translated, the word means "bayonet." It refers to a sub-unit of the secretive Metsada department assigned to carry out assassinations and special operations behind enemy lines. It consists of several squadrons. All assassinations carried out by the Mossad are the work of Kidon squadrons.

be a so-called relay station or backup relay station for an operation that, due to circumstances, had been hastily put together at the last minute.

"Cyprus is not a hospitable place for us," he said. "The fewer people we have there, the better."

Libyan leader Moamer al Qadhafi had called for a three-day summit of what he termed the Allied Leadership of the Revolutionary Forces of the Arab Nation. In other words, it was a meeting of all the terrorist kingpins. The Mossad was watching, drooling over this full house of goodies it couldn't wait to get its hands on.

A combatant had been dispatched to Libya for that occasion, posing as a reporter for the French-language paper *Afrique-Asie*. Once there, he learned that after the conference, several Palestinian terrorist leaders would fly to Syria aboard a private Gulfstream II executive jet. The Mossad convinced Israeli prime minister Shimon Peres to approve the skyjacking of the plane.

Because of the extremely sensitive nature of the operation, the Mossad chief wanted to have positive eyewitness verification that the people in question were on board. The combatant would watch the actual boarding of the plane. Then he would transmit a message via a special mobile burst-communication device. A merchant marine ship making its way to Gibraltar would receive the communiqué and transmit it to Israel. The need for a backup was due to previous communication problems with the same type of device. It depended on good weather, which in this case wasn't expected. As planned, it was really a very simple operation. The combatant, after verifying that the terrorists had boarded the Gulfstream, would activate the signaling device *and* call me at the hotel. If all was well, his message would be "The chickens have flown the coop." I would then use a beeper to send the signal, which would be picked up by a navy patrol boat close to the Cypriot shore, affirming the acceptance of the message.

After briefing me, Ze'ev wished me luck and transferred to the Dabur and back to Israel. I suspected that there was yet another backup besides me.

The meeting with the Belgian and the transfer of the key, my primary mission in Cyprus, went well. Nine days later, on February 12, 1986, the Belgian police nabbed the man and his CCC colleagues. The terrorists had in their possession over two hundred pounds of explosives and thousands of detonators. Simultaneously, Mossad's right-wing criminal partners entered several warehouses in the Antwerp area. The fascists got two truckloads of light weapons and several tons of ammunition.

It was while carrying out the secondary operation that I got into hot water. When I was at the hotel in Larnaka, I had made an approach to—or, as we called it in the field, "established contact with"—a Palestinian businessman from Amman, Jordan, who was one of the few tourists in the hotel. Such unauthorized contact was proscribed, but it was known that case officers did it all the time. Take the risk, we told ourselves. If it works, you're a hero; if not, you don't tell anyone.

It turned out that the businessman had just come from Libya and had contacts in the PLO. I learned from him that a trick would be played on us in Tripoli, Libya. He said something like, "The Israelis are going to eat shit tomorrow." I knew the Mossad had considered the possibility of a trick, but no one gave the Palestinians that much credit.

Convinced that my information was reliable, I tried to contact everybody I knew in the system to stop the operation. I struggled with the endless buffers Mossad puts on a command and control center during an operation. It was somewhat ironic that the buffers put in place to enhance security were now blocking a warning. The command center was in Mahaneh David military air base. I couldn't help thinking that someone *wanted* things to go wrong.

I eventually got the call from the combatant and relayed his message. Since I was only a relay station, I had to transmit the message as it came, without adding to or subtracting from it, even though I was almost sure the information it contained was incorrect. I never learned whether the communiqué was transmitted to the merchant marine ship. It is possible that it was, but that its reception was kept under wraps until after the operation was complete, so that if something went wrong, it could be blamed on the preselected scapegoat, namely myself. Anyway, sure enough, the plane was forced down, and the big prize was not aboard.

I left Cyprus on the yacht and eventually rendezvoused with the Dabur. Someone didn't want me back in Israel just yet, so the Dabur was instructed to stay at sea for several days. The Dabur captain was informed by navy command that he had developed "engine problems." Even as it was happening, I realized that the delay was to allow someone the time to set me up as the fall guy for this botched operation.

I couldn't see how that sort of scapegoating was possible, though, unless the combatant changed his story. Then *I* would be the one blamed for supposedly misunderstanding the message. Were that to happen, I had no doubt that the record of all my communications attempting to warn the command center would be erased, and as it turned out, that's exactly what occurred. When we finally docked in Ashdod, Oren Riff, then chief of staff for the Mossad head, was there to greet me. It was his job to fill me in on what my duty to the Mossad was. I was to take responsibility for the foul-up, accepting that I was doing it for the good of the Office.[5] I had no choice in the matter, and so I agreed.

---

5. Office: The term used by Mossad people when talking about the Mossad, which is never mentioned by name.

CHAPTER 2

By mid-February, the "Cypriot screwup," as it came to be known, was a thing of the past. I, however, was placed under constant watch. Things became very difficult with that cloud of failure hanging over me.

I was still a probational rookie, which is the case for the first four years in Mossad, except that now I was under special observation. Most other rookies didn't want to be paired with me because of the extra supervision I brought along. "You can't always be perfect," Arik, one of my colleagues, said to me. "You're bound to slip, and then they'll be all over you. Why don't you just give up and quit?" I knew he was right, but I wasn't about to give up. To me, serving in the Mossad was the highest achievement. Inside the organization, the joke went that, if there was a second coming, the man would probably be Mossad.

I found it quite burdensome, double-checking every move to ensure everything was as perfect as it could be. But I was determined not to give the higher-ups the satisfaction of catching me in a mistake. I knew that many of them would be happy to be rid of me because of my political leanings. I was center, but in Mossad terms I was left, if not extreme left.

The constant pressure was taking its toll, and my home life wasn't much better. Whatever frustration I felt, I took out on my family. As a rule, all case officers in the Mossad must be married before they can serve abroad, but few have a happy marriage. Most have a bad one, and it's usually not their first. I began coming home later than usual, spending what little free time I had sitting with the guys at one of our regular hangouts. It was like working with a bunch of old gossips: the first one to leave was the one everybody talked about and slandered. The best protection you had was to stay till the end. I knew Bella and the kids were getting the short end of the stick. But I rationalized it by telling myself this was a temporary situation, and once I became well established in the system, I'd make it up to them.

Working in the Mossad, there was always an excuse for coming home late. Instead of turning to the one person who was my real friend, my wife, Bella, I turned away from her. And she didn't like anyone from the Office; she could see through them.

Since I couldn't change the reality, I tried to change the perception. I told myself that it was her view that was wrong, that she should see things the way we did. After all, I was a member of the Mossad, the elite, the select few. At home, I wasn't Mossad, and that was all I wanted to be.

Some time into my probationary period, I found myself in the middle of a minor operation in the one place the Mossad was not "allowed" to work: Israel. Though there are no specific laws guiding the activity of the Mossad, the proscription against operations within the country is vigilantly enforced by the Shaback (Israel's internal security body). Hence, the rule regarding these "impermissible" operations is: In the event of a foul-up, make the operation look like a mere exercise.

This particular operation was to benefit an Israeli optronics company called El Op, which was developing a special device to broadcast and receive digitized photographic images (DPI). It was also developing a similar system for the Mazlat. Mazlat (the word is a Hebrew abbreviation for unmanned remote-controlled plane) was a cooperative development project between Israeli Aeronautical Industries (IAI), a subsidiary of the Israeli Military Industry (IMI), and an American company called AAI Corporation that was based in Baltimore. The development of the DPI had proven to be extremely expensive and was running into technical difficulties as well. Further, IAI was on the Mossad support list because of its enormous financial and defense potential. Hence, the Mossad devised a plan to get the proverbial wagon out of the mud.

The IMI was advised to reach a development agreement with Recon Optical Industries, an American company that possessed the technology that El Op required. IMI chose as its pawn the Israeli air force, which at the time was involved in a project financed by American military aid to Israel. The plan was for the Mossad to insinuate Israeli engineers into Recon, posing as Israeli air force observers and quality controllers, and, under the auspices of this unrelated project, steal new technology that could then be manufactured in Israel. If this technology theft was done right, the savings in research and development expenses could be enormous.

Before this exercise that I was involved in a military base in Ramat Gan, a city adjacent to Tel Aviv. Several Mossad teams had already entered the base and placed El Op personnel files into the air force reserve bank. That would smooth the way for El Op engineers to be inserted into Recon. We were there to carry out a similar operation for a company called Tadiran.

Arik and Amir showed up at the base gate in guard uniforms and with the proper documentation, in time for the changing of the guard. The real guards had been detained by other members of our team posing as military police, and the sergeant major in charge of the guard detail had received a telephone call from manpower assigning two new men—Arik and Amir. I made that call from a pay phone, and the sergeant major took it at face value. All he really cared about was having two warm bodies at the gate.

We were heading for the main office building when Yosy said to me, "I want you to meet someone."

"Now?" Yosy and I were in military uniforms, both of us wearing the insignia of corporal.

I remember him nodding and smiling. He didn't seem to think there was a problem.

"Look, Yosy," I whispered as we slowly walked up a small hill to the administration building. "We're in the middle of an exercise, and we have a job to do. How about we do this another time? We can come back whenever we want. All we have to do is flash our IDs."

"Yes." He smiled. "I know that, but we're here now. I planned it so that we'll have the time." He paused as a pair of officers came near. We saluted lazily as they passed us. They didn't bother saluting back.

When they were several steps down the road, Yosy continued, "If things go according to plan, we should have about ten minutes before we have to leave."

"What can we do in ten minutes?"

"I want you to meet someone."

"What if I don't want to?"

"I'm not going to force you to do anything. I can tell you, however, that I'm sick and tired of your long dreary face and your down-in-the-dumps attitude. I just want to pump some life into you."

"I appreciate it, but no thanks."

"I'm talking about a woman who is aching for it."

Good old Yosy, I thought. He of the one-track mind. "I don't have to break into a military base in the middle of the night for that."

"This one's different, trust me," Yosy said, making me wonder why, if she was so different, he wasn't keeping her for himself.

Yosy stopped. We had reached our target building, a three-story British relic, tan in color, square, with three rows of small windows. The eucalyptus trees that filled the grounds rustled in the wind. The floodlights along the road and on top of the high fence threw the tree shadows onto the fine stucco walls, creating swaying images to match my state of mind.

Yosy turned serious. This was work, and to my relief, he plunged into it.

"Do you have it with you?" he asked.

I slid my hand into my shirt just to feel the large plastic envelope. "Yes."

"Let's do it."

We walked straight to the small stairwell. We had to be careful as we climbed the stairs; on every second turn we could be seen from the ground. The building itself was not a high-security zone, but if a patrol had spotted us on the staircase or inside, it could be a problem. Three patrols were making their rounds.

Once inside, we moved fast, first making sure that there was no necking going on—a common pastime for off-duty military couples who were stuck on base. The room was filled with four-drawer filing cabinets. At the far end was a large gray safe. Yosy walked to the desk by the door and pulled out the drawer. "Get over there and open the safe. I'll read you the combination."

I walked to the safe and bent down, setting the dial at zero. "How did you get it?"

"That is the difference between a case officer and a burglar. I made contact with the girl working here and spent some time with her."

"Really?"

"Don't laugh. I sacrificed a lot," Yosy said.

"Sacrificed?"

"You should have seen her. Believe me, it was a sacrifice." He chuckled.

"You didn't have to take her to bed."

"It wasn't a bed. Besides, I can't help myself. For me, a woman is a woman is a woman."

"So why are you whining about it now?"

He shrugged and looked at the bottom of the drawer he was holding. "Seventeen to the right, four to the left." He went on until the lock clicked. I spun the chrome wheel and pulled the door open. There was a stack of manila files inside. We did the switch in less than five minutes, and then we were ready to leave.

Suddenly, there was a noise from the outer door. We both froze. We didn't know if the patrols made a round inside the offices or only checked to see if the outer door was locked.

"Did you lock the outer door?" I whispered to him.

"Yes, I braced it!"

We moved quietly to the window and looked outside. It was a long drop. After several seconds of testing the door, the patrol moved away. They were women soldiers. We sighed in relief as we saw them walking out of the building. Everything had gone well. All I wanted to do now was to get the hell out of there. I lit a cigarette, and we started for the gate.

Yosy looked at his watch. "We still have about twenty minutes, much more than I planned for."

"What are you talking about? We finished. What are we waiting for?"

"Dov said we should not leave before ten."

"You want to tell me they are planning a tail on us now?" The thought frustrated me. To take full advantage of the jobs/exercises we were assigned, Mossad training personnel would throw extra obstacles into otherwise simple operations. They liked to test us, to see if we knew we were being followed. Similar exercises were carried out in Europe while officers were involved in routine operations. Knowing they might be followed by Mossad testers put case officers on their best behavior.

"Anyway," Yosy said, "we're not to leave before ten, and then only one at a time. If we're clean, we'll meet somewhere. If not, then you do what you have to do. I will be leaving last, like a good commander. Now would you follow me? I have someone I want you to meet."

"Forget it, Yosy. I'm not in the mood."

"Then do it for me. Haim and I can't handle her alone; we need help. We've been double-teaming her for the past month. Haim knew her from before, in Haifa."

"Why don't you call Jerry?" I said, smiling.

"We have a woman, what we need is an extra man. Come on."

It seemed he was determined to get me out of the mental slump I was in, and getting me laid was the best method he and Haim could come up with. Did I know I shouldn't be following him? Yes. Did I follow him anyway? Yes, I'm ashamed to say.

We headed for a gray-colored prefab office structure halfway between the main building and the gate. It started to rain. I stood at the edge of the covered platform behind Yosy, who was about to knock on a door.

"Come over here," Yosy whispered to me. "I don't have time to fill you in on the cover story. Just remember we're from the Shaback. It would be better if you don't say anything. Oh yeah, we're not married, any of us, and don't use your own name, family name that is." He knocked on the door.

A soft feminine voice answered. "Who's that?"

"Yosy."

"Come on in."

He opened the door slowly, turned and winked at me, and entered.

"Dina, how are you?" He walked over to a slim, beautiful blond seated behind a large metal desk. She was wearing an oversized green army sweater with sergeant's stripes loosely pinned to her sleeves. A pair of tight faded jeans wrapped her long legs, which stretched out under the desk, almost touching a small glowing electric heater.

Yosy bent over and kissed her on the cheek. He then stood behind her, putting his hands on her shoulders, and said, "This, my beautiful candy, is my friend Dan."

I smiled at her, and she smiled back. I felt awkward, out of place, yet excited by those deep blue eyes. There was a reddish glow to the room, and I was starting to feel hot.

"What are you doing here?" she asked Yosy.

"It's an inspection. We're here to check if the place is secure."

"Is it?"

Yosy thought for a moment, leaning closer to her. "Not to worry, you're safe as long as we're here."

She stared at me, smiling. Yosy leaned over and kissed her on the lips. The kiss went on and on. As I turned to leave, I saw her slowly raise her hands and hold his head. My last glimpse was of his hand headed for her breast. I waited outside for a few seconds before I heard him say, "Listen, my flower. One of us will come over to your place, around twelve?"

"Okay. If I'm not there, you know where the key is, right?"

Yosy came out, smiling as he closed the door behind him. "Well, buddy, if all goes well, it will be Dina at midnight."

CHAPTER 3

After leaving the compound, I took steps to see if I was being followed. By now, this activity was second nature to me. After verifying I was indeed clean, I called Dov. The phone rang twice. "Yes?" Dov answered in his somewhat husky voice.

"It's Kid here."

"What's up?"

"I just wanted to tell you I'm clean."

"Positive?"

"No doubt."

"Where are you now?"

"At the Elite intersection. Will there be anything else? I want to get out of this uniform."

"On what side of the intersection are you?"

"By the diamond exchange."

"Okay. Just a minute." There was a two-minute pause on the line. When he came back, he just said, "Have a good night. I'll see you in the morning." His voice was slightly cynical; that was Dov's way. He'd picked it up from Mousa, his boss, and carried it a little further.

I hadn't even put the receiver back into place when a police car screeched to a stop by the phone booth. I watched as the uniformed policeman got out and headed for me. I slowly hung up the phone and turned to face him. I knew the routine; it was a typical training exercise to get us used to the kind of harassment we might encounter abroad. I was smirking; it wasn't a good idea to do that, but I just couldn't help myself. I knew what was coming, and yet I didn't care. I knew I could handle it.

"Hey, you!" the policeman called as he swaggered closer.

I found the situation comical. I could still remember when encounters like this got me excited and scared. "What?" I started to chuckle. "Are you talking to me?"

"What's so funny, soldier boy?"

"Are you talking to me?"

"You think it's funny, do you? I'll show you how funny this is." He slammed the booth door open to one side and stuck in his bulldog face, almost touching mine. In such situations, I'd been trained to be overly cooperative, friendly, even wimpish. Soothe the man and get the problem to shrink as fast as possible. But—maybe it was everything I'd gone through the past few weeks, maybe it was how the night had unfolded so far—for some reason, I wasn't in an obliging mood. "Are you talking to me?" The words just came out, and the smile on my face widened.

The cop grabbed my shirt collar and slammed me against the back of the booth. The metal shelf under the phone hit my lower back, sending bolts of pain through my legs. "Do you have papers?" His face was twisted with anger at my smile. He turned his head to his partner, who was slowly getting out of the car. "We got ourselves a smart aleck here. Should we take him downtown or feed him some knuckles first?"

The second cop was a giant. "Well, little soldier," he said. "I can see you want to play games."

"Are you talking to me?" I wasn't smiling anymore. The big cop's huge open hand came from behind and hit me on the top of my forehead. My head snapped back, slamming against the glass pane. I could hear the glass crack. The insides of my head vibrated; I was starting to lose consciousness.

Suddenly, both cops backed up, yanking me out of the booth. The contact with the cold air brought me around.

"You're coming with us, soldier boy," the bigger cop said as they tossed me into the back seat of the small Ford Escort patrol car.

"Where are you from?" the gorilla asked as he forced my head between my knees and cuffed my hands behind my back, closing the cuffs tight.

"Are you talking to me?"

A fast jab to my ribs brought a short cry of pain. When I tried to raise my head, he pushed it back down, hitting my lip on my knee. I could taste the blood. I stayed down. Whatever happened, I couldn't have them leave marks on my face. My face was the most important tool I had in this strange trade of mine. I could not do my job with a black and blue face. I knew they were instructed not to harm me or leave me visibly bruised, but often the cops would get carried away.

I felt like telling them, I know the routine; let's get it over with. But all I could say was, "Are you talking to me?" My mind wandered. Meanwhile, the beefy cop was slapping the back of my head and punching at my ribs. From time to time, a sharp pain would drag me out of my thoughts and force me to face what was taking place. I knew I could stop this by playing along, but something inside wouldn't let me.

Then I thought of Dina; how easy it would be to get into bed with her and forget everything, just let things happen. Even at such a low moment, the thought excited me. I tried to push the fantasy away, telling myself the encounter would never happen. But I knew it would somehow, and that became something to focus on.

It was almost a full hour of sheer agony before the police car returned to where it had picked me up. As the cruiser pulled over, the driver turned, grabbed me by the hair, and wrenched my head up. My vision was blurred, and I had a pounding headache.

The cop scowled.

"What were you doing here, you little bastard?" He spoke right into my face, tightening his grip on my hair.

"Are you talking to me?" I mumbled. I could see they were confused. This was not the way things were supposed to go. They weren't sure if I was doing it wrong or they were. The gorilla was now staring out the window, clearly worried that he might have overdone it.

"Yes, you little shit, I'm talking to you," he finally said. I didn't realize how much I'd needed that little victory.

"Why didn't you say so?" I smiled faintly.

He smiled back in relief and let go of my hair. His big friend took off my cuffs and opened the door. He then got out of the car and gently helped me out. Before he closed the door, he looked at me. "You okay? No hard feelings?"

"No hard feelings." I shrugged and staggered back into the phone booth. The cracked pane was staring me straight in the face. It seemed so long ago, I had almost forgotten how it started. I dialed, and on the second ring Dov answered.

"It's Kid," I said.

"What's up?"

"You son of a bitch. I just got off a roller coaster."

"What took you so long?"

"I don't know. I guess there was a communication problem with the operator of the amusement park."

"What do you mean?"

"I mean I'm tired, you asshole. What do you think I mean?"

"Are you okay?"

"As well as could be expected. I will live, though."

"Okay, just put it all in the report. I'll see you in the morning." He hung up.

I dialed again, this time to the phone in the academy's[1] main hall. Yosy or Haim was supposed to be there. It was a pact we had that we waited for one another until the last one was done. It was 23:40, and Yosy answered after the fifth ring. He was breathing hard, as if he had run.

"Yes?"

"Yosy?"

"Hey, Victor, where the hell are you? We were ready to give up on you."

"Who's we?"

"Haim and me, who else?"

"Why are you breathing like you just ran a marathon?"

"We've been playing Ping-Pong. So what are you up to?"

"Not much. I need a place to rest and relax."

He chuckled. "I think a candy factory would be in order."

"A candy factory?" I was still somewhat dazed by the beating and the constant pressure.

"Dina, I'm talking about Dina. Where are you now?"

"I'm at the Elite intersection in Ramat Gan."

"We'll meet you in ten minutes at the London mini-stores complex."

"See you there." I hung up and waved down a cab. Several minutes later, I was standing at the corner, staring north up Even Gvirol Avenue. The Jeep came to a screeching stop just behind me.

Haim was sitting in the back. He stuck his balding head out, looking at me. "Come on, come on, we don't have all night. We've got a job to do."

"A job?"

"There's a lawyer's office, we have to enter the building and photograph some of his files."

"When did this come up?"

"Yesterday."

"How come I never heard of it?"

---

1. Academy: Mossad training facility, located across from the country club outside Tel Aviv on the road to Haifa.

"You're not on our team. It's a nonelected setup; we didn't choose it, we were assigned."

I could feel the long blade slowly making its way through my back. Yosy, Haim, and I had been a team almost from day one. There was no reason to break us up; we complemented one another. The only thing that I could think of was that someone was trying to isolate me. I was not paranoid. Had this been a legitimate move, they would have brought it to my attention and given me an explanation. Because it was done behind my back, it was sinister. But there was nothing I could do now; accepting it was the only rational move.

"I thought we told her we'd be there at twelve?" Suddenly, I realized how anxious I was to see Dina. Funny thing was, it was the image of her smile, not her body, that fixed itself in my mind.

"What I thought we'd do," Yosy said, turning around to face Haim and me, "we'll drop Victor here over at her place, then we'll go and do the casing. Then we will come back and pick you up."

I nodded. "Fine with me."

"We'll come in with you just to get a cup of coffee, then we'll scoot," Yosy added.

I told them about my encounter with the police.

"How hard did they hit you?" Yosy asked.

"Hard enough. I was asking for it."

"I thought you could sweet-talk anyone." Haim stared at me from the dark rear of the Jeep.

"I don't know, I really don't know. All I can tell you is that I didn't feel like talking to those two."

The Jeep was on its way, crossing several lanes as we headed in the direction of Dizengoff Street. At the corner of Dizengoff and Gordon, Yosy made a sharp right, almost turning the Jeep over. It came to a stop on the sidewalk.

"Nice parking," I remarked. "I'm sure you're parallel to something." We all laughed; this was one of the perks of the job, ignoring traffic rules. The Jeep's license plate was false, and although it would show up on the police computer, it would do so only for a few days, then it would be changed. We also had a high-level special security ID card that would send a cop instantly in whatever direction we might choose. This was our God card, and we liked finding a chance to use it.

"We're here," Yosy announced and hopped out. I followed, and Haim was not far behind. It was a typical Tel Aviv apartment building.

"This is it." Yosy was at the door to the right of the dark stairwell. He turned to face me, one hand on the bell ready to press the little red button. "Just remember, we are from the Shaback, we're all single, and we live on base in . . . " He turned to Haim. "Where do we live?"

"Natania."

"Why Natania? Why Shaback?" I asked.

"Natania is far enough yet not that far, and Shaback because we can't tell her Mossad, now can we? We don't want to be police, so that is the closest thing."

"Okay, I can live with that. How often does all this come up?"

"We gave her the story once," Haim said in a low voice.

"Never spoke about it again," Yosy remarked. "Come on, hit the bell."

I was calm only because I was beat. It wouldn't have taken much for me to fall asleep at that point. The guilt associated in my mind with this sort of activity was dulled. I'd managed subconsciously to get my punishment before I did the deed.

The sound of the buzzer was harsh and unpleasant. It was followed by a soft, barely audible voice. "Just a minute."

The peephole blacked out for a second, then the door swung open. "Hey, guys, I thought you weren't coming, so I was about to go to bed." She backed away from the door, letting us in.

"Don't let us stop you." Yosy said with a sly smile. "We might just join you."

She closed the door behind us. Haim headed straight for the large bed in the center of the small living room, dropping himself right into the middle of it. Yosy made his way to the bathroom. The place was dimly lit, and the air stood heavy with the moisture of a recently taken bath and a faint scent of perfume. The smell was sensual: I could all but feel the softness of the woman's skin. The place was simple, warm, and seductive. I could feel my heart pumping harder with every passing moment. The excitement was pressing against my Adam's apple—it felt good. Dina was beautiful in her long robe. Her movements were flowing, somewhat unconcerned, casual. Except for her hair, everything about her was long. Her lazy blue eyes stayed on me after I sat on the end of the bed, still tense.

She moved slowly to the bathroom, then flicked on the light in a second room I hadn't noticed before. It was a small kitchen. She paused and asked, "Would anyone like something to drink?"

"I'll have a coffee," Haim answered, not even turning his head.

"Forget it," came a shout from behind the bathroom door. "We have things to do. We'll pick Dan up later." We always managed to find a reason for a code name, whatever the activity. It was second nature; we just did it all the time.

Yosy stepped out of the bathroom, pulled the girl toward him, and kissed her. She showed no resistance. He let go of her and said to Haim, "Let's go, we have things to do, and so does Dan." He turned to me. "Keep the bed warm until we come back."

Somehow his manner irritated me. It was as though I was taking offense where she should have but didn't. It was her submission and his abuse that angered me. She locked the door after they left and stood facing me, leaning on the door she had just closed. I felt very awkward.

"Would you care for something to drink?" she asked, smiling for the first time.

"I'll have a coffee, please."

"Make yourself comfortable. I'll be back in a moment."

She glided across the room, spreading her scent as she passed. It was a naked smell, teasing; I could feel the pressure in my loins. Dishes clattered in the kitchen. I lit a cigarette and picked up what seemed like a notebook from the small coffee table by the bed.

I opened it and saw it was filled with tight small handwriting. My first reaction was to put it back on the table. Then I looked again; there were no markings on the cover. If whoever wrote this had not wanted it read, he or she would not have left it where it was. My first guess was that it was Dina's diary. I wasn't eager to read it, but there was little else to do, and I was not going to sit there like a dummy until we got into bed like two awkward strangers doing what we both knew we had intended to do in the first place. Obviously, she didn't think my friends had dropped me off to have a friendly chat with her. And Yosy told me he had asked her if she wanted me to come after she had caught a glimpse of me at the base, and her response was positive. So there might be something in this little book to break the ice and make things a bit smoother.

I realized I was starting to feel guilty again. What the hell was a thirty-seven-year-old married man with two children doing here, seated on the bed of this twenty-three-year-old woman? I was one son of a bitch.

I started to read. At first it made no sense—short sentences that rhymed but meant nothing to me. She came back with two cups of steaming coffee and sat next to me on the bed. Her knee slid out from under the heavy robe and as though by accident touched mine. I cleared my throat. She took her coffee and started to drink, hiding half her face behind the cup.

I raised the book. "Is this your stuff?"

She nodded silently, as though she was waiting for me to say more. "Really?"

"Yes," she answered, putting the cup down and smiling at me. "Why?"

"I just asked."

She moved closer, her smile getting wider. "How do you like it?"

"I think it's great."

She leaned back, laughing softly. "What do you mean?"

"Just what I said." I told myself that a horny man should not discuss poetry. "I'm really hot," I said.

"Why don't you take a shower and change? You seem like it would do you some good."

"You mean I stink?" I laughed.

"No, no, not at all . . ."

"I would love to." I got up and started for the bath. "I have nothing to change into."

"Use the robe on the door, and then you can pick out something of my husband's."

I froze. "Your what?"

"Oh, don't worry. He doesn't live here anymore."

I let out a sigh of relief.

There was something erotic about the shower; there was something erotic about everything in the small apartment: the simplicity of things, the improvisational solutions young people find for domestic needs, furniture and appliances that had seen better days, yet were functional and comfortable. When I came out of the shower, the room was dark except for a red glow from an electric heater.

"Get into bed." Her voice came from the corner. "I'll be there in a minute."

My pulse was racing as I lay on the bed, hands behind my head, still in the damp robe I had found in the bathroom. It was anticipation that kept me awake, and I was well rewarded. She came out into the red glow wearing nothing. She walked straight for the bed and sat by me. Leaning her thin, soft-skinned body against my folded leg, she sat gently stroking my chest.

I was ready to explode. Her elbow touched me, and she could feel I wanted her. She smiled. It was clear she was happy. I sat up in the bed and cupped her small breast in one hand, slowly moving the other all over her body, which seemed to quiver to my touch. She pushed me back onto the bed and gently fondled every part of me. Then she slowly sat herself on me, bringing us together. The memory of what took place after that is hazy. I remember that when Yosy and Haim came to pick me up, I told them I would stay the night and would see them tomorrow. I had made my escape from brutal reality and wanted it to last, at least for the night.

CHAPTER 4

THURSDAY, FEBRUARY 13, 1986, 07:45

I reached the academy and ran into the building, my coat over my head for protection from the rain.

Dov, our training instructor, looked angry—not an expression regularly seen on his rounded face. He stopped me several feet from the coffeepot.

"Where the hell have you been?"

"Did we have a date?" I asked.

"I don't need a date to fuck you." He had a point, and also my attention. "I'm talking about last night?"

I paused, looking at the ceiling. "You missed me? I'm touched."

"You weren't home when I called."

"You called me at *home*?" I felt a mixture of fear and guilt. "What did you tell Bella?"

"Nothing, I just wanted to talk to you."

"What am I supposed to tell her now?"

"If you'd been there, you wouldn't have to tell her anything."

Dov had broken the basic unwritten rule of camaraderie in the Mossad: He'd called an officer's home when there was no urgent reason to do so, and it seemed he had not even covered for me once he realized I was not there. I was furious. "Fuck you, who made you the sheriff? Trust me, Dov, *coul calb bigy youmu* [every dog has his day]. I'll find a time to look for you too."

I poured myself a cup of coffee. "Okay, now you found me. What do you want anyway? I don't have all day." This was getting far more complicated than I thought.

"What did you think you were playing at last night, with the cops?" Dov was trying to keep his voice down.

"Nothing. They took me for a ride and then brought me back, why?"

"Is that how you deal with hostile police? After years of training, that is all you came up with? 'Are you talking to me?'"

"Are you talking to me?"

"Don't start with me. You're walking the edge and you know it, so don't push me."

I put my hand on his shoulder and pulled him to the corner of the room. I leaned over closer to him and spoke in a low voice. "Listen to me, Dov. You're on loan to the Mossad from internal security because of your expertise in operational security, right?"

He nodded.

"I'm a Mossad officer. In a few weeks I will be posted, and even if I'm not, I'm still a colonel [the rank I had received in Mossad]. I outrank you ten times." He tried to pull away, but I held on. "You can tell me whatever you want, that's your job. However, if you don't want me to break your neck, and trust me I will, you'll treat me with respect. Am I making myself clear?"

"Get your hands off me." He backed up.

"You'll get my report shortly, and if you don't like what you read, you can do whatever you bloody want. Now, if you'll forgive me, I have a coffee to drink." I walked back to the main area.

There were some loose ends I had to tie up, which was the reason I had come to the academy in the first place. It had to do with a conference that had taken place the previous month at the Country Club Hotel, across from the academy on the highway to Haifa. The conference had hosted the representatives of the South Korean Unification Church of Reverend Sun Myung Moon, known as Moonies, and their motley group of associates. Meetings had taken place with right-wing Knesset members and some military personnel. Also taking part on our side were representatives of the intelligence community and dignitaries such as Yehuda Blum, the former Israeli ambassador to the UN. An ex-colonel from the Korean central intelligence agency (KCIA) and several retired American generals were there too. One man I really couldn't stand was a Frenchman called Pierre Ceylac, who was a member of an extreme right-wing French fascist party. The man constantly wanted me to get him things. He thought that liaison meant having a servant or something. He had placed a request with the Mossad for a computer program that would help him communicate and store data. Ceylac needed to keep the data secure from the French secret service. I was supposed to get the program that had been modified for him by the electronics company Sitex and send it via diplomatic pouch to the Paris station. They would have the program delivered to him.

I didn't understand why we dealt with these characters to begin with. But David Biran, who had hosted the conference, said the benefits were far greater than the smell. It was not my place to question but to obey, and so I did.

Friday, February 14, Mossad Headquarters, King Saul Boulevard, Tel Aviv

"Hey, Victor." Yehuda Gill, a veteran *katsa*[1] and one of the living legends of the Mossad, called me as I was about to pass through the security post at the entrance to the building. I turned and he waved at me, pointing to a corridor that led to the photographic department. The man was involved in just about every operation that called for elaborate planning, yet he was one of the more modest people in the organization.

I smiled and walked in his direction. He put a hand on my shoulder. "Come with me. I'm going to have my ugly face photographed for a new American passport. I want to talk to you."

We entered the empty photo studio. "The photographer will be here in a few minutes," he said.

"What's with the American passport?" That was a very rare thing to get. The Mossad tried to avoid as much as possible the use of American passports.

"I'll be working in the States for the Al[2] department. We've got a big cleanup job there."

"I never heard of any screwups there. What's to clean up?"

"The Pollard thing."

"I thought that was LAKAM[3]?"

"They made the mess, but we have to clean it up. I have to contact the famous Mr. X and see to it that he doesn't get caught."

---

1. *Katsa:* Gathering officer, or case officer, in the Mossad. Only about thirty-five active *katsas* are in the field at any given time.

2. Al: A secret unit of experienced *katsas* working under deep cover in the United States.

3. LAKAM: Lishka Le Kishry Mada, the section for scientific relations, a special unit directly under the prime minister's office that was gathering intelligence in the United States. Not part of the Mossad.

I knew something about the case. The LAKAM had recruited a man named Jonathan Pollard, an American Jew working in U.S. navy intelligence, and had worked him as a spy. He was captured in 1986 by the FBI, after being refused asylum in the Israeli embassy in Washington. That refusal was the direct result of Mossad intervention, although the affair was handled outside the Mossad. There was rumored to be a link between Pollard and the Mossad, someone known as Mr. X. We never got the full story, and what did come through was buried in paper.

"So there is a Mr. X?" I said.

"In name only. Mr. X is not one person. Eitan[4] took from us lists of *sayanim*[5] when he left. He used them as sources. They would tell him where things were, and he would have Pollard bring out the hard copy."

"They agreed?" I knew it was a dumb question the moment I asked it.

"Agreed? A *sayan* is there to serve, not to question. If we don't move fast, others will end up in jail cells next to Pollard. So I have to go out there and see that it doesn't happen. How many Jews do you know in America who are willing to be branded a traitor and spend time in prison for the glory of Israel?"

I nodded in understanding. "So what can I do for you?"

"Nothing. I just want to talk to you about you."

"Me? What's to talk about?"

"I heard some things about you, and I think you should know about them."

"What things?"

"First, you have Mike Harari,[6] whom you played for a fool. He's still after your hide. The man is spreading stories about you. Then there are all the people you rub the wrong way when you talk politics." Yehuda looked at me like a teacher eyeing a young rascal. "You

---

4. Eitan: Reference to Rafael Eitan, an ex-Mossad officer who headed the LAKAM.

5. *Sayanim:* Derives from the Hebrew word *lesayeah,* meaning "to help." The reference is to Jewish helpers who do things for the Mossad. They're not paid, so it can never be said they're doing what they're doing for the money. Several restrictions govern their use. For example, a *sayan* cannot be asked to do a job inside an Arab country.

6. Mike Harari: Ex-Mossad officer involved in shady activities worldwide. Known to have been the Panamanian leader Manuel Noriega's partner.

have the right to your opinions. But since you're from the wrong side of the spectrum, you should keep them to yourself."

I believed in the right of the Palestinian people to have a country of their own in the West Bank and the Gaza Strip. I believed we were losing our humane image through this so-called benevolent occupation of the Territories. Not only did I believe all this, I said so at every opportunity. I had therefore been pegged as a leftist. In Israel in general and in the Mossad in particular, the difference between left-wing and right-wing is clearly demarcated by the question of the Territories. The right wants to keep the Territories and if possible annex them to the state of Israel, after deporting most of their Palestinian inhabitants. The left regards the Palestinians as a national entity with its own privileges and rights, including that of self-determination. Other issues, such as the economy and social policies, are not necessarily aligned along this axis. Thus, an extreme left-winger on the question of the Territories could be a right-wing conservative on all other issues.

I knew it was a myth that the Mossad, with all its power, could exist without becoming fascist. Yet I needed the myth to keep going. "So what are you telling me? That I should shut up? Isn't Israel a democracy?"

"It is, but you're not in Israel, you're in the Mossad. Until we get a chance to clean house, things will get worse before they get better. My advice to you is duck, my boy, duck until the rage passes."

"What if I don't?"

"You'll be out on your ass faster than you can believe. Or much worse."

"What is that supposed to mean?"

"What do you think it means? We deal in death and deception every day. Think about it." He smiled sadly. I wanted to ask him a thousand questions. But just then the photographer walked in.

"Thanks for coming to say goodbye," he said to me and turned to face the photographer. I knew our little talk was over.

SUNDAY, FEBRUARY 16, 08:00

I was posted to the Danish desk in Country[7] in Mossad headquarters. I reported to work first thing in the morning. After the ritualistic coffee and chatter in the corridors, I was handed my assignment for that day. For my first job on this desk, I was given a pile of Danish

---

7. Country: A department in the liaison branch.

visa applications that were shipped to us via diplomatic pouch. They were photocopies of the originals and were part of a so-called service we were performing for the Danes.

All the applicants were of Arab descent, and the procedure was to compare their names with our own database. We'd had a new system installed only some months before, and the cross-referencing of the information was extremely fast. The computer had over one and a half million names in its memory. It took only a few seconds to get a cross-reference with the new program, which was said to have been freshly stolen from an ally.

After several days, Benny S., second in command of Country, told me to contact Hombre—code name for our man in Scandinavia—and have him request a new bugging on a leading Danish judicial figure by the name of Gammeltoft Hansen. This man was a pro-Palestinian advocate and a professor in some university. The Danish police, or secret police, had installed a listening device in his office for us several years previously. "Study the file," Benny said, "then you recommend what should be done. We believe Hansen suspects his office is bugged from the way he conducts his conversations. If we bug his home, we're sure to get better results."

Monday, February 17

From what I found in the Danish secret service file, I could see that we had a "good friend" in Denmark, much friendlier and more cooperative than the Israeli Shaback was to us. The Danes had a small service that wanted to play in the big leagues but didn't have the know-how or financial backing to do so. On the other hand, they could gather information inside Denmark and do things without getting caught that we couldn't dream of. In return for getting things done for us, we made them feel important.

Hombre's answer to my request for a second bug came back the same day. They were working on it. They had placed the first one in the professor's office at the end of 1984. It was done by an agent we had inside Danish intelligence. His name was Schmidt, and he was code-named Oil Paint. He sent a police team to place the bug, making up a story that the bug had been requested by the man whose office it was, supposedly to stop some phone harassment. He gave the wrong office location, so they had installed the bug in the professor's phone. No one but Oil Paint, and Hombre of course, knew about it. The tapes were transferred directly, untouched, to Hombre every two weeks like clockwork, and everybody was happy.

The second request that I had made to Hombre was to try to get more information regarding Korean dissident activity in Denmark. This was a request from liaison to fill a promise made to the Moonies. A similar request had been made in 1982, but the Danes wouldn't give us anything then. This time, they replied that they would oblige. They also wanted us to know how sensitive the information was. They were collecting it exclusively for the CIA and didn't want to get caught in the middle.

I double-checked with Amnon Peleg, the liaison to the CIA. He said the CIA would shoot us all if they knew we were giving this stuff to the Moonies.

Peleg asked me to delay the transfer of the information. By evening, this was starting to take on a crisis format. Head of liaison insisted on giving it to the Moonies. He said the information was promised to him by Shabtai, head of Melucha. Shabtai was out of the country and out of reach. He was in Rome, a guest of the Italian head of intelligence. It was a working visit. Shabtai had taken with him Menahem Dorf, head of Sayfanim.[8] They had information tying Sabry El Bana (better known as Abu Nidal) to the December 27, 1985, attack on the Rome airport. The information was solid, although many gaps were artfully filled, tying the man to other terrorist acts that had taken place in Italy. From Rome, Shabtai was heading for France to meet with French intelligence officials about Abu Nidal's activities there.

Finally, the decision came on the side of the Moonies. Head of Country decided to go ahead and tell Hombre to activate Schmidt and have him steal the material if necessary.

WEDNESDAY, FEBRUARY 19

The information for the Moonies arrived before noon and was passed on directly to Traksin (Mashov's[9] department for paraphrasing information). Paraphrasing was done to eliminate the possibility of tracing the source of the information. I then passed it on to liaison, who sent it to Japan, where the Mossad liaison officer to the Far East—from the Dardasim section—handed it in person to his contact in Dr. Moon's church.

---

8. Sayfanim: A department in research totally devoted to PLO activity, part of the Manginot (code name for research) section.

9. Mashov: Code name for the communications department.

That same day, Hombre sent a fax through a secure line in the Israeli embassy in Denmark. He informed me that the special antiterror unit of Purples-A[10] had entered and installed a Glass[11] in the professor's house. In the fax, he said the action was made under protest by an officer named Delsgard, but the man did nothing more than that.

Friday, February 21

The Danish visa forms that were judged problematic made their way back to my desk. Several of them had names that were also in our computer, meaning that they were of some interest to us. The procedure was to double-check, because Arab names are extremely confusing. It was necessary to see if other details such as date and place of birth matched. That would eliminate almost 80 percent of the so-called hot files. The women at the typing pool had no clearance to call up the files they were working on. All they could do was enter information, not retrieve it.

Once the name was regarded as hot and verified, it was added to a roster with all the relevant information. The roster was then passed on to operations center every second day. There they analyzed the new names to see if they wanted to recruit immediately or put them on hold. If the decision was to recruit immediately, the Danes would not be given an answer regarding the person in question. They were to assume that all was well, and they would approve the visa. Once the applicant was on Danish soil and under our surveillance, the Danes would be informed he was a dangerous person. They would automatically cease refugee proceedings and bring him in for questioning. A Mossad officer would then attempt to recruit him in the Danish holding tank. If the recruiting was successful, he would be released and act as an agent for the Mossad inside the Palestinian community in Europe, or elsewhere. If not recruited, the man would be threatened and then released; usually he then escaped to another Scandinavian country where the Mossad had similar arrangements. There the process would start all over.

---

10. Purples-A: Mossad code name for the Danish civilian secret service (Politiets Efterretningsjtneste Politistatonen).

11. Glass: A listening device installed in a phone that can also listen to things said in the room where the phone is located.

"We have in this way recruited over eighty Palestinians this past year," my boss had bragged. "It's too easy to be legal."

It wasn't, but when I asked if this sort of thing could backfire on us, I got the usual answer you would get in the Mossad to just about any question: "So what?"

Over the next few days, things started to become somewhat of a haze. I was working almost around the clock preparing for my planned trip to Sri Lanka. I was to escort a large shipment of mines to the Tamil Tigers and receive payment for them. I was learning my cover story and being questioned on it by my section head.

It seemed that the whole building was going berserk. Everybody and his dog were looking for information that could stop Jordan's King Hussein's efforts for a peace initiative. The initiative caught the Mossad off guard; we had understood from sources in the United States that it was a farce. They had said it was dead in the water almost a month ago. But somehow it sprang to life again, and although Yasser Arafat would not recognize Israel, he had agreed to a meeting with Hussein. The word was that it was a ploy by Hussein. All he wanted, they said, was American approval of his request for a two-billion-dollar arms purchase. We had guaranteed the prime minister that this would not happen. The entire Jewish lobby in the United States was mobilized. The man in charge of that was Tsvy Gabay, head of the foreign office intelligence section. He was given lists of *sayanim* and pro-Zionist organizations that he could mobilize.

This was not an easy task. The Jordanians could purchase the arms anywhere they wanted. They were not begging for a grant; they wanted to spend money in the United States. They were looking for a cash deal. We knew that if they succeeded, they would have access to an American market that was more than eager to sell them anything. And so this deal never stood a chance.

The American Jewish community was divided into a three-stage action team. First were the individual *sayanim* (if the situation had been reversed and the United States had convinced Americans working in Israel to work secretly on behalf of the United States, they would be treated as spies by the Israeli government). Then there was the large pro-Israeli lobby. It would mobilize the Jewish community in a forceful effort in whatever direction the Mossad pointed them. And last was B'nai Brith. Members of that organization could be relied on to make friends among non-Jews and tarnish as anti-Semitic whomever they couldn't sway to the Israeli cause. With that sort of one-two-three tactic, there was no way we could strike out.

CHAPTER 5

Thursday, March 27, 1986

Two months had passed since the Cyprus fiasco, and the system was in torment over how to deal with me. On the one hand, the Mossad leadership had invested a great deal in bringing me to this point. And I *had* responded well—meaning I was a good product of the system's training and modeling process. However, several high-ranking officers had come to regard me as a divisive influence. One I barely knew, a man named Ephraim, made it his personal crusade to expel me from what he called the first family of the state.

He had somehow been made my assessor and was not happy with things he had found in my file. He said that I was inflammatory and that my political outbursts were a menace to morale. He agreed that I had the makings of a good case officer, but since I leaned to the left, I would be a danger to the system.

The Mossad is a small organization with thirty to forty case officers, each an important member of the field family. Whatever happens to one affects the rest. My situation was well known and was a topic of discussion at almost every gathering where I wasn't present. I learned about it from friends, but I didn't have a so-called horse (a brass member who wanted to advance me as part of his clique) who would speak for me.

By now I knew I was going to get the boot. I stood outside the large wooden doors of the academy, at the edge of the staff parking lot. I stared at the winter sun sinking slowly into the Mediterranean. A slow drizzle had started, and the light was fading fast.

"Victor," came a call from inside the main hall. I turned. It was Dinur, someone I had regarded as a friend. I was sure he still was.

"What?"

"They want to talk to you." He nodded in the direction of the offices.

"Is the chief there?" As a case officer on his way out, I had the right to speak one-on-one to the head of the Mossad. If that was denied, I would activate my second privilege and ask for a hearing with the prime minister.

"No, the boss isn't there. David Arbel is."

"I have the right to speak to Rom." I used the code name for the head of the Mossad.

"Why don't you listen to what Arbel and Gideon Naftaly have to say?"

"Naftaly? What the hell is Naftaly up to?" Naftaly was head of the psychiatric department and someone I didn't respect. In the cadet course, one cadet who was a psychologist had made manipulating him into a sport.

"Look, Victor, don't ask me all these questions. Get in there and ask them."

I nodded and started for the hall, stopping by the coffee table to take a cup and use some napkins to partially dry my hair, which was still damp from the rain. Dinur was walking by me. I felt like a man on his way to the gallows.

Gideon popped his head out of the office. "Victor, we're waiting for you. Can you please come in here now?"

"Go ahead," said Dinur, pushing me toward the office. "Go, man."

I nodded and entered the room. "You called?"

"Yes," said Arbel in his heavy, self-important voice. "We want to talk to you about the termination of your contract with the Mossad."

"When will I have my talk with the boss?"

"You won't," he said in a casual tone, as though he were telling his secretary to get him someone on the phone. "This will be your final talk."

I felt a sudden burst of anger. I could see that they wanted to get this over with as fast as possible. I had ceased to be one of them, and they didn't want me around anymore. They had cheated me out of my country and my belief in a cause. I was clutching at straws. "What are you talking about? You're not the boss, and this clown shouldn't be here anyway."

"Watch your mouth, Victor," Arbel said.

"Nor could you ever be."

"That's enough." Arbel's eyes were shooting sparks. I could see that he felt the control slipping between his fingers. "I wanted to talk to you before you left. If you don't want to answer, that will be okay with me. In fact, I would be grateful if you didn't. Now listen to me, and never forget what I say to you."

I leaned back in my chair. I found his manner offensive, but the power was his. "Once on the outside, you'll forget everything you have learned, done, heard, or otherwise understood is taking place here."

"I thought I'd get a chance to tell the boss what I think is wrong," I returned. "I know that what I say might not amount to much, but at least he could make a face like he's listening, the way he does when Brains here talks to him."

Naftaly shook his head but didn't say a word.

Arbel went on. "Well, as you can see, that isn't going to happen. Why don't you just spit out whatever it is you want to say? I'll pass it on to him."

"How about talking to the prime minister, if the boss won't talk to me?"

"You'll talk to me and that's it." He was losing his patience.

"In my employment contract, it says that upon involuntary termination of the contract, I will have a meeting with the head of the Mossad and/or the prime minister. It says the meeting will take place before final termination of employment." I moved closer to him, subconsciously defying his unlimited power.

He smirked at me. "I don't give a shit about your contract. Who are you going to complain to?" His voice was low. "Can't you see? We made that promise, and we can break it. We can do with you anything we want. I could put you in jail now and throw away the key. You know it's happened to others. You're like a mosquito on my head. You're starting to become a nuisance, and I'm about ready to crush you. So listen, Victor, get moving while you still have time."

"So does that mean no?" I knew I was pushing it.

"Are you hard of hearing? I said you're not talking to anyone. You're out of the loop, you're out of the game, and if you don't watch it, you'll be out of this world."

"What are you telling me?" I was almost whispering. "You'll kill me if I don't play it your way? If that's what you said, it's a first. I might have flunked an exercise, and, if you want to believe the stories, even screwed up an operation. But you know as well as I do that I'm one of the best field people you have, and I'm still a patriot, whether you like it or not, and it's starting to look like you might not be one. You might be responsible for the security of our country, but nobody has yet made you king." I got up and headed for the door.

"Don't you walk out on me." Arbel was now on his feet, shouting after me.

"Fuck all of you," I answered, not even turning around.

When I reached the door, Naftaly was at my side, breathing hard. The short run was too much for the little couch potato. I stopped and turned to face him. "What is it?"

"There is something I have to tell you, shall we say out of professional courtesy."

"I'm listening, but hurry up. I have a life to start."

"When I met you in the final testing stages, I wanted you out of the game. I knew you would be trouble, but I was overruled; they saw great operational potential in you, as they put it."

"Well, I'm out. That should make you very happy."

He turned red. "I'd like to take the credit for this, but unfortunately I can't. You turned several of the leadership against you all on your own."

"So what do you want from me?"

"I have a good psychological profile of you by now. After all, I have been observing you for several years. I know you have learned a lot in the courses and the short time you have spent in the field. Now you're an expert on how to kill, steal, forge, recruit, and break into places. Having learned all that, you're sent into the world with no real use for it."

"Does that scare you? Are you worried that I'll be coming for you or something?"

"Don't be ridiculous. I just want to tell you that you have a basic problem, and you should look after it or it will kill you." He paused, then went on, "You have what I call in novice's terms a fear deficiency."

"What?"

Not one muscle moved in his pudgy face. "I'm not kidding. It was one of the main reasons they picked you in the first place. Most people in the system have the same problem, but they have the system to take care of them. You don't have that anymore. Before you learned all the things you did in the Mossad, it didn't matter." He paused. "You have gotten and will get into trouble because you're not afraid of the consequences. If you would consider the fact that fear is a protective mechanism we have, the lack of it is a deficiency. What you should remember is to analyze everything you are about to do. You don't have natural fear to rely on."

"So what you're telling me is, Find a job doing something that doesn't call for what I've learned here?"

"Yes, that will be preferable." He lowered his head and looked at the tips of his shoes.

"Tell your boss it didn't work. You're probably right; nothing seems to scare me."

"It will kill you if you don't watch out, Victor."

"And a good day to you." I headed for my car. I was angry.

Once I was inside the tiny blue box, my car, it hit me. This is it. Once I start my car and drive the three hundred feet to the gate, it will all be over. Everybody I knew in the Mossad will now be a stranger to me. From this point on, all my access to information and the power that comes with it will be gone.

I couldn't comprehend it. Life after the Mossad—it sounded like an oxymoron. I felt like a figure plucked from one of Dali's surrealistic paintings and set down in the real world, a world where people are only the size they were born to be and can do only what is allowed, a place where rules are meant to be followed, not broken.

I felt like throwing up, and at the same time, I wanted to punch someone. I started the car and headed for the gate. I remembered entering this place a happy cheerful man, curious and anxious, like a child allowed into Aladdin's treasure cave. Now here I was heading in the other direction, bitter, beaten, and betrayed.

I stopped at the gate, waiting for it to open. I was staring ahead when I heard a knock on my window. It was a perimeter guard. I rolled down the glass, not even looking at the man. "What?"

"I was told to get your entry card, please."

I wanted to say something mean, but his expression was apologetic. He wasn't sure what to do or say. I drew the white card out of my pocket and handed it to him. "Now could you guys open the bloody gate and let me out of this shit hole?"

The gate moved quickly. Not waiting for it to open all the way, I slammed the gas pedal to the floor. The small wheels spun, and I sped into the night.

I knew I should be heading home, but I just couldn't go there yet. I knew that once I told Bella I was out, it would become a full reality.

The rain did not let up. I drove slowly through the streets of Tel Aviv. Everything seemed gray and dull. Before, there'd been a challenge in everything; now there was nothing. No one was following me, and I had nowhere to report. I was mortal again, kicked out of heaven. It was time to go home and try to put my life back together.

CHAPTER 6

It was almost midnight when I pulled into my parking stall under my apartment building in Herzelia. As I locked the car, I heard someone calling from inside the storage room, "Victor."

I stepped back.

"Don't be alarmed, I'm here to pick you up and take you to a meeting."

I tried to see who was talking to me, but all I could discern was a dark figure leaning on the wall inside the storage room. I reached over and flicked the switch to turn on the light. I wasn't surprised when it didn't work. "Who are you?"

"Only a messenger. I can't answer any of your questions, but you have nothing to worry about. . . ." He stopped talking for a minute, listening to something through a receiver he had in his ear. "Like I said," he went on, "you've got nothing to worry about. You weren't followed on your way here. Except for myself, there was no surveillance on this building either." He opened the screen door and stepped out closer to me. "Shall we go?"

"Is this some sort of joke?"

"Believe me, it's no joke. Look, if we wanted to harm you, we could have done it even before your meeting with Arbel, okay?"

Nobody outside the Mossad could have said what this man just did. I could feel adrenaline rush into my system. Deep inside, I hoped the Mossad was calling me back.

"There's a black Lancia parked across the street. Get in the back seat. They'll take you to the meeting."

"Why can't I take my car?"

"Don't worry, they'll bring you back."

"Okay, but first I need to tell my wife I'm going. She'll be worried if she sees my car and I'm not around."

"As long as it doesn't take too long."

"Look"—I was ready to get mad at anything at that point—"it will take as long as it takes. You on the other hand can go back into that little room over there and lay an egg as far as I'm concerned."

"Sorry, go ahead. We'll wait for you, but please make it fast, okay?"

His tone sounded much better; for a moment there I thought I'd found the face I was supposed to slug that day.

I rang the intercom. "Yes?" Bella's voice sounded tired.

"It's me."

"Aren't you coming up?"

"I will in a while. Some people from the Office were waiting for me here. We're going for a short ride. I'm okay."

"You don't sound okay. Are you sure you should go?"

"It's nothing to worry about."

"Why don't they come up? I'll make some coffee."

"I don't think that would work. They're waiting. I have to go. I'll be back soon. Don't worry, everything's fine." She didn't answer. I knew she'd given up. No other woman would have put up with me as long as Bella had. I loved her but at the same time found it very difficult to show her that. Telling her was easy enough; showing her was something else again. I stood there, staring at the silent black intercom. I wanted to run upstairs, hold her in my arms, and show her how much I loved her. Instead, I turned and headed for the car.

As I settled into the front seat of the man's car, I felt nothing. It was what we'd call operational numbness. You have a small pain in the base of your chest, more like a slight discomfort. That's your personal feelings. They're compressed into a small controllable zone, your so-called tragedy spot, while your consciousness is in receiving mode, pumped up and ready to take in information that will decide how you should react.

It was as if I had awakened from a dream and then, while still awake, stepped back into it. At this stage, there could be only two options: either they wanted me back, or they were going to have a "talk" with me. By "talk," I mean straighten me out so that I wouldn't start something that could damage the Mossad.

After a ten-minute drive, we came to a stop behind an abandoned warehouse in the industrial area of Herzelia. A car was parked by the building. I spotted two men seated in it when our car shone its lights on them momentarily. "They're waiting for you over there," said the driver, not turning his head.

I got out and headed for the parked car. One man was now standing by it, his back to me. When I got to about five feet from him, he turned to face me. He then opened the car door just enough to turn on the interior light. What I saw was not registering. It was Ephraim, the officer who had constantly tried to get me fired. Seated next to him was a uniformed officer I recognized instantly. It was a brigadier general from the tank brigades. I had respected the man for a long time and had had several opportunities to work with him during combined exercises involving the armored divisions and the navy.

I climbed into the backseat. The driver closed the door behind me and headed over to the other car.

Introducing himself as if we'd never met, Ephraim extended his hand and said, "I'm very happy to meet you again."

I was dumbfounded, a situation I don't find myself in very often.

"Well, aren't you going to shake my hand?"

"No, I don't see why I should. You're a liar. You said things about me that weren't true, and they believed you."

The general was silent, relighting his pipe every few minutes, filling the car with a sweet cherry smell. Ephraim was a heavyset man—about five foot nine. His hairline was receding, and his thin light hair was neatly combed to one side. He wore gold-rimmed glasses that he kept tucking back up into place with his index finger as they slid down his nose.

His voice was soft, and he made a pleasant first impression on most people. "Okay, I'll get straight to the point, then you can ask all the questions you want. Are you up to thinking?"

"Is this a trick question? Can I stop thinking?"

"No, but after what you went through today, you might not be thinking too clearly. Never mind." He offered me a cigarette and took one himself. With a friendly smile, the general held out his lighter.

"You didn't get yourself thrown out," Ephraim went on, "you were set up. Don't kid yourself, though. You would have gotten kicked out sooner or later. It was better all around that it be sooner." He paused, looking at me over his gold-rimmed glasses. "Before we go any further, I want you to know that there's nothing you or I can do about it. So whether you help us or not, you can't go back."

"Wait, you're going too fast for me. Who set me up, and why? What the hell do you mean, I can't go back? If you know I've been set up, you could turn it around. I will bloody insist you fucking do that. Do you have any idea what being a Mossad case officer means to me? What are you, some sort of a god?"

"Cut the crap, Victor. What you want is the life that comes with the job. You want to keep your dick employed and have the glory like the rest of us, and that's okay."

"So how come when it's the rest of you it's okay, and when it's me I'm out?"

"You're not out because of that." The two men exchanged glances. Ephraim went on. "There are those who believe the Mossad exists for them to use. We have to stop them, before it's too late."

"Too late? Too late for what?"

"They'll lead us into a war, just as they have done already in Lebanon."

It was no secret that the relationship the right-wingers within the Mossad had with Bashir Gemayel, the charismatic playboy leader of the Christian militias who was elected president of Lebanon, had developed into a full-fledged love affair. In the sea of hatred that surrounded Israel, the Mossad had supposedly found an ally in the Christian thugs of Lebanon. The irony was that the hatred others felt was bolstered by the Mossad to maintain the status quo, forcing Israel to maintain a strong military machine instead of succumbing to the weakness of peace and its so-called dividends.

"One minute, please." I raised my hands as if I were trying to stop a ball headed for my chest. "What does all this have to do with me? I'm out of the game or, as Arbel said, I'm out of the loop."

"Don't believe everything you hear, or see for that matter. There is a lot you don't know. You're going to have to trust me."

"Trust you? I don't know you from a fucking hole in the wall, and what I do know of you, I don't really like. You lied about me and you were probably the reason behind me getting kicked out of the—"

Suddenly it dawned on me: He did get me kicked out. He wanted me for himself, for something he wanted me to do outside the system. I'd heard of things like this done in other agencies. When there's a problem in the system, you get a man kicked out, then you use him to do things for you—he's well trained, knows the business, and remains ditched.

"Look, I know how you feel, but you'll have to trust me, which is why I brought the general. You know him, don't you?"

I looked at the rugged face staring at me from the front seat. The general's eyes pierced through me. I nodded.

"Good, now listen carefully. We don't have much time."

"Why, what's the rush?"

"Your friends are not so sure about you. Some think you might be back, others think you might become very noisy, with what you know."

"What are you telling me?"

"They want you out of the way. You know, dead. You wouldn't be the first one."

"So, what, they'll shoot me? Or run me over?"

"No, they'll have you called for reserves and posted as a liaison officer to the South Lebanese army. How long do you think you'll live in South Lebanon?"

"They know me there as Mossad," I said with a bitter smile. "Probably a few hours. Sure would be a neat way to do away with me. There is only one flaw in that plan."

"Really?" Ephraim said.

"Yes, according to regulations, I can't be called up for reserves before I cool off for one year. Then I can only be posted in what is regarded a safe environment."

"You have friends in the navy, don't you?"

"Yes."

"Why don't you call one of them and see if you're being called up or not. Just so you know, the paperwork is already on the way. If you're not out of the country in a day or two, you're a dead man."

It was starting to sink in. Up to this point, it was as though we were talking about someone else, a hypothetical situation. But we weren't. We were talking about me and about my demise. I didn't feel scared. I was tense, the muscles in my neck stiffening. I stared out the back window into the black night. In my mind, I could see myself in a ditch on the side of the road leading to Marj Uyun.

"What can I do?" I was calm. "If the papers are already in preparation, the military won't give me a release. Without that bloody paper and computer confirmation, I can't get out of the country. I would appreciate if you could take me home now so I could spend what little time I have left with my family."

"Do you really think we'd drive out in such a night and sit in a car and wait, just to tell you what is going to happen without some sort of a solution?"

I smiled. "I'm listening."

"When you get home, you'll tell your wife that you were kicked out of the Mossad. You will then tell her that you just met with some friends who told you that you should get out of the country fast."

"What do I do for money?"

"Sell that clunker of a car."

"What can I get for that?"

"Just to get out of the country, you'll need about five grand."

"The car isn't worth more than two."

"Put a sign on it and sell it for six. Trust me, you'll sell it. Then get a ticket on Tower Air to London. You will arrive at Gatwick Airport. Stay at the Skyway Hotel. I'll contact you there."

"Why are you doing this? What's in it for you? What do you want from me?"

"You have my offer. I recommend you take it. I'll tell you the rest when we meet in London—that is, if you get there." He got out of the car and walked around to the driver's seat.

"Do what he asks you to, Victor," said the general in a rasping voice. "Trust him, it'll be good all around."

"What about the military release?"

Not turning his head, Ephraim handed me a small manila envelope. "The papers are in order and registered on the computer. They will expire in seventy-two hours. And if you're not on your way to London before that, so will you."

CHAPTER 7

I walked silently back to the parked Lancia and got in. I ignored the two men in the front and lit a cigarette. I could feel my temples thumping. I'd been given a lot of information, yet there was little time to analyze it. One thing was clear: If I decided to go along with Ephraim and his people—and it was obvious to me that there were more people involved than just Ephraim and the general—I would have to see it through to the end, whatever "it" was. This was the ultimate decision: If you're right you live, if not you're dead.

If what Ephraim had said was true, and I had little doubt it was, then there was a good chance that even *his* help wasn't going to get me out of this mess. He headed a powerful clique in the Mossad, but his power was apparently limited. Otherwise there wouldn't have been any need for me to run away. Of course, there was always a chance that this London trip was a setup to get me to run so the Mossad could nail me. The possibilities seemed endless.

The car came silently to a stop about a block from my building. Staring ahead, the driver said, "Last station." He didn't want to be seen near my house, should it now be under surveillance.

I stepped out into the cold night, put my hands in my pockets, and walked slowly home. What was I supposed to tell Bella now? Honey, they kicked me out and now they want to kill me, so I'll be leaving for England.

I stopped by the intercom, my insides churning. What was I supposed to say to someone I loved and at the same time had kept out of everything until now? My excuse was always that I wanted to protect her; what bullshit—I knew that it had been easier not telling her, until now.

I found myself standing there, looking for a new story, rather than the truth. I was beginning to think that there was no truth left in me.

Maybe it would be better just to go up there and say nothing, do nothing, and wait for the call from the army that would solve everything. I would answer my country's call, put on my uniform, and go where they sent me. By the weekend, it would all be over. A military funeral with all the honors. It was even possible that the prime minister would show up for that; after all, I was a colonel. He would have it exactly the way he wanted it; he could talk, and no one would answer.

Why go through the hassle of trying to stay alive? What was the point? This might just be the best thing that had ever happened to me; I would do something right, permanently.

But I was not the type to lie down and play dead. If there was a chance I could make it, I was going to go for it, no matter how slim that chance was. So there I was, my cigarette almost at its end, and still with no idea what I would tell Bella.

I prayed she wouldn't give up on me. I threw the cigarette butt into a small puddle and headed upstairs. I knocked on the door, and Bella, after peeping through the spy hole, opened. She left the door ajar and walked into the living room. She was in a soft white robe, her dark hair shining. Her fresh clean smell made me feel even more like a swamp monster.

There was no smile on her beautiful face; it seemed as though there hadn't been a smile on it for quite some time.

She sat on the sofa, pulling up her legs and folding her arms across her chest. I was uneasy, yet at the same time I knew this was my place; I belonged. Everything that was dear to me was in this cozy apartment.

I remembered the first time I had laid eyes on her. I was sixteen, and she was walking toward me on the sidewalk with a good friend of mine. She wore a dark blue sweater with a white stripe across the chest and a white ribbon in her black wavy hair. Before she said a single word, I was in love. Remorse for the agony I had caused her was gnawing at me. I knew she could see through me.

"So what was that all about?" she asked, her voice carrying an ironic tone, as if to say, Why don't you tell me another story?

I sat across from her; my mind was already made up. "They kicked me out." I felt the lump in my throat as I said the words. "I'm no longer with the Office."

She stared at me, not knowing how to take it, her legs lowered as she leaned forward. "If they kicked you out, why did they come and talk to you downstairs?"

"Someone came to tell me that it would be a good idea if I got out of the country."

She was up on her feet, one hand running through her hair as if to find a solution to a problem that suddenly was hers to solve. "What are you talking about, leave? Leave where, why, when?"

I got up and went over to her, took her in my arms. There was something radiating from her that soothed the dull pain in the base of my chest. She was drawing me out of the melancholic coma I'd been in for so long. "Calm down, it's going to be all right."

She pushed me away. "Where will you go? What about us? I told you this would happen. It's all those so-called friends of yours, Yosy and Haim and all the others. What will they do to you if you stay?"

"I don't know. You know what they can do."

Bella was well aware of my politics; in fact, her own opinions were a beacon to me when, as a result of peer pressure, I occasionally strayed toward the right. However, not wanting to show her how correct she was when it came to my "friends" in the Mossad, I kept from her most of the details of the political turf wars at the Office.

She dropped back into the sofa. "Where will you go?"

"I thought about flying to England and from there to the States. I'll stay with my dad for a while and then we'll see."

"Why England?"

"That would be the cheapest flight. And then I could get a charter from England to the States."

"So when will you be leaving?"

I sat next to her on the sofa and pulled her toward me. "The day after tomorrow."

She threw her head against my chest. She was crying. I wanted to pull her face up so that I could kiss her, but she wouldn't let me.

"I love you, Bella," I said, the lump in my throat growing, choking me. I hugged her as hard as I could. I wanted the moment to last. I knew reality was going to tear us apart, and I had no idea for how long. In the back of my mind, I wasn't sure I'd get to see her again. I didn't even want to think about what Ephraim had in store for me. Had it been merely terrible, he would have told me about it and given me a chance to volunteer.

We sat there on the sofa for a long time, holding each other. We were married when we were nineteen and had gone out since we were sixteen; I always saw us as two parts of a single human being, I the yang and she the yin. I knew she loved me in a way I never deserved, and I loved her more than anything.

We had two beautiful daughters who were now—I hoped—asleep. The apartment we were living in was rented, and except for the car and a few pieces of furniture, we didn't have much. The Mossad salary was good, but it didn't allow for a lot of luxury. That was reserved for the case officers in the field, not for their families.

Friday, March 28, 1986

I got up early and showered before my two daughters were up. I wanted to wake them with a kiss and start their day off on the right foot. I had the state of mind of a man who is about to die and has accepted the fact.

It was the memory of a loving father that I somehow wanted to burn into their minds. I wanted to do it fast, in an instant with one big hug, because there was no way I could reach back into the past and hand them all the time I had stolen from them. I swore that should I make it through this, whatever "this" was, I would never leave their side again. Guilt over not spending more time with them was always with me. Nevertheless, we were very close. It was extremely important to me that they know how much they meant to me.

Less than an hour after I had put the For Sale sign on the car and parked it on the curb across from my building, the phone rang.

"I'm calling about the car," said what sounded like a young man.

"What would you like to know?"

"How much are you asking for it?"

"Six thousand American," I said, trying not to laugh.

"Can I come and take it for a spin?"

"Sure, when did you have in mind? You see, I have things to do and . . . "

"In about twenty minutes."

"Great, I'll meet you by the car."

"My name is Boaz, and you are . . . ?"

"Victor, my name is Victor."

"See you, then." I had no doubt it was one of Ephraim's people coming to take the car and give me the money so that I could leave. This whole charade had to be played out because the home phones of Mossad officers were frequently monitored by Mossad security. I knew that if they were listening, they too would laugh at the price, but they'd probably just think I'd landed a sucker.

By noon that day, I'd purchased my tickets and was back home, stuffing a reduced version of my diary and a set of photographs of almost all Mossad field officers into a stash I'd prepared in my suitcase. It had to be perfect. I couldn't afford to be caught with such a stash on hand. I'd kept the pictures after using them to prepare a comical graduation photo for our case officers' course. This was going to be my insurance; if Ephraim turned out to be not what he seemed or if anyone at any stage tried to stop my family from joining me, I would strip the Mossad of all its field personnel in one day, forcing it to cease operations for a very long time.

There was more explosive material packed into that suitcase than had ever hit the Mossad in a single blow.

My flight was Sunday at noon. Bella and I decided to tell the children the morning of my flight; she would keep them home until she knew my flight had taken off. There was no point in spreading the news; many of my ex-comrades were living in the same area as I was, and I wasn't sure who might try to stop me if they could.

Sunday, March 30

I got out of the cab at the airport. I licked my lips and tasted Bella's perfume, which had rubbed off when I kissed her tiny earlobe. The girls were sad to see me go again, but they didn't notice a difference from the other times I'd packed and gone on duty. I took solace in that.

I had two suitcases and a carry-on bag with me. I headed for the Tower Air counter, at the eastern end of the Ben-Gurion terminal. The flight was to leave at 14:00 and it was now only 11:30. It was standard procedure in the Israeli airport to request that passengers arrive two to three hours before departure. Most passengers dropped off their luggage the night before at the special counter adjacent to the North Tel Aviv train station. There was no way, though, that I was going to leave my luggage somewhere overnight with the papers I had stashed in it, nor would I want to give anyone the opportunity to plant something in it.

The Tower Air ground crew wasn't there yet, and there were no more than five passengers standing in line waiting to check their luggage and get their boarding cards. In fact, there were two lines, and I was the first in one. I sat on the stainless steel table used by the security people to go through the luggage. I usually felt good at this airport.

I knew most of the security watch commanders, and most of them knew me. I had brought into the country and taken out scores of people, most of whom could say they were never in Israel. And except for some photos stored in the Mossad filing system, no one could prove them wrong. The feeling I had that day was very strange. Here I was in a place where only a few days ago, had I business there, I would have walked around like a peacock in heat, an arrogant snob, with the ability to have things done at a snap of my fingers.

Today, however, was different. I was already on the run, and even though no one was visibly after me, I knew it was a race against time. It turned out I was extremely lucky; at the beginning of the month, I'd had to get a real passport for a job, and had picked it up only a few weeks before. Since I'm a dual citizen, I'd also requested a new Canadian passport and had received that about a week later. This totally fortuitous circumstance would allow me to leave the country at the speed that I was about to attempt.

Feeling some apprehension, I looked across at the other line, where a heavyset blond bearded man was standing at the head of the line, nervously tapping on his pigskin attaché case.

The security watch officer's face was beaming as he walked in my direction. "Hey there, how are you?"

I guess he doesn't know yet, I thought—not that telling the security at the airport was high on anyone's list. "I'm fine. How are you?"

"Good, good." He paused. "Are you on business or pleasure?"

"A little of both, I guess. Why do you ask?"

"I want to ask you a favor." This was starting to sound bizarre.

"How can I help?" I was trying hard to keep smiling. I was also grateful for the short conversation that bridged the abyss of self-doubt and fear. I knew I didn't have to put on a show for him. He knew I couldn't really refuse him, even if I wasn't thrilled.

He leaned closer to me and said in a low voice, "We're breaking in a couple of new security people, a guy and a woman." He winked at me. "She's really something, you'll see." He leaned even closer. "Actually, I understand she's quite friendly, if you know what I mean."

"So you want me to seduce her or something?" I felt a deep dislike for the man and wanted him to get the hell away from me as soon as possible. On the other hand, I couldn't alter the fact that I had with me a wad of top-secret Mossad documents dealing with several foreign intelligence agencies, a stack of Mossad officer photos, and a detailed list of more than two thousand *sayanim* in Britain, France, and the United States. What was in my suitcase could get me a life sentence in a dingy prison, and he was leaning on it.

He laughed. Apparently, he found what I said amusing, not taking the offense intended in my tone. "No, no, I can do that. In fact, I probably will very soon. What I'd like you to do is exchange your passport with that guy over there." He nodded at the big guy heading the other line. "And then we'll see if the two of them realize what has happened, or for that matter if they notice anything."

"Did you talk to him?"

"What, you think he'd say no?"

I looked at the man. "No, I guess not. Sure, what the hell, I'll do it." As he was about to turn to the other man, I held him by the shoulder. He faced me again, smiling. "What?"

"If I do it, I want you to run me through to the other side like I was here on business." What I meant was that he should take me through all the stations, flashing his ID card and clearing the way for me.

"Sure. No problem."

I smiled, feeling the blood drain out of my face. A cold sensation took hold in my chest, as though a chill breeze were blowing through it.

This teeter-totter of emotion was something we were trained to deal with in the Mossad, since an officer always has personal feelings that could get in the way of the job he has to do. You learn how to create new feelings that will compensate for the ones you lack.

Less than one minute after the security officer had handed me the passport belonging to the big guy and given mine to him, the new crew arrived. I glanced quickly at the passport I'd been handed. It was an American passport, and the photo was a color close-up of the man standing next to me. The beard he now wore was not on the passport photo. That could stump the new crew. I read the name and tried to remember it. This was extremely amateurish; my real name was on my suitcase, and my ticket was in my real name. They would have to be extremely daft not to notice—unless there was something else behind it.

"Sir, your passport, please," said the woman. Her attitude was cordial and quite professional for someone who was the first time on the job. I could see what the officer had meant. She was indeed very pretty, which may have accounted for the nasty rumor someone had circulated, most likely out of envy. I stepped forward, leaving my luggage behind, my arm outstretched, passport in hand. I smiled at her. Her expression didn't change as she took the passport.

From the corner of my eye, I caught sight of Ephraim, leaning on the counter some forty feet from where I was. He was watching me. I couldn't make out any expression on his face. Was all this a charade to get me in the slammer; was the Lebanon story a ploy to get me to run and then catch me in this stupid exercise at the airport? I could hear it now as I tried to explain in court that a security officer had asked me to help in an exercise, etc., etc., and there would be no such officer to verify my story.

She took the passport, and I could see the big man handing in my passport to the other security officer.

"Your name?" she asked me.

"Robert Freidman."

She closed the passport and put it on the metal table in front of her. "Could you please place your luggage on the counter?"

"Sure, no problem." I turned to pick up my suitcases when I heard the other security man raise his voice at the big fellow. "Don't move, raise your hands above your head." He drew his gun, and within seconds several police were on the scene.

"What's the matter? What's going on?" asked the first to arrive, gun in hand.

"This man is traveling on a false passport." He turned to the big fellow, who was now feverishly searching for the security officer. His face was wet with sweat, his eyes staring down several gun barrels.

"This is a big mistake. Please don't shoot. This is only a game, ask him." He nodded to me, and at that moment the duty officer came back on the scene. "Everybody calm down. David, put your gun away." He turned to the policemen. "Everything is under control, this was only an exercise. You, sir." He was now talking to the man whose passport I was holding. "You can put your hands down. It's all over. Good work, David." He then turned to the girl. "Well, Sarah, would you mind giving that passport another look?"

Her eyes opened wide with the realization that she had done something wrong. She slowly picked up the passport and looked at the photo and then at me. I knew at that moment that no matter what might happen in the world over the next one hundred years, I wouldn't be able to get that girl to look on me kindly. She was silent.

The officer returned my passport to me and handed the big fellow his. He then said to Sarah, "I want you to report to me after work at my office in the prefabricated building. You know where that is?"

She nodded; there seemed to be a tear ready to roll out of the corner of her eye, but somehow she managed to hold it back. When the officer and I turned to head for the ticket counter, I saw her wiping her eye with the sleeve of her dark blue sweater.

The officer stuck to his promise, and after my ticket was in order and I got my boarding card, he escorted me through all the stations, getting my passport stamped and avoiding the body search that everyone else was put through. We had a cup of coffee on the second floor in the departure lounge, and after I'd bought myself a fresh pack of cigarettes and a copy of *Time* magazine, he got up to leave.

"Have a good flight, man, and thanks for the help."

"You're welcome, any time." About then, some of the other passengers made it to the departure area and were sitting down, getting ready for the almost two-hour wait for takeoff.

I began to feel a slight sense of relief. It wouldn't be over until I was actually aboard the plane and above the Mediterranean, but it was quickly getting there. Ephraim was seated at the far end of the departure lounge, reading a paper. It seemed to me at that stage that he was like a mother hen watching over her young, wanting to be sure that I got out safely. For now, his presence gave me a sense of security.

I called Bella from the pay phone on the outer wall of the duty-free store. I could hear from the tone of her voice how she was holding back the tears. The sound was more painful than if she had sobbed openly. We had a lot to say, but this was not the forum, given that we were probably not alone on the line. I knew they were not set up for a trace; as long as we didn't say where I was calling from and talked as if I were merely on my way to Elat, we were okay. Again I wanted to reach through the lines and hold her tight in my arms.

"I'll call you when I get there, okay?"

"Do it right away. I'll be waiting for your call."

"I love you."

"I love you too," she said. "Look after yourself and pay attention to what you wear so you don't look funny."

I chuckled. "Okay, I'll do that. Don't worry, I'll call you then."

"Bye."

I waited to hear her hang up; I couldn't hang up on her. Why such a precious woman loved me was far beyond my imagination. Looking back on our life, I really hadn't done much for her; I had never bought tickets to a show I knew she wanted to see or taken her on a surprise trip or had a surprise birthday party for her. In fact, I wasn't even there for her when she needed me, when she had an operation. Somehow, I had other things to do that seemed so much more important. They involved the security of our country. What bullshit, and not only did I dish it out, I believed it myself.

Two police officers entered the cafeteria where I was sitting. I could feel my blood pressure rising. Had someone noticed me and advised someone else? Were they here to stop me? I could smell the disinfectant used in Israeli prisons, having spent time in the cells as part of the exercises. Then there was that time in the military when I was caught without a hat and made to spend ten days in the military brig. I could hear the echo of the locking doors as metal hit metal. The policemen ordered coffee. Ephraim tensed too as he followed them with his eyes. I knew he was nervous and wanted to see me out of the country already.

I didn't catch the first announcement of the flight, but by the second, I was already in line, moving in the direction of the gate.

Within twenty minutes, we were aboard and taxiing to the runway. I closed my eyes. I didn't want to look at the tarmac and worry that every car crossing the runway would be the one that was there to stop the plane and take me off.

The person seated next to me seemed to be consumed by the view from the window. The person on my right was reading a newspaper article about the Swiss rejecting their government's proposal to join the UN. Nobody was bothering me, and that's the way I wanted to keep it. In general, I'm quite a talkative person, but in airplanes, trains, and buses, I prefer to keep to myself; the captive audience syndrome always jumps into my mind.

Seeing the sky through the window was very much like staring into paradise. I was free—for a few hours at least, beyond the Mossad's reach.

CHAPTER 8

MONDAY, MARCH 31, 1986, GATWICK, ENGLAND

Twenty-four hours had passed, and still no word from Ephraim. His restriction, that I should not call home before we talked, was making my life difficult. I hadn't spoken to Bella since calling her from the Ben-Gurion airport. By now, she must be climbing the walls with worry about me. Ephraim was concerned that my home phone might be bugged (there was little doubt it was) and that the Mossad would know I had made a prolonged stopover in England on my way to the States. Should something go wrong, Ephraim's also coming to England might not sit well.

I scanned the television for something to pass the time, but found it difficult to concentrate. At about ten-thirty in the morning I decided to head for London and get my mind off things for a while. I needed to loosen up, walk around, get something to eat. When Ephraim came, he would just have to wait.

I took a train into the city. The thirty-minute ride brought me to Victoria Station. From there I took the underground to Piccadilly, changing at Green Park. I wandered the streets aimlessly, eventually returning to the tube station. I had a couple of hamburgers at Wimpy, the British answer to McDonald's. Afterward, I headed back to the hotel.

In the elevator, I noticed the sweet aroma of cherry tobacco. It got stronger the closer I got to my room at the end of the pale green corridor. Standing at my door, I could all but taste the pipe. The only smell as strong as the cherry was the smell of the freshly painted walls, hanging heavy in the air.

I stood by the door and listened: Ephraim and the general. It was more the smell of the tobacco than the sound of their voices that brought recognition.

I entered the room quickly. They sat staring at me, bewildered.

"Why are you so surprised to see me?" I said. "Who were you expecting?"

"I asked you to wait for me at the hotel." Ephraim's voice was on the harsh side.

"I don't work for you, my friend. I'm here as a favor."

"I saved your life, remember? May I remind you of Lebanon?"

It was true that he had gotten me out of Israel before I could be sent to South Lebanon and a certain death. No doubt he would be reminding me of this over and over again in the future.

I tossed my coat onto the bed and sat on the edge.

"You only got me out of something you put me into, and probably in order to get me into something else." I smiled at him. "For the time being, I'm here to listen, then I'll make up my mind who I work for. So what I suggest you do is come out with it."

"Look here, Victor—" Ephraim started. The general put a hand on Ephraim's shoulder. "The man's right, why play games? We know what we want and why we want it. You've got a job for him, fill him in, bring him inside."

I could hear the tradition of the Israeli military speaking out of the brigadier general's mouth: An informed soldier is a good soldier.

Ephraim stared at me silently for a few seconds. He then leaned back and glanced at the general, who was relighting his pipe. "Let's start from the beginning, then."

"Just a minute," said the general, producing a large thermos from a brown leather tote bag at his feet. "Get some glasses from the bathroom. I need a coffee."

"I could use one too," I said, moving quickly to fulfill his request. Coffee was served.

"I'm listening." I said, sitting back on the bed.

"This all started in '82. You were still in the navy then. You probably know we were all preparing for the war in Lebanon. At that time, the operation was still called the Cedars of Lebanon, and we in the Mossad had a close relationship with Bashir Gemayel's Christian Phalange. Our man dealing with Gemayel was Nevot. Nevot was in the midst of getting Israel involved in what he and other right-wingers called the best war we'll ever have.

"They saw Israel as the policeman of the Middle East. Prime Minister Begin loved the idea of appearing to be saving Christians from the savage Muslims, which fit in well with his right-wing colonialist ideology. Ariel Sharon, then minister of defense, was all for it."

He paused to sip the hot coffee. Then he drew on his cigarette, letting the smoke out as he spoke. "Hofi, then head of the Mossad, was against the ploy, saying that the Christian Phalange in Lebanon was not a reliable ally. Military intelligence agreed with him. But Hofi, who'd been in office for almost eight years then, was on his way out.

"Many people in the Mossad were hoping that this time they would get an insider to run the show. As you well know, until that point it had always been an outsider who was parachuted into office."

I nodded. I knew this was the only way the outside world could ever have any control over the Mossad. A new chief from the outside—meaning the military—was a way to clean house.

"Many were hoping that an ex-Mossad officer would be brought in—someone like David Kimche, who was then director general of the foreign office and had been a department head in the Mossad before he had a clash with Hofi. Then there was Rafael Eitan, whom Begin admired but thought was too close to Ariel Sharon. Begin was worried that Sharon would have too much power if his friend was head of Mossad.

"Begin decided that he would keep with tradition and have an outsider take office." Ephraim paused. When he started to talk again, there was something different in his voice; he sounded angry, restless.

"At that point, when the war was about to start and Hofi already had one foot out of the Mossad, the right-wing element managed to place many of their members in positions of power.

"In fact, all of us in the Mossad were getting tired of having our future plans shattered and changed every time a new boss came. And the right-wingers especially were not going to give up what they'd grabbed. It was a coup d'état, the only difference being that there was no état to coup at the time.

"General Yekutiel Adam, or Kuti, as he was called by his friends, was appointed head of the Mossad and was supposed to take office some time at the end of June 1982. The war in Lebanon started on June 6, and by the second day of the war, Kuti had a run-in with Sharon regarding the attack on the Syrian antiaircraft missiles in the Beka'a. Kuti believed and stated clearly that this might lead to all-out war with the Syrians. He was undermining the effort the Mossad, in combination with Gemayel, had worked so hard and so long to mount. Certain elements realized what was coming if this man became the new chief. Someone decided that it was not to be."

"Kuti was my best friend," the general spat out.

"He had friends in the Mossad," continued Ephraim, "people who were preparing working papers analyzing the situation so that he could take drastic action once he took office and not spend time wasting the lives of young soldiers who were at the time being used as cannon fodder for the right-wingers' dream of a Mossad-run state in Lebanon. Using the philosophy known as the 'balance of weakness,' they believed that they could be the power behind Gemayel's puppet regime, forgetting what every Lebanese child knew—that anyone could swallow Lebanon but no one could digest it.

"It was clear that the power of the right-wingers was threatened; once Kuti took control, he'd pass an honest assessment of the situation to the government and to Sharon, who wouldn't want to be the first Israeli minister of defense to lose a war." Ephraim paused, sipping his coffee. "The opportunity came on June 10. The army had entered the outskirts of Beirut, and there was a cease-fire in effect. Kuti, appointed to head the Mossad but not yet in office, requested a farewell visit to his troops in Lebanon. It was the Mossad's job to organize it."

"Why the Mossad? Why not the IDF?[1]" I asked.

"Because he was already the responsibility of the Mossad security and out of the hands of the military."

"If he *had* been our responsibility," the general interjected, "he would still be alive today."

"They planned the visit for the next day." Ephraim's voice was low. "When Kuti arrived at the location, he was killed in an ambush. The attacker, a fourteen-year-old kid, was killed on the spot by the guards."

"You're crazy." I got up. "That's crazy." I could not believe what he was implying. It was too weird.

He looked straight at me, his voice low and hoarse. "They found a photo," he said, "a photo of Kuti on the kid. Who else would have known Kuti was there except the people who planned his sudden little trip? The Mossad—or rather, elements within the Mossad—killed him, there is no doubt in my mind."

"So you wait four years and then tell me about it?"

"No, you're the latest step that we are taking. You have to realize that working against the Mossad from the inside is not the easiest thing in the world to do."

"So no one asked how come that photo was found in the killer's pocket?"

"That particular piece of information was kept from the investiga-

---

1. IDF: Israeli Defense Force.

tive committee—the one piece of evidence that proves beyond a shadow of a doubt that it was not a coincidence, but in fact a calculated murder."

I sat back on the bed. I could feel the cold sweat on my forehead. What he was telling me was unbelievable. Mossad members conspiring to kill the newly appointed head? This was far too much to accept.

"You're crazy."

"He's not crazy," said the general. "I know, because he's not the only one who told me. I found out more about it when I interrogated a captured Hizballah fighter in the south of Lebanon in the beginning of '85. He was talking about how, when he was in Nabih Berri's Amal Shi'ite militia, he was supposed to go with a kid on a mission to kill an Israeli general, and let me tell you, the man was not lying."

"How do you know?"

"Because he knew he was going to die, and the question was whether it was going to take all night or just a few minutes. And he thought that I knew about it anyway."

While I didn't want to believe what I was hearing, it was hard to argue with the facts. Yes, it was possible for a terrorist group to obtain a photograph of an Israeli general and give it to one of their assassins, prefatory to staging a hit. But it was inconceivable that a photograph could be obtained and a plan concocted on such short notice—all while the Mossad napped. I stared at the general for a few seconds, then turned to Ephraim. "How come you didn't go to the prime minister?"

"And say what? Sir, right-wing elements within the Mossad have just killed the appointed head. What do you think he'd say? Thanks for telling me. I'll call the bastards and fire them. Besides, there was a war going on at the time, remember. Within the next day or two, at the most, I would have had an accident of my own."

"How do I know you're not just setting me up, and it's you who wants to stage a coup d'état?"

"You have to trust me. We can't do this without someone on the outside."

"I'm listening."

"I think this would be a good time to have something to eat," Ephraim said.

I wasn't hungry and wanted him to go on, but I decided to play it his way for now.

"The hotel has a restaurant," I said. "I just hope their dinner is better than their breakfast."

The two men laughed. "No," said Ephraim. "I don't think leaving

the room would be a good idea. There's always the chance that someone will spot us, and that we cannot afford. Ramy will go out and
bring us something." He turned to the general. "If that's okay with
you?"

"I'm on my way," Ramy said slowly, the pipe in one side of his
mouth as he spoke from the other. He put on his coat. I couldn't help
noticing how unimpressive he was in civilian clothing.

After the general left, I turned to Ephraim. "You screwed up my
life," I said.

"I did no such thing. All I did was pick you out of a specially
selected group of people, just before you were going to self-destruct
anyway. And you were right for the job."

"But you never asked me. How do you know I wouldn't prefer to
be on the other side of the barricade, fighting people like you who
supposedly want to relinquish control of the Mossad into the hands of
parachuted amateurs rather than leave it in the hands of professionals
who rose through the ranks?" I stopped and stared into Ephraim's
almost skull-like face, with its thick pale skin deeply lined, like that of
a veteran sailor parched by the salty sea air.

"I have your psychological profile, remember. I know you probably better than you know yourself, Victor. You would not fit into that
category."

"The Mossad's psychological profile of me isn't worth the paper
it's written on."

"If you turned out to be a psychological mistake, I'd go to phase
two."

"And what is that?"

"I can't tell you yet. But let me tell you a short story, before our
friend the general comes back."

"Why? You have secrets from him too?" I was as sarcastic as I
could be.

"Yes. In fact, I probably have more secrets from him than I have
from you. He's not from the inside, and there are a lot of things he
cannot understand. I don't want to destroy the Mossad, which is
something he would be happy to do. I want to fix it."

"Why?"

"Because I believe our country needs a Mossad, a strong Mossad
with teeth that can tear our enemy apart. But above all, it needs a
leash so that it can be kept under control."

"You were going to tell me a story."

"In '82, before the war in Lebanon, we had a man working the
turf, trying to get some sort of a dialog started. He was one of my

group then. I wasn't the leader of the group, but we had the blessing of Hofi and some people in the foreign office who were waiting for a breakthrough. We had the Palestinians so scared of what we might do in Lebanon that they were willing to start talking."

"So you were attempting to make a link?"

"Yes, not with the Christians, with the Palestinians. We put one of our better men forward. His name was Yakov Barsimantov. He was stationed in Paris, working liaison."

"He couldn't make contact and be trusted by any Palestinian. If he was liaison, they had to know he was Mossad," I interjected.

"He wasn't working directly with them. We had an American go-between who had volunteered to give this thing a nudge. Barsimantov presented it to him as a sort of dare, during a cocktail party at the French foreign office."

"And he agreed?"

"He jumped at the opportunity. Mind you, he himself was not in the best position to talk to the Palestinians. It was against State Department regulations, but he went for it anyway."

"Why didn't you use some other contact, like the Romanians or something? They were working both sides of the fence, and you had dealings with them."

"They were tied directly to the top clique. All they wanted was to back up the Phalangists and Bashir Gemayel."

"Who was the American?"

"His name was Charles Robert Ray. He was assistant military attaché and a very dedicated man. He believed that peace in the Middle East was in the strategic interest of the U.S."

"There's a twist on military thinking."

Ephraim chuckled, "Right. But that was the case. Someone in the foreign office must have leaked it out, and both Barsimantov and the American were shot before they could make the first contact with the Palestinians. So we know for sure it wasn't the Palestinians." He ran his fingers through his hair, then over his face. He suddenly seemed older, more tired than before. "They killed Ray in January, and when Yakov was about to make a new contact, they killed him too. Yakov was a good man, yet on April 3, outside his apartment, he was gunned down like a dog by his own people. Our own hit team took him out."

"But the Kidon wouldn't kill an Israeli."

"They didn't know who the target was, and later it was said to be a mistake. After they killed Yakov, they stashed the Czech-made gun in the apartment of a Lebanese revolutionary, pointing the finger at him. They went so far as to claim responsibility for the hit under the name of the Lebanese Armed Revolutionary Faction, informing the French intelligence that the LARF was a faction of the pro-Syrian SSNP, the Syrian Social Nationalist Party." He turned and gazed out the window. "Do you know, they had the audacity to try and use the killing as the provocation they were waiting for to start the war in Lebanon. If there was ever something you could call chutzpah, that would be it."

What surprised me most was the fact that what I'd just heard didn't surprise me one bit. I believed him, and yet I almost said, So what? What I did say was not that different. "Okay, you told me a short story. How is that supposed to explain why I should want to do anything for you?"

Ephraim sighed. "What I wanted to tell you is that I can't use someone from inside because I don't have a clue who I can trust. The general has been a buddy of mine for years, and he was a close friend of Kuti's. So he's clean as far as I'm concerned. You I have taken straight from the womb, you're not yet tainted, and unlike most of your friends, you didn't come in on the back of a horse but through the normal recruiting process. You came in because you were a patriot and not because you wanted to make a career."

"Well, I wanted that too. I wanted the job, the life, the fun."

"If you want the life, stick around. You'll get more than you can handle."

"So what now? Are you going to offer me a job?"

"That is exactly what I'm doing. Your cover will be you. Everything you do will be on your own; you have no net and no tether. I will hand you an assignment and help you as much as I can, but you will be out there on your own."

"Doing what?"

"You'll be putting the present Mossad out of business."

CHAPTER 9

There was a knock on the door. Ephraim stiffened. I walked to the door and stared through the peephole. It was the general. I swung the door open, and he entered as though the corridor were on fire. He clearly didn't enjoy playing the spook.

For the next hour we ate. Very little was said, and the atmosphere was like the beer: lukewarm. I was trying to place myself in the scheme of things, but I didn't see a purpose or an end result. Sure, I knew he said he wanted to fix the Mossad, but what did that mean?

From what I could guess, he was out to destroy it first, and that I could relate to. What I wasn't sure of was whether the Mossad he wanted to build out of the ashes would be any better than the one we had. Was his notion of a cleaner and better Mossad the same as mine? And if not, why should I align myself with him? I was out on my own; why not stay that way?

I decided to listen to whatever Ephraim had to say and then do what I wanted. I was a Canadian citizen with a valid Canadian passport, and at this point he could not intimidate me.

At the same time, there was a voice inside me that said I had tasted the life and I liked it; it was hard to turn your back on it. I was like the soldiers whose war ends on them too soon, before they've had a chance to get it out of their system, so they roam the world looking to keep that war alive, to live on the edge, and the sharper the edge the better. Was I one of them now, testing the limit?

"So what next?" the general asked, wiping his hands. Smears of fish and chips and ketchup stuck stubbornly to his fingers. Ephraim stood up. "We'll be leaving shortly, and Victor here will leave tomorrow."

"I will?"

"Yes, you are going to New York, and then you will go visit your dad in Nebraska."

"Why New York?"

"Because that way we'll know if someone is on to you or not."

"You're not sure? What do you mean?" The general sounded alarmed. This was one thing he hadn't considered. Suddenly, fighting the Mossad had taken on a whole new meaning.

"We're never sure, but there is a way to find out."

"How?" the general asked. I had a feeling I wasn't going to like the answer.

"Victor here will go visit the PLO office in New York. If all the lights and bells go off in headquarters, we'll know that he has a tail."

"I thought you people could check these things yourselves?" The general's face was serious.

"We can," Ephraim said, "but we can never be sure. There is a limit to what we can do. If the team on our tail is big enough, we cannot detect them. That is something we cannot risk."

"What if someone in the PLO office is working for Mossad, what then?" I asked.

"We don't have anyone working there. And even if we did, it would take time for the message to get through, and by then you'd be out of there."

"Okay." I tried to strengthen my point. "What if someone runs with the information and volunteers it to the embassy? I'll be history before I can leave the city."

"You will not tell them who you are. What you will do is go in and tell them you are an Israeli sympathizer, something along those lines."

"But how will that help what we want to do?" The general was now sucking hard on his pipe as if he wanted to turn it inside out. He kept looking at the door. I could see this wasn't his game; he liked to see his enemy and measure him up. A brave man, no doubt, but somewhat afraid of the dark.

"Victor here will be asked to do things in the near future that are extremely dangerous. He will have to do them in places much less hospitable than New York. Before I send him to those places, I want to be sure. If there's a problem with his cover or if someone suspects him of wrongdoing, this is the time to find out about it—when he is in the United States, where it is more difficult for the Mossad to operate. If they're watching us now, they will want to see what comes next. So we'll hand it to them on a platter; if they're on our tail, as soon as he enters the PLO office, they'll almost instantly arrest me and you." Small beads of perspiration appeared on the general's forehead. Ephraim continued, "If that happens, then of course we won't contact Victor. That will be his sign that it's time to get lost, and I mean lost. But if nothing happens, we know that we're clean."

"How will he get lost?" The general's voice quivered slightly.

"He shouldn't have a problem with that. After all, he did get what probably amounts to the best training for that in the world, or at least we'd like to think so."

The general cleared his throat, then asked, "What will they do to us?"

"We went through that before." Ephraim was getting annoyed. "I thought you understood."

"I do. It's just that I didn't . . . " He hesitated.

"Didn't what? Do you want to back out? Because if you do, say so now, before we make one more move. After today, there won't be a way out. We are rapidly approaching the point of no return. Once Victor leaves for New York, we're committed."

"That's very nice of you," I said, raising my voice at Ephraim. "You're letting him back out, and you didn't even let me decide if I want to get on board."

"You don't understand. I was talking about *him*. If he wants out he can get out, but we are committed. In fact, if he leaves now and we are under surveillance, then he'll be put away just like I will, and like they'll try to do to you. He can, however, walk away if it turns out we're clean."

The general got up, shaking his head. I had a feeling he was starting to get my drift, and was worried it would not be reversible in a matter of seconds. "I don't want out. It's just that it's starting to get very real to me now. I never played this game before, and I had no idea what I was getting into. It's not what we are about to do that gives me the creeps, it's how. What I want to know is this: If they catch us, what do you think they will do to us?"

"You can relax if you're worried about standing trial, because you won't. They can't afford that. They'll settle matters with us behind closed doors; an accident perhaps, or maybe we'd be admitted to an asylum for an undetermined length of time. Almost anything is possible, except a trial."

"Not a very promising future," said the general, smiling.

"Well, that is *if* we are caught before we finish what we have set out to do. I believe we won't fail; the cost to our country, let alone ourselves, would be too great."

For the next few minutes, we were all silent. Then I got up and turned to Ephraim. "There is something I want from you before I plunge into this."

"You're in it already," he replied.

"I might be, but I promise you I won't do one more thing for you until you do one thing for me."

"And what might that be?"

"You have to put me in contact, right now"—I pointed to the phone—"with someone I know personally from your clique in the Mossad."

"*What?*"

"You heard me. Someone that I know. I want to be sure you're not setting me up."

"What about the general? I thought you trusted him."

"With all due respect, we both know that you could have tricked this man ten ways from Sunday. I want someone from the Mossad, someone who knows the ropes."

"I can't just expose someone to you like this."

"In that case, I'm walking."

Ephraim paused. "You know I can't let you do that, not with what you know."

"Kill me then, but if you want me to work with you, you better call somebody on that phone now."

Ephraim stared at me silently for several seconds. He then walked over to the phone, got a line from the operator, and dialed a number. He waited with the receiver to his ear. "Reuven?" he finally said, and waited. "Hold it for one minute." He turned to me. "Do you know Reuven Hadary?"

"Yes."

He spelled it out to the man on the phone that I wanted verification that there were others in the Mossad working with Ephraim. Reuven, a man I knew and liked, confirmed it. I insisted on getting Reuven's number so that I could call in the event of a mishap and not be totally dependent on Ephraim. They agreed, and by the time we hung up, I was satisfied. This was not a setup but a legitimate effort to bring down the Mossad, to make room for something we all hoped would be better.

I opened the window—I badly needed some fresh air. After the cigarettes, the pipe, and the fish and chips, the smell was getting to be overwhelming.

"Just one more thing." I said. "How many are involved in this?"

"About ten people. But only the three of us know what is really going on, or should I say four. No one outside this room, except for Reuven, knows about you, if that's what you're asking."

I didn't answer. I sat by the open window and stared out at the gray concrete housing project that was the best view this hotel had to offer.

"You'll arrive in New York on April 2. From that point on, you'll be on your own. I won't recommend a hotel for you. In fact, I don't want to know."

I nodded and kept my eyes on the view outside.

"Are you listening to me?" Ephraim asked softly.

I nodded.

"Here's the number I want you to call after the meeting in the PLO offices." He handed me a business card. "There is a number like that in New York; it's a bakery. Dial the same number in Tel Aviv, and I'll be there."

"And if you're not?"

"Call back three times, once every four hours, never from the same place. After the first time, start your disappearing act; by the last call, you should be gone."

"What should I do if they get you?"

"Just try to stay alive and out of their hands. This I can tell you, you'll be better off than we will."

"That's cold comfort for me. What about my family?"

"If we're caught, you don't have one. Or rather they don't have you; for them you'll be as good as dead."

"Does it have to be so drastic?"

"No, I'll be there to answer the phone. I won't lose you."

Several minutes later, they both left. They did so without fanfare; a simple handshake sent me on a journey that at times I wish I'd never taken.

CHAPTER 10

WEDNESDAY, APRIL 2, 1986, NEW YORK

I arrived in New York feeling like a wreck. I was exhausted, plastered from the endless stream of little rum bottles and half-filled plastic cups of Pepsi I had consumed on the flight.

The large terminal at the end of the long gray corridor leading from the docking bay came suddenly. The smell of a hot dog in a fresh bun replaced the smell of jet fuel and recycled air, causing my mouth to water. I automatically lit up a cigarette to kill the craving that could only be satisfied somewhere on the other side of the United States of America's bureaucratic defense line, also known as Customs and Immigration.

I could barely keep my eyes open, kicking my small carry-on bag forward every time the line moved up. I eventually found myself facing the immigration officer, who at that moment looked as though he would be more than happy to kick me back to wherever I came from.

"Passport, please." His voice was mechanical.

I put my Canadian passport on the counter, having returned to being a Canadian from the moment I landed in Gatwick, England. It was a good feeling indeed; that little blue document with the gold Canadian crest on it gave me a sense of relative security.

"Business or . . . "

"Just a vacation. I'm going to visit my dad."

"Canada?"

"No, he lives in Nebraska. He's American."

"How long will you stay?"

"I don't know yet. Why, is there a problem?"

The man handed me my passport back after stamping it with a red seal. "Have a nice time, sir." He signaled me to continue.

Customs was not much of a problem either. It seemed that even though I was slightly drunk, I managed to make a fairly good impression on the officials. Besides, I didn't have anything to hide, that is if you didn't count the documents hidden in the special compartment in my suitcase.

After a short taxi ride, I ended up at a small motel not too far from the airport. I dropped on the bed fully dressed, apart from one shoe I'd managed to get off, and fell asleep.

Thursday, April 3

The first light coming through the loose top of the curtain jolted me into consciousness. I realized instantly that it was almost a week since I'd talked to Bella. Considering the way I'd left, and the state I'd left her in, I felt like a heel. I slowly got off the bed, trying not to move my head too fast since the pain above my eyes was killing me. The alcohol was taking its revenge.

I stared at myself in the peeling mirror and realized I actually felt much better than I looked. The alarm radio on the small wooden table by the bed glowed seven A.M. I tried to figure out the time back in Israel but couldn't concentrate enough.

Ephraim had told me that I could call home after six A.M. on the third. I badly needed to make that call.

I lit a cigarette and sat at the end of the bed, clutching my head in my hands. I put the cigarette in the chipped glass ashtray and noticed that several of the previous patrons of this establishment had missed the ashtray altogether, leaving short burn lines on the wooden tabletop. Some had even managed, it seemed, to put out their cigarettes on the thin, worn-out greenish carpet. How the hell did I find this place? When I'd told the taxi driver "inexpensive," I should have qualified it. On the other hand, it was a good choice since no one would look for me here—unless of course they were already on to me.

I made the call collect; should they be listening, this was something I wanted them to hear, it was something Ephraim wanted me to verify. "They must have confirmation that you are in New York if we're to find out anything." It had made sense when he'd said it, but at the moment, I couldn't reconstruct the logic. All I could manage was the mechanical action of dialing the number.

Her voice was fresh, like a breeze of cool air dissipating the clouds of pain in my head. I wanted to keep listening to her voice; it was soothing. It didn't matter much to me what she said as long as I could cling to the sound. Her image flashed in front of my tired eyes: her dark wavy hair, her feminine body, the spark in her deep brown eyes. I could hear she was tired, worried, pained that I hadn't called before. She complained only briefly and then, once she realized that she wasn't going to get a full explanation, she asked, "So what are you going to do?"

"I'm going to be in New York for a day or so, and then I'll go visit my dad."

"What are you planning to do there?"

"I don't know yet. Maybe I'll get some sort of job or something. Don't you worry, everything will be fine."

"They came here yesterday with your call-up for military reserves."

"Who did?"

"An officer from the navy. They hand-delivered it to me."

"Really? I never heard of it being done that way before."

"I told them you were abroad. They didn't believe me at first."

"What did they say?"

"They asked how you left without getting a release form from them."

"I got a release from them. The bloody bureaucrats don't know their hands from their legs."

"Did you call your dad yet?"

"No, I'll do it right after I hang up with you."

"I hope he's home. He might be out of town or something. What will you do then?"

I could feel she wanted to talk almost as much as I did. "Don't you worry. Things will be fine," I lied. From where I was at that point, things were not looking up. Suddenly, I wanted to end the conversation; I was afraid I might say something that would irritate her. I couldn't handle it now. As far back as I could remember, I'd always managed to place the blame in her lap for whatever failure I was responsible for. I promised to call back the next day.

After a quick trip to the diner next door, then a long, hot shower back in the room, I felt sufficiently revitalized to embark on the day's errands. I called the front desk and told the man I wanted to keep the room for a few more days. Then I asked him to call me a cab.

In less than half an hour, I was in front of the UN building. From there I walked to the PLO offices. I knew I could get most of the way back by subway and then use the cab for the last leg, but *going* there I wanted to be relatively quick and make sure I did not lose any tail I might have. After all, if they were after me and I took the subway and then a cab, there was a good chance they might lose me. And then we'd think we were clean because they didn't report me entering the

PLO offices. That false sense of security could bring worse calamity further down the road.

The sun had come out, and it was slowly turning out to be a nice day, in New York terms, of course. There was still a slight chill in the air, which kept whatever amount of freshness the city would allow.

I knew what was expected of me, and I wasn't about to fool around. This was something I had to do, and I wanted to get it over with. I entered a small coffee shop across the street from the PLO office. I had to take my time. As before, if the team following me was slightly behind, I wanted to give them time to catch up and take position so that they could see exactly what was going on.

After another coffee and an excellent croissant, I started slowly across the street. I was nervous. I had dealt with Palestinians before, but always from a position of strength, with the entire military or Mossad mechanism close behind me. Today was very different. It was possible that the Mossad was still behind me, but for totally different reasons. And the PLO people I might meet were not in any way subject to my power or will. I was armed only with self-confidence and the hope that things would go smoothly.

The reception area of the suite was lined with brochures and posters, the light blue and gray colorings giving the place a sophisticated aura. The front room was deserted for several minutes until a tall, well-dressed man entered. His gold-rimmed glasses dropped slightly on the bridge of his nose as he looked at me over the top of his bifocals. He was about six foot two, on the heavy side. His black suit was well tailored, and he smelled of an expensive aftershave. I felt slightly out of place in my jeans and black leather jacket.

"Can I help you, sir?" His voice was deep, friendly, and without any traceable accent.

"I'd like to talk to someone in charge, please."

"I'm in charge. My name is Yasin. What can I do for you?"

"Well, can we talk freely here?"

"That depends on what you want to say. I'm sure that there are more people listening in on this room than are present," he said, smiling.

I drew my Israeli passport out of my pocket and handed it to him. "I wonder if you might join me for a coffee," I said. "There is a nice little place just across from here."

He seemed somewhat surprised as he leafed through the document. He then handed it back to me, smiling. "Actually," he said, "I was just on my way out. There is an even better place down the street. Would you care to join me?"

"I'd be delighted." I smiled back, feeling great. I'd made contact, and if the Mossad were in fact watching me, they'd see me with a man whom I had no doubt was known to them. We would know for sure in a very short time what was going on, if anything.

"Let me just get my coat," the big man said and disappeared down the hall. I looked out the window at the scene below. Even though the streets were not overly crowded, there was no way I could spot any surveillance. I had no doubt that the Americans were watching this office—the feds, certainly, and probably also the city police, wanting to observe any subversive activity stemming from this place and at the same time attempting to stop any attacks on it.

The only thing that worried me was the possibility that someone might get a photo of me with the PLO man and send it to the Mossad. Then I'd be in deep trouble. Even though Ephraim had promised me that this particular aspect of the operation was covered, I knew that the graveyards were full of irreplaceable people, lying next to those who had good intentions.

This was the point of no return for me, and I was happy to have passed it. From now on, it was the life again.

We didn't speak on the way to the small restaurant, which was about a block away from the office building. The place was badly lit and looked like a scene from a Bogart B-movie. I ordered coffee, and he did the same. I got the impression that he wanted to get this meeting over with as fast as possible.

"So what was it you wanted to talk about?"

"As you know, I'm an Israeli."

He nodded. "What do you want?"

"I just wanted to give you a warning." His eyebrows arched slightly, hardening the look in his eyes.

"Nothing personal or imminent, just a general warning, that's all."

"About what?"

Ephraim had made it very clear that I was not to go into any detail, only give the general information and then throw in an example or two to make them realize I was not some loony off the street.

"It's important that you tell your top brass that everything they say, on any phone they use, is listened in on. Just to give you an example, when your people were talking to Felitsia Langer[1] before the war

---

1. Felitsia Langer: A well-known Israeli attorney who stood up for Palestinian human rights.

in Lebanon, right up to the actual invasion, it was all recorded. So were the talks between Arafat and the king of Saudi Arabia during the siege on Beirut, and so were the calls made by Arafat from Tripoli, Lebanon, to Damascus during the Syrian siege of Tripoli. And today all the calls from Tunis to wherever."

"We know that. What do you think we are, stupid? Who are you, anyway?"

"All I can say to you is that not everybody who is against you is your enemy. There are those who think that even though we are on two sides of the barricades, we will have to live together, or at least next to each other, in peace."

"Look, we have many enemies, and the various authorities in this country are looking for any excuse to kick us out of here and make a mockery of our cause. I will have to end this conversation with you for that reason."

"I understand. Only one more thing that you must take back, and that is that only in Tunis is Arafat safe."

"You people are funny." He smiled. "You know more about us than we do; you know our history, our customs, our daily habits. You know the location of every tree in the Palestinian forest, but you can't see the forest. You can't comprehend us as a people, nor do you understand anything about us." There were several seconds of silence. The man stared directly into my eyes, as if he were trying to solve some puzzle or find a way out of some darkened maze. "All I can tell you is that there are many on our side of the barricade who feel the same. We want to live in peace and be a free people. There are those who think that this can only be achieved over the dead bodies of your people. Most of us do not, but we will never break ranks to be slaughtered by you. We ask for respect, and a place we can call our home. Let me send a warning to you, and it is nothing personal. But, trust me, it is imminent. There will come a time, and it is not that far off, when the street will dictate to us what we are to do and the extremists will take our place. And then all you will have to talk to will be your ancient wall. Tell whoever sent you to seize the moment." He got up and held out his hand across the small table, his face still frozen. I stood up and shook his hand, noticing the small smile on his face as I did so. He nodded. "Tell them," he said, "if they want to see who we really are, all they have to do is look in the mirror." He turned and walked out.

CHAPTER 11

fter Yasin walked out of the restaurant, I remember feeling a strange sensation, having met a PLO man face-to-face on an equal footing and realizing he was a nice person.

I kept looking at him as he made his way outside, past the restaurant window. I leaned to one side and saw him turn the corner.

I had about two hours to kill before making my scheduled telephone call. Ephraim had calculated that two hours were more than enough time: if the alarms in Mossad headquarters didn't go off by then, we were safe. This was a crucial and dangerous point in the operation. If anything went wrong, the entire program would be eliminated, Ephraim would probably rot away in some jail cell, and I would make it to the top of the Mossad hit list.

Time, it seemed, was at a standstill. Under normal circumstances, when a Mossad case officer is working in the field, either he is on his way to another appointment and has barely enough time to get there, or he has a safe house to go back to, where he writes reports or gives an account of the meeting to his superiors. With the exception of the short time a case officer is on his way to or from a meeting, he is rarely alone.

I'm not one for window shopping, which always made this part of the job more of a burden to me. While waiting, I had very little patience for anything. I walked slowly, searching for something to take my mind off things, while time passed at its snail's pace. I considered making a call to my dad in Nebraska. The time was right, since there's a one-hour time gap between Nebraska and New York. But then I decided against it. Should something go wrong, there was no point in implicating him in all this. I would call him once I knew I was clean. I trusted Ephraim to do the right thing, and I'd do whatever—

My thoughts snapped abruptly. Across the street, a man in a long black coat caught my attention. He was standing by a street vendor and busily dumping mustard onto a hot dog. I had seen him before, entering the restaurant where I sat with the PLO man and seating himself at the back.

He was clearly trying to avoid looking directly at me, a true mark of an amateur. I moved closer to the wall, out of the pedestrian traffic, and watched him. By my estimation, he should have started on that hot dog already, unless he was loading it with mustard simply to buy time at the stand. I remembered that he hadn't been alone in the restaurant: He was with another man. I began to scan the street slowly, searching for his partner. The man with the long coat and the hot dog had a Middle Eastern complexion. That could make him just about anything from a New York cop of Italian descent to a Syrian intelligence officer—or a Mossad man, for that matter.

I kept turning slowly, scanning the street, moving casually. I noticed a man standing by the entrance to a bookstore, holding a small bag in his hand. He stared at me through the reflection in the store window. The man was less than ten feet from me. His presence jolted me: I hadn't expected to find him so close. It was the other man from the restaurant. In a strange way, the unprofessionalism of his positioning offended me—he wasn't playing by the rules. I assumed that they were either amateurs or members of a lesser organization.

I stepped into the bookstore, passing right by the man. I had to find out who these guys were working for.

I leafed through a book for several minutes, running options through my mind. I had to forget most of the things I was trained to do in situations like this, such as call for backup or set up a surveillance locator exercise.[1] I was on my own. It all boiled down to not having protection from the local authorities, or from anyone who felt like taking a shot at me.

From the bookstore, I saw the man toss the hot dog into a trash can as he rushed to cross the street. The one by the door moved toward the intersection, waiting for his partner to arrive. They spoke for several seconds, then the man in the long coat gestured at the bookstore. The man with the bag pointed down the street and shrugged his shoulders. The man in the long coat nodded and moved

---

1. Surveillance locator exercise: A preplanned activity that places members of a security team along a predesignated route. Once an officer detects a tail, he calls it in, and the team takes position. The officer then passes through the testing area, and the tail is verified and identified.

closer to the store door, while his partner headed in the direction he had just indicated.

What do you know? The dummies actually think. Not good enough, though. I felt like walking out and talking to the one in the long coat, straightening him out, giving him a short lesson, and sending him back to try it again. There was a part of me that would get a kick out of doing something like that. This, however, was neither the time nor the place to do it; for all I knew, they were planning to snuff me out, for whatever reason. It doesn't take a genius to kill someone. I had to concentrate and make my move, and I didn't have all day. I was just hoping the two were not some fancy decoy someone was setting up for me to grab.

I knew for certain that they had been tailing me at least since I entered the restaurant, and it was more than likely that they were on to me from the time I left the PLO office building. Time was suddenly moving very fast. I had only an hour before I had to make my call, and by then I had to have some answers.

The plan came to me in a flash. I walked out of the bookstore and headed south for about ten minutes, occasionally stopping to look in a window, just to make sure I didn't lose my new friends. I walked at a slow pace to make sure of that. Around Forty-seventh Street, I made a sharp turn and stepped into the first store I came to. It was a large electronics discount store. I was now out of sight. If there were more than the two of them, my constant movement in a single direction would more or less put them to sleep, operationally speaking, and string them along behind me. There was a slight chance that someone would move ahead of me, but it was very slim. In fact, I didn't really believe there were more than the two I'd seen. Now I was ready for the second stage.

I waited for the man with the bag to pass the store and stop, realizing he had lost me. He was looking in all directions until his coated friend arrived. They stared into the electronics store but didn't see me. As I had anticipated, the man in the coat sent his friend to search for me down the street while he started in the other direction. I had split them up. One down and one to go.

I stepped out of the store. The one with the coat had his back to me and the bag man had just entered a store in the other direction. I walked briskly, passing the coated man at the crosswalk, heading west on Fortieth Street. If he didn't want to lose me, he would have to come on alone, and he did.

I had only gone fishing once in my life, and that was with my dad on a short visit I made to the States—and then it was my dad who caught the fish. But I could feel the pleasure now as the fish took the bait and I slowly reeled him in. We walked in single file for another five minutes. I wanted to put as much distance as possible between him and his partner. We were almost at the Port Authority Bus Terminal, not the best neighborhood in the world, with its endless array of adult bookstores and peepshow parlors. The terrain was extremely good for my purposes, though, and I prepared to do my second disappearing act.

At the corner of Seventh Avenue and Forty-first Street, I made an abrupt stop at the pedestrian crosswalk. I wanted to make sure the coated man was still with me. It was lucky that I'd stepped to one side, or my fish would have swum right into me. Speaking of operational sleep, this man was absurd. He was an amateur if ever I saw one. But he had determination.

Even the most backward agency in the Middle East had the privilege of learning basic surveillance techniques from either the French, the Soviets, or the Americans—not to speak of the ones we had trained in our time. This guy was private,[2] and he must have gotten his training from TV movies or cheap paperbacks.

I wasn't happy about having to deal with amateurs; they're so unpredictable. I would have preferred to encounter professionals any day—at least it's not personal with them. You feel much better if you know that whoever you're confronting is after something, and once he gets what he came for, he's off your case. Should your termination be what he's after, at least it will be done quickly and neatly.

The little green man appeared in the traffic light and I crossed the street, my tail close behind. I made a fast left into the first street after the light, and then a right. I stood at the entrance to a large adult book and video store. I waited for my tail to show up on the corner, and once I was sure he had noticed me, I entered the store.

I knew he would stand outside for some minutes before entering, since at this point he had time to think, and he knew he was alone. This was a one-on-one now.

In a glass showcase that doubled as a counter, I saw a large array of kinky sex paraphernalia, from strange-looking male organs to spiked condoms. In the corner of the showcase was a pair of silver handcuffs. I bought a handful of movie tokens and the cuffs from the clerk, who handed me my change and was happy to return to his dirty magazine. Who said shoemakers go barefoot, I thought, smiling to

---

2. Private: Not part of a professional intelligence agency or trained by one.

myself. I walked to the back, where the red neon sign read "Movies," and turned down a long dim hall lined on both sides with a row of small booths that looked much like the stalls in a public washroom. Each booth had a number on it and a small framed picture by the door depicting a scene from the explicit sex movie showing inside.

I walked in such a way that my tail would think that I knew my way around and therefore might use a back door to slip away, or maybe meet someone inside. He had to come in after me. The fact that I didn't know the place and was not meeting anyone there didn't change a thing.

I entered the booth at the end of the hall and latched the door behind me. I put a token in the slot and pressed the start button. The booth was not much bigger than a toilet stall and had a small three-legged chair tucked against the corner. The walls were painted black, and opposite the door, about four feet from the ground, was a television screen almost flush with the wall. There were no controls on the set, and as it turned out, the sound was not adjustable. The show started while my thumb was still on the start button. It began with a threesome involved in an elaborate act of lovemaking. The male was extremely well-endowed and seemed to impress the two women in the movie very much—their moaning was quite loud. I looked around the small cubicle, searching for a crack of some sort through which I could look out and see what my friend was up to. The plywood wall had a small cavity in it where a nail had fallen out at the joint.

I stood on the stool and peered out—just in time too. I saw the man in the long coat look around; after going all the way to the back and realizing there was no door, he tried the door of the cubicle just across from me. Finding it occupied, he tried my door, and then settled for the one just ahead of me across the hall.

He entered, and I could see that he had left the door slightly open and was watching the dim hall. I had to admit it wasn't a bad move at all, for an amateur.

I waited for several minutes, letting him get comfortable. Then I opened my door and walked out, staying in his blind spot. I closed the door behind me, clutching the small batch of tokens in my fist. I was alone in the hall, but I had to move fast—someone could pop into the hall or out of a booth at any moment. I took a deep breath and stepped across the hall, grabbed the knob of his door, and pulled it open hard. I could feel him lose his grip and his balance too. It seemed that he had been crouched by the door, staring at the hall ahead, completely taken by surprise.

There was no gentle way to do this; I had no gun or other weapon with which to impress on him the seriousness of the situation. I walked right over him into the cubicle, closing the door behind me. I hammered my coin-filled fist on the top of his head before he had a chance to utter a single syllable. My quick action had the expected stunning effect on him; he was on his knees in shock, facing the dark screen.

I latched the door, grabbed his hand, and twisted it high behind his back, pinning his face hard against the screen and placing my knee on his shoulder. I was now in total control.

I dropped a token into the small slot under the screen and pressed the illuminated red button with my thumb. The movie started instantly, but I could hardly see what was taking place on the screen, as my friend's face was smeared over most of it. He was motionless—not that he could have done much even if he'd wanted to, but it was very clear to me that he didn't want to. Things were happening far too fast for him even to think. I leaned forward closer to his ear so that he could hear me above the moaning of the big-breasted woman on the screen, who was being rocked back and forth by someone I couldn't see.

"What's your name?"

The man was silent. I could see he was closing his eyes tight in expectation of a blow.

"You can close your eyes, asshole, but your ears are open. I'll ask you one last time. What's your name?"

"Marvin." His voice trembled.

"Who do you work for, Marvin?"

"Nobody, I don't work for nobody."

"Why are you following me, Marvin?" My voice was steady, low, almost friendly.

He tried to turn his head and look at me, so I pushed his hand up as high as it would go without breaking, and he let out a sigh of pain. "Were you with the guy from the PLO?" he said.

"Who are you working for, Marvin?"

"I told you, nobody. I'm a detective. I'm on a case."

"What case?"

"I can't tell you. That's privileged information. Let go of my hands. I have rights, you know."

I realized that the man thought he'd been caught by a policeman. I pulled out the cuffs I'd purchased and cuffed the hand I was holding behind his back. Now I held the empty cuff in the same hand with which I grabbed his hair, so that when he pulled his hand down he was pulling on his hair. With my free hand, I took out a Bic pen from my coat pocket.

"Would you like my autograph, Marvin?"

"What?"

"Do you want my autograph?"

"What would I do with your autograph?" His body was starting to move as he attempted to get up, so I pressed my knee harder on his shoulder. Now I could see the big black man who was rocking the woman on the small screen, her moans getting louder. Someone tried to open the door. I applied a little more pressure to the hand. I didn't want him to start screaming.

"You're breaking my hand, man, you're breaking my hand. Please let go of my hand."

"This is a pen, Marvin." I spoke again in my monotonous voice as I placed the nib on his cheek. The big-breasted woman was starting to move faster. "I will now place this pen in your ear, and then I will push it in slowly until such time as I autograph your brain. Think about it, Marvin."

"What are you talking about?" Panic was getting into his voice as he felt the tip of the pen in his ear. I knew that at this point he was sure he was dealing with a psycho who would derive pleasure from his pain. "Whaddaya want? Whaddaya want from me?"

"You followed me, Marvin, and I really don't like that. I want to know why, and who sent you." I pushed slightly on the pen, holding tight on to his hand. The little room was getting hot, and the heat was making me nervous. I wanted an answer, although I already had an idea of what I was dealing with.

"I told you." His voice was whiny. I could see a tear, shining in the blue light of the TV, rolling down his face. The woman was reaching her orgasm, the black man just kept on going, and it was hard to make out what Marvin was saying.

"I told you. I am a detective."

"And I want to know who you are working for. Hercule Poirot?" I pushed the pen deeper: a few more millimeters and it would start to cause damage.

"Let go of me. You can't do this."

I moved the pen, and he pushed hard against the screen as he tried to get away from it. The little red light started to flicker, reading "Add token," so I did. The show must go on. "I will be very clear with you, Marvin. If you don't start talking to me, I will take this pen out of your other ear, and I'll still get my answers from your friend. In fact, my friends are probably getting those answers right now."

I could see he was thinking. His eyes were wide open, and he was terrified. Any thought that his friend might save him was gone. He realized I knew more than he did. He was trying to analyze the situation—this was not what I wanted. I had to do something to move things along faster. I left the pen sticking out of his ear, raised my hand, and hammered him over the head again. This shocked him—it was totally unexpected. Then, when he thought he would start talking, I hit him over the head yet again.

"I'm from the JDL, you know? The Jewish Defense League. We're watching the offices of the Palestinian scum. We saw you come out and we thought you worked for them or something so we wanted to know . . ."

"Know what?"

"Who the fuck you were, we wanted to know who the fuck you were. How were we to know you were a cop?"

"Who sent you?"

"The rabbi, he tells us what to do. Nobody cares what happens to us, we have to take care of ourselves. Jews have to take care of themselves or the goyim will eliminate them. Are you Jewish?"

"No," I answered.

"Well, you don't know that the Palestinians have a plan to exterminate all Jews. And the American government is a party to the scheme."

"What the hell are you talking about? I think I hit you over the head too hard."

"We will not let that happen! You just wait and see! We will kill them all first, we will." The man was starting to lose it. I eased some of the pressure on his hand. By keeping my knee hard on his shoulder and pinning him down, I could put some distance between us.

I stood up, took my knee off him, and pulled him up by his twisted arm, the pen still in his ear. There was nothing in the room to tie him to, and I couldn't render him unconscious without risking killing him. He was not a threat to me, so killing him would not be even a consideration.

I let go of the pen again and undid his belt.

"What are you doing?"

"I'm undressing you, my boy."

"What for?" There was fear in his voice. "What'll you do to me?"

"Nothing, if you behave yourself. Now undo your pants and drop them."

His pants fell to the floor. After about five minutes of wrangling, with my keeping his hand pressed behind his back, he was buck naked. I put all his clothes inside his big coat and held the bundle under my arm. He was down on his knees, facing the screen, his hands cuffed behind his back.

"I will leave you now," I said, and put several tokens in the slot. "You have about ten more minutes of entertainment, then you're on your own."

"You can't leave me like this. Please don't take all my clothes. Please." He was begging. The place was extremely hot, yet he was trembling. I was worried that he might start to defecate on the floor and on my shoes. He smelled bad enough as it was.

"Well, it's either that or kill you. You understand that I can't just let you walk out of here with me, so which would you prefer?"

There was no answer; he was now sobbing silently. I got out of the cubicle and slammed the door behind me. I heard him drop to the floor, moaning—or was it the woman with the big breasts? I wasn't sure. I felt pity for the guy; after all, this wasn't the best neighborhood in which to walk around naked. But I knew I couldn't have done it to anyone more deserving. I hated the JDL people or, as they were called by many, the Judeo-Nazis (somehow the biggest paradox of our time). I passed by the clerk at the counter and spoke to him without looking in his direction. "There's a man in number four who is bugging people back there." The clerk stared at the closed curtain leading to the hall. From the door, I said, "He's naked and is asking to be punished or something."

He didn't even stand up—he was not about to leave the cash register for nothing. He picked up the phone and started to speak. No one paid any attention to me as I blended into the lunchtime crowd now moving through the streets like a human torrent. I dropped the bundle of clothes into the hands of a street person huddled in a narrow alley between two red-brick buildings. His glazed eyes didn't realize what had fallen into his lap until he slowly started to unfold it. As soon as he felt the wallet, he moved faster, thrusting the whole thing into a shopping cart and disappearing into the alley.

I hopped on a bus and was back at the Chrysler Center just in time to make my call. It was afternoon in Israel; I got through without a hitch, and Ephraim was almost instantly on the line. The sound of his voice came as a relief—someone familiar. And the fact that he was there to answer said it all. Only then did I realize how nervous I was about the consequences of what we were doing, should we be caught at such an early stage of the game.

"I guess you did what you had to?" He was inquisitive; there was always the possibility in his mind that the reason he hadn't been arrested was not that I wasn't being tailed, but rather that I hadn't made the move I was supposed to.

"Yes, I did. I went into the office and met the man that was working there. Then we went out for a coffee and I gave him the message."

"What did he say?" Even though the phone line Ephraim was talking on was secure and I was calling from a randomly picked pay phone, we were still playing it safe.

"Well, he wasn't surprised by what I had to say. He knew all that and so does his boss, apparently."

"Anything else he said?"

"Just that we should know that in his firm there are people that want what we want, but the time to do business might be limited. What he was hinting at was that the market has a say in the matter, and that he might undergo a hostile takeover which would leave us to deal with someone we might not like."

"I see, I had expected as much. At least he knows there are those in our firm that want to do business too." I could hear him smiling; he was clearly as relieved as I was. "Did you run into any problems?"

"Well, I had a visitor, and it turned out to be a member of this radical group here."

"From our people?"

"You could call them that. They were Meir's people." I was referring to their leader, the so-called rabbi Meir Kahane.

"You're kidding me."

"No, I'm not. I got rid of them, it's okay. Did any of our people see anything?"

"Apparently not. I found out we don't have the place watched at all, and if someone else does, they're not reporting to us. It's regarded as a political location, nothing we really care about."

"I guess that's why those loonies from the JDL are watching."

"Okay, so much for the first step. Now get out of sight, just get lost," Ephraim said slowly, over the phone. "Do you know what I'm talking about?"

"Yes."

"Will you be going to visit someone now?"

"Yes. I'll call him later today and fly there tomorrow. When will I hear or see you?"

"Have patience; it won't be long. I'll call you there. Just remember what I told you; stay there until I say you can leave. Is that clear?"

"Yes, but give me an estimated time," I pressed. "When I come to visit, I need to know a timeframe, something."

"I can't tell you."

"What? Days, weeks, what?"

"Shouldn't be more than a couple of weeks."

"That's a hell of a long time."

"We have a hell of a big job. I'll call you there."

"How about I call you to check how we're doing?"

Ephraim knew the importance of a live link for someone out in the cold; the fact that you had a place to call and didn't have to sit and wait made all the difference. "Call and leave a message if I'm not here, the message we agreed on."

"I will." The line went dead. I was alone again in New York. It was night in Israel. I headed back to the motel. I could feel the numbness the afternoon's activity had given me starting to dissipate.

CHAPTER 12

I called my father from the motel. He was happy to hear from me and surprised to learn I was in New York. He offered to pay for my ticket so that I could come out and visit with him (my dad always offers to pay for everything, and quite often does). But I said I could handle it and that I planned on arriving in Omaha the following day.

I was not exactly enthusiastic about this visit. Not really knowing where my life was parked at that moment and not being able to tell my father how long I actually planned to stay put me in an odd situation. I told him that I was actually between assignments and was waiting for a call from a friend who was also my boss. As an ex-officer in the Royal Canadian Air Force and then in the Israeli air force, he knew not to ask too many questions.

Once my friend called, I explained, I would know where I was supposed to go. I told him and his wife, Gigi, that my friend would be arriving in Washington shortly, and if there was any problem about my staying with them, I could wait for my man in Washington. I found myself apologizing almost constantly, even though there was no need to.

I had never really spent much time with my dad before. My parents had separated when I was about five, and my mother had taken me with her to Israel. It wasn't so much that she wanted to raise me, but rather she didn't want my father to do so. In fact, my maternal grandparents were saddled with that job, which was made all the harder by my mother's attitude. In that household, she behaved more like my sister than my mother, constantly competing with me for the affection of her parents. Even though I was only a small child at the time, she made me feel as though she were the younger sibling.

It was my grandparents who ingrained in me the love for Israel and the Zionist movement. I also received a heavy dose of Judaism for which I'm grateful to this day, although they were not what would be considered Orthodox Jews.

At the same time, fearing that if my father had any direct contact with me he would want to take me to the United States, they made sure that such a connection did not exist. All communication with him was severed until I reached the age of seventeen and found a letter from my father addressed to me, hidden in a drawer, along with a monthly child support check. Up until that point, I had been led to believe that he didn't want to have anything to do with me. It is hard today to quantify the pain that belief caused me through the years. Nor can I express the anger I felt when I discovered that this was not the case, and that all those years had been wasted.

Years later, I would learn that such a letter had arrived monthly for years and that my father, having seen that the check was cashed without any reply, was sure I wanted nothing to do with him. He never imagined I was not made aware of his letters.

Shortly after finding that letter, I phoned him, and later I visited him just before joining the army. Since then, we had met several times for short periods, but somehow we were never able to bridge the gap that time had put between us.

On this visit, I didn't feel much different. I could feel his frustration at not being able to get through to me. Nor could I get through to him. We seemed like two opposing magnets trying hard to lock. I couldn't sit him down and run the truth by him, much as I wanted to and probably should have.

The quiet, harmonious life my dad was living, in an affluent neighborhood in Omaha, with all the trappings of a success story and the serenity of living the American dream, only intensified my feelings of frustration at being ripped away from Bella and the kids to dangle on a thin string over a bottomless pit.

Tuesday, April 8, 1986, Omaha

I made a call to Ephraim from the pay phone at the mall. I'd been in town for almost a week and hadn't heard from him yet. I'd held back as long as I could, but it was starting to get to be too much.

"I'm glad you called," he said. "I have something I want you to do."

"Why didn't you call me, then?"

"I was about to. I want you to make a call to a man in New York."

"Do I know him?"

"I don't think so. His name is Avraham Bar-Am. He's a reserve brigadier general."

"Another one of your friends?"

"Not at all. The SOB is trying to sell arms to the Iranians. He submitted the names of his contacts to us and is waiting to hear if they're approved. He actually brought one of them here for a visit a while back."

"So what do you want from me?"

"I want you to call him in New York and tell him that it's all been approved. He might record the call, so be brief."

"What do you mean, it's all approved? If it is, why don't you people call the shmuck?"

This didn't feel right. It seemed more as if I was doing the Mossad's work for them than going out to get the bastards. I had a strong feeling that Ephraim was using me for other things, as if to say, Since you're already there . . .

But he was my link to "the life." He was also restoring a purpose to the long years I'd given to the Mossad. What's more, he was enabling me to fulfill my desire for revenge. I never learned to like Ephraim or to regard him as a friend, but I always knew that I was using him just as much as he was using me.

"I can't call him," Ephraim replied. "The man knows me; it's a setup. The Office started this situation. I was the one who made the contact for him. What I learned today was that the contact was turned by the FBI and is now an informer. He used to work for the CIA before."

"So why don't you warn your man, this Avraham guy?"

"I would, but that wouldn't serve our purpose."

"Why not?"

"I want him to get caught. It's going to be a blow to the Office. If they try to help him, they will look dirty in the eyes of the Americans, and if they let him hang out to dry, I have no doubt he will sing and implicate them. And since it's my call, I'm going to let him hang."

"I see. So that is what I'm to expect from you too, when the time is right?"

"Don't be ridiculous. This is a different matter; the man is in it for the money, and he deserves what he gets."

"Okay," I said.

There was a short silence on the line. Then Ephraim's voice sounded like a snake on sand. "Call him and tell him that you're a friend and that the connection is cleared. He's to go ahead as planned." He gave me the number to call and the rest of the information that I might need. "And I'll call you soon," he said.

I just hung up. I stood there thinking for several seconds about what I was going to do. Then I picked up the receiver and made the call.

The phone rang several times before it was answered. A woman's voice came on the line. "Yes?"

"Can I speak to Avraham?"

"Who wants him?"

"A friend of his."

"Do you have a name?"

"No, just a friend with an answer."

She didn't say a thing. After several seconds, there was a click on the line. "Hello?"

"Avraham?"

"Yes, who is this?"

"A friend with a message."

"Who is this?"

I started to speak Hebrew. "I have a message for you from your friends. They say that the contacts you have submitted check out and that it's a go."

"Are you sure?"

"I'm only a messenger. It's not my father's company. Take it or leave it."

"Thanks."

I hung up. I was sweating. I knew he was walking into a trap. I had an urge to call back and shout at him that it was all a hoax. I didn't.

I drove back to the house and went to my room. It wasn't really my room; it belonged to my half brother, Mike, but he wasn't living there at the time. The housekeeper had the day off, and both my father and Gigi were out. I sat there staring at the silent pictures on the television screen.

On April 23, 1986, twelve men were busted by the FBI in a sting operation for attempting to sell arms to Iran. The story was all but lost in the big bang that followed the Americans' bombing of Libya and the nuclear accident in Chernobyl that same month. I heard that General Bar-Am pleaded not guilty and presented the documentation that had supposedly authorized him, in the name of the Israeli military industry, to deal on their behalf. The official Israeli response was that the man was a liar and that the documents he presented were issued indiscriminately to anyone who wanted to deal in arms. They added that such a document did not grant him the authority to finalize a transaction, only to act as a sales representative. In short, the man was hung out to dry. But there was no shakeup in the Mossad, and the end of the tunnel was nowhere in sight.

I do suspect, however, that this was part of a bigger plan that Ephraim and his clique were part of. I knew that Ephraim's channel to power was Amiram Nir, adviser to the prime minister on terrorism. While this dirty affair with Avraham was taking place, Nir was traveling to Teheran with a Bible autographed by President Ronald Reagan, without the knowledge of the Mossad or the CIA, in what later became known as the Iran-Contra affair. Using the general as a patsy to pacify American intelligence was ingenious; it took the focus away from Amiram Nir's secret dealings, and once he was out of CIA view, there was no way for the Mossad to find out. Since the CIA was the Mossad's only contact in this escapade, having the CIA in the dark meant the Mossad was out of the loop too.

The telephone talks I had with Bella were getting to be more and more frustrating; she wanted to know when things were going to start moving. I could not fill her in on what was really going on, and so I had to build up a cover story for her. I kept telling her I was looking for a job and had a plan that I was about to present to a friend of my father's. The friend in question was the owner of a national travel reservation company based in Omaha.

I did in fact talk to this man. My plan was to offer a secured flight package to passengers, since air piracy was affecting the industry. I suggested we set up several teams that would rotate between various major destinations and would escort and secure specific travel routes. For instance, there would be a chartered flight every day or every second day leaving New York for London or Paris and one returning. We would not establish an airline as such, but only the security package. I would train the teams, and we would work out a schedule. I had no doubt that during these times of fear and uncertainty the flights would be full even if we charged a slightly higher fee. We could then turn to the major airlines and offer them a similar service on a per-flight basis.

It sounded great, but I had a distinct feeling my father's friend was going along more to appease my father than anything else. I sensed that nothing would come of this, but it served my purpose as a cover for Bella.

There was one thing I had not considered, although I should have. I'd always expected that Bella would not pass on any information about us, simply because she was a very private person who believed that the less anyone else knows about you, the better off you are. She regarded our little family as the center of the universe, and it was almost impossible to get anything out of her unless she wanted to say it, and that was very seldom indeed. I should have remembered that she too was running through a very dark and scary tunnel, probably darker and more frightening than mine. I at least had the benefit of knowing what this was all about, or so I thought. She was disconnected from me and yet could read me like an open book. She knew something was not exactly as I was telling it and that there was more to it than I was letting on.

One day, she called me in Omaha. Gigi, my father's wife, answered the call. Having always gotten along, they struck up a conversation in which Bella, thinking that everybody in Omaha knew I was out of whatever I'd been doing before and that I really was looking for a job there, made a statement to that effect, asking if Gigi knew how things were going. I had never told Bella not to ask that, nor did I tell her that it was not common knowledge that I was looking for work. It turned out that the two women surprised each other.

I had been to the shopping center, where I had called Ephraim from a pay phone to let him know I was fed up, and if he wasn't about to get moving, I was.

I didn't reach Ephraim, but there was a message for me to meet him in two days in Washington. He would be waiting for me in a hotel somewhat out of the way: the Holiday Inn in Silver Spring, Maryland.

Back at the house, I received a call from Bella. She was both wrathful and concerned; she told me about her conversation with Gigi and warned me that my secret had been revealed. She demanded an explanation and started to cry on the phone; the faint hope I had built up in her regarding our future was dashed again. I tried to explain, and at the same time, I was thinking about what to do. I knew that when I faced Gigi, she would not be the pleasant, gracious hostess I'd encountered before. My dad would probably be incensed at my having lied to him. He had assumed, and I hadn't corrected him, that I was still working for whoever it was in Israel, and that I was waiting for a call from a colleague who was coming to the States. This was not a situation I was looking forward to. As things were shaping up, I could do very little explaining. The only consolation I had was in that message Ephraim had left me: Things were in fact starting to move.

I pulled myself together. "I can't tell you anything now," I said. "You will just have to take my word for it. Trust me just this one more time, please."

"But how can I? What do you want me to do? If only I could sleep until all this is over, whatever 'this' is."

"Please trust me, everything will be fine. I'm leaving here tomorrow and I will call you when I get where I'm going, okay?"

"I know this is the end," she said, her voice as sad as a human voice could be over a wire stretching thousands of miles. "I will never see you again, will I?"

"Don't talk like that. What are you talking about?" Deep down, I had the feeling she might just be right; there was a strong possibility that whatever Ephraim was getting me into had no way out. I knew of a few men who had crossed the Mossad and were now sealed away in unidentified prison cells in high-security facilities—living corpses with no names. And there were others, more fortunate, who had perished in a hail of gunfire or been torn apart by a hidden bomb. Would Bella ever know what it was that killed me, or would they leave her to wonder, to think that I had chosen to vanish and was living somewhere?

That thought was too hard to handle. I could feel the tears running down my cheeks as I tried to control my voice. "That is not true. We will see each other sooner than you can imagine." I wanted it so badly, it must have come through in my voice, because when she answered me, she sounded somewhat relieved.

"So what are you going to do about what they know now?"

"There's not much I can do. I'll just have to face the music and make as fast an exit from this place as I can."

My dad came in as I hung up. We had a brief exchange of words; I could see in his face that he didn't exactly know how to handle this. On the one hand, there was the lie he couldn't understand, and on the other, there was the fact that I had made him look bad in front of his wife.

It was clear to both of us that the sooner I left, the better for all concerned. He took me to the airport just as soon as I could get my things together. He put a thousand dollars in my hand and, trying to keep his voice from cracking, told me that no matter what, he was my father and he loved me. I told him I loved him too and left him sitting in his car as I entered the terminal.

I was hoping he'd come after me and try, in whatever way he could, to drag out of me what the hell was going on, and say he could help or get me out of it or something. But he didn't; I was a mystery to him, a memory of a relationship that had gone sour many years ago.

CHAPTER 13

SUNDAY, APRIL 20, 1986, WASHINGTON, D.C.

It was raining in Washington when I landed. I was a lonely stranger in an unfamiliar place, feeding on my own silence.

I took a cab from the airport to the Holiday Inn in Silver Spring. Being registered in the hotel under my real name during an operation made me feel naked. I was there to do strange things, and would have felt much more comfortable had I gone under an alias from which I could walk away if things got hairy.

My cover story in the hotel was that I was looking for a site on which to build a restaurant. I represented a group of investors who were into building specialty gourmet restaurants, getting them to run and become profitable, and then selling them off at a large profit. I said I would probably stay in the hotel for several days, if not weeks. Not knowing what exactly was going to be my assignment, I decided to remain in my room except for meals, for which I came down to the dining room on the main floor.

I called Bella and gave her the number of the hotel; if someone was listening, they would not suspect a thing. It was not unusual for someone with my background and knowledge to be in Washington in search of work in the field of security. After all, how many people around could provide the level of protection I could for executives and other high-profile personalities?

There was a relief in being alone, almost as strong as the feeling of safety I'd had at my dad's house. I didn't have to keep up appearances. I could smoke as much as I wanted and drink myself to sleep, which I did.

MONDAY, APRIL 21, 09:00

The phone rang. Ephraim was on the line. "So I see you arrived early," he said, not bothering with any niceties.

"Yes. When did you get here?"

"I just came in from the airport. Did you have company?"

"No, I'm fine. How about you?"

"I'm fine too. Why don't we have breakfast? I'm starving."

"Sure, give me ten minutes or so. I'll meet you in the dining room."

He hung up. I jumped out of bed. At last things were starting to move. The sooner I did what had to be done, the sooner it would be over and I could get on with my life, whatever was left of it. I wasn't expecting to be out of the game just yet, but I wanted a secure base from which to operate, with my family by my side.

I made my way directly to Ephraim's table, which was across the dining room in a corner, just by the door leading to the hotel bar.

He greeted me with a big smile. He was alone with a cup of coffee. As I sat down, the waiter arrived with our breakfast.

"I took the liberty of ordering for you. I didn't want to wait; we've got things to do."

I stared at my plate with the bacon and eggs over easy and raised my hand. "No problem. I see you ordered exactly what I wanted anyway." I found the place a bit dark for breakfast, but the aroma of fresh coffee and country bacon brought on an appetite I didn't think I had.

"So, what are we going to do?"

"After breakfast, we'll go to my room and talk."

I nodded and dug into my food.

We took a couple of large Styrofoam cups of coffee with us so that we wouldn't have to call room service. His room was on the sixth floor. In the corner, I saw a small carrying bag. "Where is your luggage?" I asked, curious, since I knew Ephraim was a dresser, and there was no way he could get more than one day's worth of clothing into that little bag.

"There." He pointed at the bag. "I'm not going to stay long. I'm here to instruct you, and then once you're on your way, I'm out of here."

"I'll have no backup?"

"You have me, and the training you got. What more do you need?"

"How do I have you if you're back in Israel?"

"I'll get to that. Once you understand what your first assignment is you'll—"

"Whoa, whoa," I interrupted. "First assignment? Did you say first assignment?"

"Yes, what did you think it was going to be: Bang, and it's over?"

"Don't give me the lecture, okay? I need to know a timetable." I knew I could walk away anytime I wanted, but Ephraim was betting that I wouldn't, that with the drive I had to get this done I couldn't, and he was right. I was like a junkie promising himself this was the last fix.

"What difference would that make? You have a job to do, it will all be over when the job is done, and that will be whenever it will be. You weren't promised a rose garden when you joined."

"I know, and I'm not asking for one now. When I joined the Office, they put Bella through a grueling security check, and they gave her a clearance just as high as mine. We were always told that the wife was part of the team and that there were no secrets from her." As I spoke, Ephraim was nodding at me over his glasses. "Now you say that I can't even tell her I'm still working for the Mossad." I paused. "Am I still working for the Mossad?"

"No, you're not working for the Office, you're working for me. And about Bella: You're one hundred percent right. But the rules have changed; this is a different ball game." He leaned back and pushed his glasses into place. "Does Bella know about Dina or Rachel or all the others? Does my wife know everything I do? No, they don't. Do they know the risks we take out in the field? Do you come home from a job and tell Bella, 'You know, I was almost killed last night in Austria,' or 'There is a good chance they will get me on my next trip to Spain?' No, you don't. When you're called out on patrol in the military and you're given an assignment from which you might not come back, do you call your wife and tell her about it? We make decisions every day that affect their lives, and we do not consult them. We say to ourselves, 'If something happens to us, they will understand we had to do it.' That's the way it works. Now can we put this aside and get down to business?"

"I need a timetable," I insisted.

"Three weeks and you're on your way," he finally snapped, clearly not pleased at having to tell me that.

"On my way where?"

"What difference does that make? You will be with your wife and children, I promise you that."

I felt a wave of optimism taking over, rejuvenating me. You never realize how bad things are in your mind until a moment like this.

"Okay, I can live with that." I now wanted to put a lid on my high. "So what is it we're getting into this time?" I could feel myself grinning.

"You'll volunteer to work for a foreign country."

"Work?"

"Intelligence. You will volunteer as an ex-Mossad officer. You'll offer to work for them, tell them how we do things, structure personnel, and so on."

"You mean sell out, become a traitor." I found saying the word hard.

"Yes, that's exactly what you'll do."

"Who for?" I raised my hand as if to say, Let me guess. He didn't say a word. "Okay, who could it be? The NSC? No, they wouldn't deal with me. CIA? I don't think so. Must be FBI; for sure it's the FBI. I could be valuable to them regarding the Al department."

"No. You're going to have a chat with the KGB." He got up and faced the large window. The glass was wet; it hadn't stopped raining for the last twenty-four hours.

I was stunned. It hit me like a ton of bricks. "No, really?" I said, trying to keep my composure. I was barely able to talk.

Ephraim stayed by the window, only turning his head slightly. I could see his profile; he wasn't smiling. "I told you. The KGB, the Soviets. What's so hard to understand?"

"I don't get it, that's what. Why would I want to do that? I mean, what makes you think they would buy me?"

"If you do it right, they will. Think about it. How could they turn you down: Fresh out of the Mossad, you're an asset. With all the Arab partners they have, they will swallow you like gravy."

"What if they want me to go to Moscow or something? They might just work like we do."

"So you go. Just remember you are doing it for the money, always think about that or they'll suspect you. You will use your real name and your real story to back yourself up."

"What if they just pump me for information and then throw me out? I mean, what will we have gained then? Think about it. I have no access to information anymore. What good will I be to them?"

"Well, you tell them you are still working."

"What are you saying? You want me to tell them about you?"

"No, of course not. Tell them your story, but instead of saying you were canned, tell them you're on probation, just so they think you still have a way back. Then they'll try to recruit you."

"Ephraim, listen to me." I wanted to do the job if it would cripple the Mossad, an organization that as it stood was a danger to the state of Israel as a democratic entity. But, on the other hand, I was not going to walk blindly into anything anymore. If I was to be killed or locked up forever, it would be because of something I agreed to do. "I need to know what it is I'm doing." I knew he was listening. "You must trust me, Ephraim. My life is in your hands, and you say yours is in mine, so let me in on the secret."

He thought about this. I got up and headed for the washroom. I had to get rid of the coffee that was filling my bladder. When I came back, Ephraim was opening a new pack of cigarettes. We lit up.

"Okay," he said finally, placing the smoldering match in the overflowing ashtray, "Okay. We'll do it your way."

"Thank you." I was watching his expression as he spoke. It was very possible he had anticipated that I would react this way and had a story ready that would make me feel good. If that was the case, there was little I could do about it, but at least he would have to make up a good story; that elevated me in my own eyes from a robot to a human being, although how vulnerable remained to be seen.

"To be honest with you," he began—I was never happy when people said that, but I reserved judgment—"this job is not as hard as you might think. The only obstacle is the FBI observation station overlooking the Soviet embassy. They will photograph you and then send the photo to reference. They will try to match your picture to their files, and if there is no match they'll file it away electronically." He shrugged. "That's no big deal. If it were an Arab embassy, they might send the photos to us; I mean the people we have there would do that, nothing official of course."

"So there won't be a need for a disguise or anything?"

"No, no, you can just go in. Don't forget, the Soviets are looking too, so don't take your time casing the place; once you get there, just go in."

"Well, I'd probably do that anyway."

"Good. Now to answer the question of why. I know from a friend I have in the FBI that they've found information they gave us in the hands of the Soviets. My friend was sure the Americans gave that information only to us. We were the only possible source for the Soviets."

"A mole in the Mossad?" I couldn't believe what I was hearing; I never believed that could be possible.

"Well, that's what it looks like. And if we could flush him out, the scandal would force the top brass of the Mossad to resign."

"Okay, but how will my volunteering to work for the KGB help with this? All we'll be doing is giving them more information. You don't expect them to tell me that they have a mole and who he is."

"If you come to them with a good story, and play your part well, they'll want to verify whether you're out of the Mossad or just on probation like you said." Ephraim was starting to get excited; I hadn't seen him like this before. He was turning red in the face. "You see, if they think you're still in the Mossad, then you're a very valuable asset."

"But you said they have someone in the system."

"So what's wrong with having two? That way they can spread the risk. We don't know how many they have. We're only assuming they have one. And, to be honest with you, I doubt very much that who they have is a case officer; I would think he is some clerk or something like that." He paused and stubbed his cigarette into the ashtray. "A live case officer: If they can verify that, it will be the catch of the year for them."

"How will they verify?"

"They'll go ask their mole." He was pleased with himself. I could almost hear him purring like a big cat. It suddenly all came together.

"So I'm the bait?"

He nodded. "Does that bother you? I thought you wanted to know."

"What did you expect me to say? That I'm thrilled?"

"So what will it be?"

"I'll do it. What else is there to do?" I leaned over in his direction and said in a low voice, "Just one thing. If you're not telling me the truth, Ephraim, and you're playing some game with me, you better think about it some more and maybe even consider taking me out. Because if you're not one-hundred-percent above-board with me, I swear to you I will kill you, if I have to dig my way back to Israel with my bare hands."

There was a soft smile on his face, as if a window had momentarily opened onto the man behind the facade. I had a feeling that this was the side of him his family and friends knew. "I would never do anything to hurt you. I know what I'm asking for is hard, and I can only imagine what you're going through. But this is not a game, and I'm not pulling anything. This is the real thing, and we're losing ground by the minute. I don't want to start waving the banner, but there is a far bigger thing at stake here than just you and me. If we lose, everything is lost, and if we win, we might not get to eat the fruits of victory; you know that."

"I figured as much." I wasn't sure how to feel. On the one hand, he had gone a long way toward winning me over with that outburst. On the other, I was fearful of being a patsy. I knew I could put on just as good an act as he could, at a moment's notice. Still, I chose to buy in. I was smiling. I could feel the fog clearing out of my head. Now I knew what the game was and therefore I could play it. A clear directive was always easier to execute than some vague instruction that you had to work out yourself.

CHAPTER 14

The game plan was simple. I would go to the Soviet embassy and make contact with the resident KGB. We knew, in general, what takes place when someone comes to volunteer in an embassy. After all, it's a daily occurrence in just about every Israeli embassy in the world. We had to assume that it wasn't much different with the Soviets.

"I'll wing it," I said. "What the hell can happen? The worst-case scenario is that they'll keep me there and try and ship me to Russia in a box or something."

We both laughed; this method had been used by the Mossad to smuggle people back to Israel several times.

"When do you want me to go in?"

"I have to get back to Israel before you make your move. I do have someone in archives who will report to me before he answers any request for files or anything, but still I'd feel better if I was there."

"Why? If you're covered, wouldn't it be better if you stayed here in case something went wrong?"

"What if the inquiry comes in from an unexpected direction? What if our mole is a case officer after all? Besides, the reason for my visit here is almost over." He smiled at me. "I'm here to ensure we get the bid for the Mazlat with the American navy. I'm here to make sure that the right man gets the money and the other one is scared enough to do what he has to." This was a reference to an operation run by the Mossad from Israel, using a crooked Israeli air force officer who was connected to someone in the office of the American naval secretary.

Ephraim lit another cigarette; the room was hazy with smoke.

I nodded. I knew about the Mazlat deal, and I knew we were getting some help from the inside. I would have preferred to have Ephraim stay. But I could manage without him.

"So when will you be leaving?"

"I'll leave right after I buy you a meal."

"Where are we going?"

Ephraim picked up the receiver. Turning to me, he asked, "What would you like?"

"Not bloody room service," I whined.

"That's all I have time for."

"Fine," I grumbled. "Get me a hamburger. Or, no, I'll have a club sandwich."

We were halfway through the meal when he looked at his watch. "I have to run. I have a dinner appointment with a very greedy young man."

"I'll make my move the day after tomorrow," I said. "That should give you ample time to get everything in order and stand ready."

"Right. Now, you watch yourself. This is not some exercise in the academy, you know." I could sense a genuine concern in the man's voice.

"Don't worry, just make sure things are tight on your end. One more thing, what do I do for money? I'm running out very fast."

"We'll see about that." He handed me an envelope. "Here's some money to tide you over, for the time being. We'll figure something out later. Let's just get this one under our belt."

I nodded and headed for the door, bringing my half-eaten club sandwich with me. I stood there for a moment, wondering if there was something I had forgotten. I couldn't think of anything. I opened the door and walked out. I was alone again.

There was very little for me to do in Washington. I didn't know anyone. This was the worst kind of operation imaginable. My cover was my real identity; I had no elaborate expense account. All Ephraim had handed me in the envelope was five hundred dollars, barely enough to keep me in the hotel. I was starting to feel down again; the whole thing was more of a *partach*[1] than anything else.

I was trying to act like a combatant in enemy territory, totally disconnected from his country and family. But I was worse off than any combatant. A combatant's job is clear and very well defined; he knows for whom he is working and against whom he is fighting. Besides, he has no financial problems, and his family matters are, as far as he knows, in good hands. The fact that the people who are supposed to

---

1. *Partach:* Slang for screwup.

take care of his family back in Israel will be busy trying to get his wife into bed if she looks only slightly better than Godzilla is something that can't bother him because he's not aware of it, and probably never will be.

To kill time, I walked the streets of the city, somehow always ending up in a large square where yuppies and homeless people sat together on wooden benches, the yuppies trying to get some fresh air as they munched their sandwiches, the homeless staring at them, hoping they would not finish so that a meal could be picked out of the garbage.

I had an urge to pass by the Soviet embassy, just to see where it was and how I should approach it. But I knew that it would be exposing myself to whoever was watching the place. It was better that I come there on foot at the last minute and just walk straight in.

I took the subway to Silver Spring, heading back to the hotel, only to find that I was far too restless to sit in the room and watch television. Tomorrow I was to make my move; I wanted it to be that time already.

In the evening, the downtown city took on a different look. The men were still wrapped in suits and ties, although most collars were worn slightly open. But the women had changed, going through a total metamorphosis, unless, as was very possible, it was a whole different breed of woman out there. They were long and sexy and moved more like cats than like any other animal, and the so-called watering holes (better known as meat markets) were full.

I made stops at some of them and sat for a while in conversation. But I was too edgy to feel comfortable, and by eleven I realized it was time to head back.

WEDNESDAY, APRIL 23, 1986

I got up early, and by the time I was dressed and into my third cigarette, I was starting to get over my habitual hangover.

The sky was cloudy and there was a constant drizzle; the weather couldn't have been better if I'd ordered it myself. I was wearing casual pants and a simple shirt with a yellow sweater. I was also wearing a gray wind jacket with a fold-in hood. I would wear the hood when entering the embassy; that way, no surveillance could actually see who I was or photograph my face.

By eleven, I was in front of the embassy. The weather had started to clear, but there was still reason enough for the hood. The iron gate was open, and the surveillance cameras didn't move in my direction. I walked quickly up the marble stairs and entered the main door.

The place was virtually empty; there was no one but me and an unimpressive blond woman behind the counter. She looked at me, smiling. I walked straight up to her.

"Can I help you, sir?" she said with a heavy Russian accent. I knew that the Soviets preferred to employ Soviet citizens in their embassies whenever possible.

I was fairly sure that the waiting area was bugged by the Americans since the access to it was so easy. "I would like to get some brochures on the Soviet Union," I said.

"What sort of brochures?"

"Whatever you have."

Her smile faded somewhat. "Just one moment, please." She turned and disappeared behind a small wall. I saw a notepad on the counter and a pencil on a string. I took the pencil and scribbled the words "I want to talk to security" on the notepad. When she came back, she handed me a thin booklet that looked as though it came straight from a printing house in the fifties. If this was a travel brochure, it wasn't very appetizing. I turned the small pad to face her. "Thank you, is this all you have?" I said.

Her smile was not there when she raised her eyes and stared back at me. "Why don't you have a seat, sir. I will see if there is anything else I might have."

"Thank you very much." I turned and headed for the wooden bench under a poster of Lenin's tomb at night. The woman disappeared behind the small wall again. When she came back, several minutes later, she sat down in her chair, ignoring me. I couldn't see what she was doing behind the counter, but it took all her concentration.

I had to wait patiently; at least she hadn't asked me to leave. I was hoping that they hadn't misinterpreted the note as a threat to their security and called the police. Well, if they did I had a story ready for them, albeit one I'd prefer not to use.

After about fifteen minutes, a well-dressed, solid-looking man came in from a door behind the receptionist. He leaned and spoke to the woman and then left. She stood up and, smiling again, signaled me to come over.

I moved fairly fast and leaned on the counter. "Yes?"

"We need your passport for identification if you want more information."

Without hesitation, I pulled out my Israeli passport and handed it over. "Here."

"Thank you." She got up. "Please have a seat." She nodded in the direction of the bench I had just left. I was tapping the side of the bench this time, not as calm as before. The woman reappeared shortly, and several minutes later, the man came out and beckoned me over. When I reached the counter, he raised the flap and allowed me to enter. Then he signaled me to follow him. Not a word was said.

We walked into a narrow hall and then climbed a flight of stairs. The carpet was worn, and the banister was slightly loose. Our steps echoed loudly on the squeaky floorboards—not at all what you would expect in an embassy of a world power.

I was ushered into a small bright room with a large mirror on one wall. I realized I wasn't nervous; in fact, I was very calm and quite cheerful. So far, I was doing well.

At last, my host smiled at me and pointed to a wooden chair on the other side of a plain wood table facing the mirror. "Would you please sit down, Mr. Ostrovsky."

"Thank you."

"So what brings you here today? Is there some threat to our security?"

It was turning out to be almost identical to the routine we would follow in our embassy. "No sir, no threat."

"So, what then?"

"I want to work for you people."

The man slowly sat down and leaned back in his chair. His smile was warm and friendly.

"And who exactly do you mean by 'you people'?"

"KGB. I want to work for the KGB."

"In what capacity?" The man was doing extremely well in keeping a straight face. He must have been the first buffer, as they probably got their fair share of intelligence nuts per day.

"Well, you will have to help me there. I can only tell you where I'm from. Where I'm going, we'll have to plan together."

"I see that you're an Israeli, Mr. Ostrovsky."

"I'm a member of the Mossad." I paused. "Have you heard of the Mossad?"

His smile turned into a grin. "I have indeed. How do I know you're not just making this up? The world is full of, shall we say, funny people." The man's English was excellent, but his accent was heavy. I had to concentrate to get every word, since he was talking fast.

This was the part that Ephraim and I had worked on, and I was ready. "Well, there is not much in the way of documentation that I could show you, as you can well imagine. But I could probably prove it to you by going into some details regarding methods of operation—without of course revealing too much that I might later want to be paid for." I smiled at him.

"I understand."

"Are you at a level where you can make any decisions, or should I talk directly at the mirror?" I said, a slight irony in my voice. The man smiled. There was an unspoken understanding between us, as if we belonged to a strange cult that had bizarre rituals. And although we might have been on different sides of the barricade, we were still somehow related.

"No, it's not up to me. But I will get the information from you, and then we will see."

We talked for almost a full hour. He made little notes on a yellow paper block. "I will be back in a short while," he said as he got up. "Could I get you something to drink or eat, maybe?"

"Coffee, just some coffee, if that is not too much trouble."

"Not at all." He nodded and walked toward the door.

"One more thing."

"What?" He stopped and turned back.

"Please don't mention my name on your communication to the Motherland."

"I don't understand."

"The Mossad broke your embassy code a long time ago and is updating itself every time you make a change. So if you don't mind, I would very much appreciate it if you didn't use my name in your broadcasts."

"What you're saying is impossible." He raised his chin in defiance.

"Ben-Gurion, the first prime minister of Israel, once said, 'The most difficult we'll do at once, the impossible might take a little longer.'"

"I'll see what I can do." He seemed very unhappy when he left the room.

Several minutes later, the receptionist walked in with a hot cup of coffee on a silver tray with a creamer and a sugar bowl. I wasn't sure at first if I should drink the coffee, since it could be laced, but then I realized that if they wanted to knock me out, there was very little I could do about it in this place. All I had to worry about was the possibility that the man I was talking to (or the one behind the mirror) was working for the Mossad, or CIA, or the FBI, or all of the above. And that he wouldn't decide to defect minutes after I left the building. But that was the risk one had to take in this business. I grimaced to myself as I wondered whether I was still in the business or on the outside being used.

I stirred some drops of cream into the coffee and raised the cup in a gesture toward the mirror. I had no doubt that I made someone behind it either smile or feel uncomfortable.

When my friend came back, he had a series of questions.

"Is the coffee okay?" he asked, playing the gracious host.

"Surprisingly so."

"Why surprising?"

"I would expect the tea to be good, but the coffee I find a very nice surprise."

"Very well then." He sat down. "This shouldn't take too long."

I lit a cigarette and offered him one.

"Thank you." He took the cigarette. "Americans never offer a cigarette."

"That's because they all have plenty if they want them."

He nodded, smiling. "Well, what my friends would like to know is, are you still in the employment of the Mossad or are you now on your own?"

"I'm on my own in the employment of the Mossad. What do you mean, 'friends'? Is this in front of some bloody committee or something?" I was playing a part I knew well from contact with Mossad agents. No one wants his name or the fact that he is involved in a situation like this made public, and a group of several people is regarded as public.

"No, no. It's as you say, a figure of speech. Just my boss and me." He looked at the mirror and said to me, "He says cheers to you too."

"Okay, so I'm on probation. The bloody assholes think they are God. I made one small mistake and they shafted me. Let me tell you, I'm going to show these bastards where the fish pisses from."

"How long is your probation?"

"Six months. That way, I lose my rotation turn this year, so I'll have to sit in headquarters for another three years before I'm rotated abroad."

"So what are you doing in America?"

"Visiting my father and trying to get recruited by a foreign agency."

This seemed to amuse him. "What do you expect to make doing this?"

"What are you people willing to pay?"

"That will depend on what you bring in. If, of course, we decide to make a deal."

"I'll be very frank with you. Your reputation is not very good as a source of income, but it is said that you do take care of your own. I mean, I wouldn't want to work for somebody who would have nothing to trade if things went wrong."

"That is a very valid point." He nodded at me and at the mirror. It seemed that I was giving all the right answers. The conversation went on for almost a whole hour, during which time I learned the real reason that the Americans would not offer the man cigarettes. He almost finished mine without once offering me any of his, which were in his shirt pocket and in plain view. He was one of the types we in the army used to call the Yours Filter smokers.

"Okay, my friend," he said, "one last thing. We know that your company puts everyone in its staff through a lie detector test every six months or so."

I nodded in approval. The man knew his stuff. Ephraim hadn't been sure if this would come up. "Don't worry about that. I thought about it before I set foot in this building."

"Okay then, what's your solution?"

"What they ask is fairly routine. You have to be sure not to lie, so when they ask me if I have made contact with an enemy agent, I will say yes."

"And?" He frowned.

"After the questioning, they will want me to explain. I will tell them about the brochures. It's a thing in the Mossad to bring brochures. You bring as many and from as many places as you can. They end up in the library and help officers to build up their cover stories. I had placed your country's name on my list of promised brochures several weeks ago."

The man was clearly amused by the solution. I, on the other hand, was very happy he bought it because I had no idea if the trick would have worked. I knew, though, that they wouldn't much care if it didn't; as long as I was satisfied and willing to take the risk, it was no skin off their backs.

"We will think this over and contact you at your hotel room. How long will you stay there?"

"Not long, I hope. Once I get your answer, I'm out of there. If you don't call me in three days, I'll know there is no deal."

"Here." He scribbled a number on a small piece of paper and handed it to me. "Before you leave, call me. We don't want to lose you just because of a technical problem in communication."

"Thanks." I took the paper and followed him down the steep staircase. Before letting me out of the building, he handed me a pile of brochures. "Don't forget what you came for."

"Thanks again." I took the brochures and headed out into the rain, my hood pulled tightly over my head and my face to the ground. I was happy to be out. The fresh air was a blessing. After turning the corner, I started a testing course. I wanted to see whether I was being followed. You can never be too careful.

I was very hungry. After realizing that no one was tailing me, I stopped at the Dupont Circle. I had my traditional hot dog and headed back to the hotel. The subway station in Silver Spring was almost deserted. I stopped at the pay phones on the station wall, taking the last one in the row and facing the empty hall. I dialed the operator, gave her the number, and asked for a collect call. Ephraim was on the line almost instantly.

"Well, what do you have to say?"

"I visited my uncle from the Old Country." I knew there was no need for speaking in code since my line was picked at random and therefore clean, even if I was being followed, and his was a secure line—he had to make sure of that. Still, it was a hard habit to kick.

"How did it go?"

"If there is no way for them to check at your end, I have no doubt I'm their next Philby."[2]

"It went that well?"

"What did you expect?"

"So now we have to sit and see what happens next. I have a good feeling about this."

"I'll get back to the hotel. I don't want them to call and not find me."

"Well, you shouldn't sit there all the time. If you played it the way we decided, they'll be expecting a playful person, not one who will pass up a good time in the city for his work. Go out and enjoy yourself. After all, you have a reputation to keep up. We have a series of jobs for you after this one."

"With the few dollars I have, it's not easy to play the playboy."

"That's okay; you'll be getting money soon. Just use what you have to build your image."

"When will I see you?"

"Once this little episode is finished, I'll come over."

"What will you do if you find what we're looking for?"

"That's a problem in itself. I can't just waltz in and accuse someone. I'll have to manipulate someone I know in the Shaback and put

---

2. Philby: Kim Philby, a Soviet mole in British intelligence.

them on the trail without letting out much. But don't you worry about that. If he's there, I'll nail him, and we'll chalk one up for you."

"Yeah," I replied. "A lot of good that will do me, that chalk mark."

"It will mean a hell of a lot when you come in from the cold."

There was silence on the line. I could feel myself choking up. I had figured that I would do whatever I had to do, and then I would fade into oblivion, living with Bella and the kids somewhere in Canada, doing something or other. Coming in from the cold had not been in the cards for me, not until he said it over the phone as if it were a given, something he'd always thought would happen. "You never said anything about coming back."

"What did you think?"

"I don't know. To be honest with you, I didn't think about it."

"Do your job, my boy, and we'll talk about it later. This call is getting too long for my system. I'll call you if anything happens. You call me if there's anything new too."

The line went dead. I stood for several minutes, receiver in hand, trying to comprehend what I had just heard. There *was* a way back into the life; suddenly things were not as black as I had believed they were.

I was in a very good mood when I left the station. I decided to have a good time that night. It was part of the job, as Ephraim had said.

CHAPTER 15

My spirits were high when I got back to the hotel. It amazed me how I could be on an emotional high while walking so close to the edge. It was probably the old sense of power, which I hadn't felt for some time. But the doubts I still had were giving me a pain in my gut. I was a pessimist by nature, though I led my life taking risks. I was curious to know what was happening in the Soviet embassy.

I had little doubt they'd sent a communication to Moscow, passing on all the information collected in our meeting and asking for instructions.

After spending some time in the hotel bar, I decided to stay in that evening and not head out to the city. It was the first time I'd stayed at the hotel after the happy hour, and I was surprised at how the place filled up. There was more to do in this little place than I could have found in the city. I was sitting at a table meant for five, and it didn't take long for some newcomers to join me. I made a new group of friends: normal regular people, the kind you find in any American city: honest, fair, and very vulnerable. One was a painting contractor and another a slightly odd guy who had a part-time job with the city's gardening department; he was newly divorced and extremely high-strung.

The contractor, a big burly guy, was friendly and very protective of his odd friend. He spent most of his time telling anyone who'd listen how much money he had made that day—not working too hard. In fact, when he described what he'd done, it seemed to me he'd earned every penny he made. After he was finished telling about that, he went on to talk about what was planned for tomorrow. Somehow the simplicity and basic integrity of these people was like a breath of fresh air. I envied their uncomplicated lives, the fact that they could plan for tomorrow with some certainty. Being in their presence rubbed some of that off on me. I couldn't help wondering what they would have said had they known who I really was and what I was up to.

For the next four days, there was nothing. I was starting to get restless and called Ephraim. He wasn't there, and the answering machine didn't take my call. By the fifth day, the line was disconnected. This could mean nothing but trouble. Were they on to Ephraim at headquarters?

Reacting to such a situation is the hardest thing to do. You are in what you might regard as a relatively safe situation in a fairly comfortable place. Suddenly, without knowing whether there is a real danger or just some mistake or mechanical problem, you must get up and leave it all behind. The odds are even that it is a mistake. The price for not reacting to a real problem, however, is high.

That morning, I had paid my hotel bill and realized that I had about fifty dollars left. I was starting to get very worried. It was one thing to be disconnected, but it was far worse to be totally broke while it happened.

At that point, I had to consider the possibility that the gamble hadn't paid off. Even though there was nothing new when I had spoken to Bella, and that was somewhat reassuring, I had no doubt that if the Mossad learned about my trip to the Soviet embassy, they would not want to tip me off. I could see it in my mind's eye: Ephraim, now trying to get his ass out of the fire, getting on the bandwagon and suggesting ways to bring me in. If there was anyone I should worry about, it was he.

At this point, if the Mossad was aware of my contact with the KGB, they'd want above all to have a talk with me and measure the amount of damage my escapade had caused. That's a normal procedure called damage control. On the other hand, if it were left up to an exposed Ephraim, he'd want to have me eliminated. That was natural and very understandable; I knew I would have done the same. I had to disappear and stay in contact at the same time. I wanted to see what might happen in the hotel, but not be around if anything did.

There was a small plaza in front of the office building across the street from the hotel. Remembering that the Mossad had access to the reservation setup of just about every hotel chain in the world, I had no doubt that my exact location could be found in a matter of hours with nothing more than a few phone calls. I decided to spend my days in the hotel and the nights on a bench on the edge of the small plaza overlooking the hotel. If they were going to come for me, it would be at night, and if that happened, I wanted to see it not from the confines of my room but from a safe distance.

Because of the delay in communications, I had to consider the option that when Ephraim renewed the contact, he might be attempting to trap me. I could feel that I was becoming paranoid, but for good reason. I tried Ephraim's phone again. The line was still disconnected. If things didn't clear up by tomorrow, I had two choices: I could just fall out of sight for a while and see what happened, or I could call my friend Rolly, the Mossad liaison to the CIA stationed at the Israeli embassy here in Washington. I would meet with him and bring everything out into the open. I had it all planned out in my head; I'd bring along a newspaper reporter so that I wouldn't just vanish, and my problem would be solved somewhere outside Tel Aviv.

But there was time for that later. Now I had to make sure I was out of the hotel once it got dark. During the day, I'd gone to a Salvation Army store and bought myself a long ragged overcoat. I brought it back to the hotel wrapped in a regular shopping bag. I also placed a supermarket cart at the end of the outdoor parking lot by the hotel's back door. I didn't shave that day and had a mickey of Cutty Sark rum in the shopping bag along with the overcoat. Once it got dark, I took the elevator to the underground parking lot, and there I took the coat out of the bag. By the time I came out of the back door of the hotel and threw a pile of laundry into the shopping cart, I was indistinguishable from any of the other homeless people who invisibly filled the streets.

I positioned myself on the hard bench and got ready for the night, warming myself with an occasional sip of rum. It was cold and lonely. More than anything, the night out on the street is long. I wanted to make sure that I didn't fall asleep so that I could see if there was any activity around the hotel, the kind of activity someone with a Mossad hit team after him might expect.

Nothing happened—nothing that was of any interest to me, that is. Drugs were bought and sold on the street, a car was stolen not twenty feet from where I was located, and another homeless person wanted to get into a fight with me over what he claimed was his bench.

By four-thirty in the morning, I realized they were not coming, or if they had come, I hadn't seen them. There was always the chance that they were waiting for me in my room, so I wasn't going to go back until I could get someone to come up to the room with me. There were at least another four hours to go before I could do that. The bench was getting much too cold. I walked the few blocks over to the subway station, where I spent the rest of the night on the floor, leaning against the large ticket dispenser. I'd left the shopping cart outside the hotel and was sure I wouldn't have it in the morning when I came out.

At seven-thirty, I woke up, realizing that I had been asleep for some time with commuters rushing all about, ignoring me as if I weren't there. It was as though I had clocked myself out of existence. This was something I would not soon forget; that sort of device could come in extremely handy in the line of work I was involved in.

Thursday, May 1, 1986

I slowly staggered back to the hotel. The cart was untouched. I left it by the back door and went into the underground parking, where I got back into being myself. I entered the lobby. Using the house phone, I called for someone to please come and fix the tap in my room because there was no water. I watched as the service man walked out of his tool room. I joined him in the elevator. I waited at the end of the hall while he went to my room and knocked on the door. When he got no response, he opened the door with a pass key and entered. I ran to the door and went in after him.

"Did you call with a problem, sir?" he asked, looking somewhat bewildered.

"No water," I said, pointing to the closed washroom. I scanned the room; it was empty. The service man checked the taps and informed me that all was well. I apologized, and he left. I needed to use the washroom and badly wanted a shower. Afterward, I called room service. At that point, I could have just about eaten a horse.

There were no messages for me and no sign that anyone had been in the room. I'll call the embassy at eleven, I decided; I'll try Ephraim one more time, then it's over. The big breakfast I'd ordered could very well be my last. The waiter was at my door. I opened it and turned back into the room. Before he could close the door, I heard him talking to someone behind me. "Excuse me, sir, you can't just—"

I turned on the spot, moving slightly out of the way, ready to duck around the corner. I was expecting to see a gun pointing in my direction; instead, I caught the big grin on Ephraim's face. "It's okay, it's okay," he was saying to the surprised waiter. "The man is expecting me, right?" He turned to face me.

"Sure, it's okay. Would you care to join me for breakfast?"

"No thanks, I'll just have a coffee."

The waiter put the tray on the table and handed me the check. I signed the paper and ushered him out. I turned on Ephraim. "Do you have any idea how close you came to blowing the whole thing? Can you even imagine what would have happened if I'd decided that yesterday was enough?"

"Things were out of my hands. I couldn't get in touch with you."

"What about the bloody phone? Who disconnected the phone?"

"What are you talking about? The phone is fine."

I handed him the receiver. "Show me."

"Not from this phone. We'll go out later, and I'll call from a pay phone."

"You call now." I wasn't backing off. My tone was harsh. I wasn't ready to take any more bullshit.

He grabbed the receiver and dialed direct, using his calling card number. After listening for several seconds, he seemed flustered. "You're right! What the hell is going on?" He dialed another number and waited. "What the hell is the matter with number twelve?" he snapped at someone on the other end. He listened for several seconds, then said, "Do you know that could have cost us a life? If something happens to my man because of you, then you'd better not be there when I come back."

I could hear the incoming voice but couldn't really make out what the man was saying; all I could get was the panic in his voice. "No," Ephraim went on, "I don't want the line restored, you get me a new one and I want it now, and it better be working if I call it in the next hour."

He listened, then grabbed the pen from the night table and scribbled a number on the hotel pad. While he was still talking, he handed me the pad. When he hung up, I was already seated, buttering the toast and taking the cover off the order of eggs and triple bacon.

The only comfort I could draw from what had happened was the fact that, had this been a Mossad operation and not one run by a rogue element within the Mossad, it never would have happened: It's not like the Mossad to screw up on the hardware and technical side. I could trust him now, but it was funny that it was trust by default.

He poured coffee into the glass I had brought from the bathroom.

"Did the Russian call you back?" he asked.

"No," I snapped at him. "And don't change the subject." I was still angry about the phone screwup.

"I'm sorry," he said, trying to catch my eye. I was staring into my plate, dipping the toast into the soft egg yolk. "Someone screwed up. These things happen."

I looked at him. "You should have made sure they didn't. If you were only a few hours later getting here, the whole thing would have been over."

"What were you going to do?"

"That's none of your business. I was going to take care of myself. What did you expect?"

"We're on the same side." He had a slightly embarrassed look. "What did you plan to do?"

"What brings you here?" I asked, ignoring his question.

"I just got saddled with the tail end of an operation," he said.

I wasn't going to say anything until he was finished.

"It's the old Trojan dick trick." He lit a cigarette.

"What's that?" I couldn't help smiling; I'd never heard it called that before.

"I knew that would get your attention," he said, grinning. "Shimon activated Operation Trojan in February of this year."

I nodded. I'd still been in the Mossad when that order was given, and because of my naval background and acquaintance with most of the commanders in the navy, I participated in the planning for the operation as liaison with the navy.

A Trojan was a special communication device that could be planted by naval commandos deep inside enemy territory. The device would act as a relay station for misleading transmissions made by the disinformation unit in the Mossad, called LAP,[1] and intended to be received by American and British listening stations. Originating from an IDF navy ship out at sea, the prerecorded digital transmissions could be picked up only by the Trojan. The device would then rebroadcast the transmission on another frequency, one used for official business in the enemy country, at which point the transmission would finally be picked up by American ears in Britain.

The listeners would have no doubt they had intercepted a genuine communication, hence the name Trojan, reminiscent of the mythical Trojan horse. Further, the content of the messages, once deciphered, would confirm information from other intelligence sources, namely the Mossad. The only catch was that the Trojan itself would have to be located as close as possible to the normal origin of such transmissions, because of the sophisticated methods of triangulation the Americans and others would use to verify the source.

In the particular operation Ephraim was referring to, two elite units in the military had been made responsible for the delivery of the Trojan device to the proper location. One was the Matkal[2] reconnaissance unit and the other was Flotilla 13, the naval commandos. The

---

1. LAP: LohAma Psicologit. Psychological warfare, or, as it's known in the West, disinformation.

2. Matkal: Top military reconnaissance unit of the Israeli army.

commandos were charged with the task of planting the Trojan device in Tripoli, Libya.

On the night of February 17–18, two Israeli missile boats, the SAAR 4–class *Moledet,* armed with Harpoon and Gabriel surface-to-surface missiles, among other weaponry, and the *Geula,* a Hohit-class missile boat with a helicopter pad and regular SAAR 4–class armament, conducted what seemed like a routine patrol of the Mediterranean, heading for the Sicilian channel and passing just outside the territorial waters of Libya. Just north of Tripoli, the warships, which were visible to radar both in Tripoli and on the Italian island of Lampedusa, slowed down to about four knots—just long enough to allow a team of twelve naval commandos in four wet submarines nicknamed "pigs" and two low-profiled speedboats called "birds" to disembark. The pigs could carry two commandos each and all their fighting gear. The birds, equipped with an MG 7.62-caliber machine gun mounted over the bow and an array of antitank shoulder-carried missiles, could facilitate six commandos each, while towing the empty pigs. The birds brought the pigs as close to the shore as possible, thus cutting down the distance the pigs would have to travel on their own. (The pigs were submersible and silent but relatively slow.)

Two miles off the Libyan coast, the lights of Tripoli could be seen glistening in the southeast. Eight commandos slipped quietly into the pigs and headed for shore. The birds stayed behind at the rendezvous point, ready to take action should the situation arise. Once they reached the beach, the commandos left their cigarlike transporters submerged in the shallow water and headed inland, carrying a dark green Trojan cylinder six feet long and seven inches in diameter. It took two men to carry it.

A gray van was parked on the side of the road about one hundred feet from the water, on the coastal highway leading from Sabratah to Tripoli and on to Benghazi. There was hardly any traffic at that time of night. The driver of the van seemed to be repairing a flat tire. He stopped working as the team approached and opened the back doors of the van. He was a Mossad combatant. Without a word said, four of the men entered the van and headed for the city. The other four returned to the water, where they took a defensive position by the submerged pigs. Their job was to hold this position to ensure an escape route for the team now headed for the city.

At the same time, a squadron of Israeli fighters was refueling south of Crete, ready to assist. They were capable of keeping any ground forces away from the commandos, allowing them a not-so-clean getaway. At this point, the small commando unit was divided into three details—its most vulnerable state. Were any of the details to run into enemy forces, they were instructed to act with extreme prejudice before the enemy turned hostile.

The van parked at the back of an apartment building on Al Jamhuriyh Street in Tripoli, less than three blocks away from the Bab al Azizia barracks that were known to house Qadhafi's headquarters and residence. By then, the men in the van had changed into civilian clothing. Two stayed with the van as lookouts and the other two helped the Mossad combatant take the cylinder to the top floor of the five-story building. The cylinder was wrapped in a carpet.

In the apartment, the top section of the cylinder was opened and a small dishlike antenna was unfolded and placed in front of the window facing north. The unit was activated, and the Trojan horse was in place.

The Mossad combatant had rented the apartment for six months and had paid the rent in advance. There was no reason for anyone except the combatant to enter the apartment. However, if someone should decide to do so, the Trojan would self-destruct, taking with it most of the upper part of the building. The three men headed back to the van and to their rendezvous with their friends on the beach.

After dropping the commandos at the beach, the combatant headed back for the city, where he would monitor the Trojan unit for the next few weeks. The commandos wasted no time and headed out to sea. They didn't want to be caught in Libyan waters at daybreak. They reached the birds and headed at full speed to a prearranged pickup coordinate, where they met with the missile boats that had brought them in.

By the end of March, the Americans were already intercepting messages broadcast by the Trojan, which was only activated during heavy communication traffic hours. Using the Trojan, the Mossad tried to make it appear that a long series of terrorist orders were being transmitted to various Libyan embassies around the world (or, as they were called by the Libyans, Peoples' Bureaus). As the Mossad had hoped, the transmissions were deciphered by the Americans and construed as ample proof that the Libyans were active sponsors of terrorism. What's more, the Americans pointed out, Mossad reports confirmed it.

The French and the Spanish, though, were not buying into the new stream of information. To them, it seemed suspicious that suddenly, out of the blue, the Libyans, who'd been extremely careful in the past, would start advertising their future actions. They also found it suspicious that in several instances Mossad reports were worded similarly to coded Libyan communications. They argued further that, had there truly been after-the-fact Libyan communications regarding the attack, then the terrorist attack on the La Belle discotheque[3] in West Berlin on April 5 could have been prevented, since surely there would have been communications before, enabling intelligence agencies listening in to prevent it. Since the attack *wasn't* prevented, they reasoned that it must not be the Libyans who did it, and the "new communications" must be bogus.

The French and the Spanish were right. The information *was* bogus, and the Mossad didn't have a clue who planted the bomb that killed one American serviceman and wounded several others. But the Mossad was tied in to many of the European terrorist organizations, and it was convinced that in the volatile atmosphere that had engulfed Europe, a bombing with an American victim was just a matter of time.

Heads of the Mossad were counting on the American promise to retaliate with vengeance against any country that could be proven to support terrorism. The Trojan gave the Americans the proof they needed. The Mossad also plugged into the equation Qadhafi's lunatic image and momentous declarations, which were really only meant for internal consumption. It must be remembered that Qadhafi had marked a line in the water at that time, closing off the Gulf of Sidra as Libyan territorial waters and calling the new maritime border the line of death (an action that didn't exactly give him a moderate image). Ultimately, the Americans fell for the Mossad ploy head over heels, dragging the British and the Germans somewhat reluctantly in with them.

Operation Trojan was one of the Mossad's greatest successes. It brought about the air strike on Libya that President Reagan had promised—a strike that had three important consequences. First, it derailed a deal for the release of the American hostages in Lebanon, thus preserving the Hizballah (Party of God) as the number one enemy in the eyes of the West. Second, it sent a message to the entire Arab world, telling them exactly where the United States stood regarding the Arab-Israeli conflict. Third, it boosted the Mossad's image of itself, since it was they who, by ingenious sleight of hand, had prodded the United States to do what was right.

It was only the French who didn't buy into the Mossad trick and

---

3. La Belle discotheque: The terrorist attack on this location was said to have been linked to the Libyans and was the catalyst for the April 14 bombing of Libya by the Americans.

were determined not to align themselves with the aggressive American act. The French refused to allow the American bombers to fly over their territory on their way to attack Libya.

On April 14, 1986, one hundred and sixty American aircraft dropped over sixty tons of bombs on Libya. The attackers bombed Tripoli international airport, Bab al Azizia barracks, Sidi Bilal naval base, the city of Benghazi, and the Benine airfield outside Benghazi. The strike force consisted of two main bodies, one originating in England and the other from flattops in the Mediterranean. From England came twenty-four F-111s from Lakenheath, five EF-111s from Upper Heyford, and twenty-eight refueling tankers from Mildenhall and Fairford. In the attack, the air force F-111s and the EF-111s were joined by eighteen A-6 and A-7 strike and strike support aircraft, six F\A-18 fighters, fourteen EA-6B electronic jammer planes, and other support platforms. The navy planes were catapulted from the carriers *Coral Sea* and *America*. On the Libyan side, there were approximately forty civilian casualties, including Qadhafi's adopted daughter. On the American side, a pilot and his weapons officer were killed when their F-111 exploded.

After the bombing, the Hizballah broke off negotiations regarding the hostages they held in Beirut and executed three of them, including one American named Peter Kilburn. As for the French, they were rewarded for their nonparticipation in the attack by the release at the end of June of two French journalists held hostage in Beirut. (As it happened, a stray bomb hit the French embassy in Tripoli during the raid.)

Ephraim had spelled it all out for me and confirmed some of the information I'd already known. He then went on. "After the bombing of Libya, our friend Qadhafi is sure to stay out of the picture for some time. Iraq and Saddam Hussein are the next target. We're starting now to build him up as the big villain. It will take some time, but in the end, there's no doubt it'll work."

"But isn't Saddam regarded as moderate toward us, allied with Jordan, the big enemy of Iran and Syria?"

"Yes, that's why I'm opposed to this action. But that's the directive, and I must follow it. Hopefully, you and I will be done with our little operation before anything big happens. After all, we have already destroyed his nuclear facility, and we are making money by selling him technology and equipment through South Africa."

"That still doesn't explain why you played hide-and-seek with me."

"I was incommunicado in Belgium, explaining to an Iraqi how to hit the oil pipeline in Kuwait. As you can imagine, I wasn't alone there, and no one was coming or going until the man was on his way."

"One man?"

"Yes, one. He'll instruct his friends when he gets back there."

"And you trust him to do the job?" It sounded fishy to me. It was almost standard procedure in the Mossad that acts of sabotage were carried out only by our people, and that the locals were set up for the fall if something went wrong. Sending a team to get secondhand training was suicidal.

"He'll do the job."

"I'm willing to bet that he either blows himself up or gets caught."

"I sure hope you're right, because that is exactly what I'm banking on. What I mean is, he'll probably get caught, and by the time he's finished spilling the beans, the Kuwaitis will be positive that the man is working for the Iraqis, and that he's there to try and help overthrow the Kuwaiti royal family."

"And what the hell would be achieved by that?"

"Agitation, my boy, agitation, what else? Then we'll see where we can take it. After all, there's still a war going on between Iran and Iraq, and the Kuwaitis together with the Saudis are paying for most of it."

I was grateful to Ephraim for talking to me in such detail about things I had no direct connection with. It made me feel I was still part of it all. Within the Mossad, everybody told everybody else about everything. Had Ephraim not done that, we both knew he would have lost me.

I was now dumping large quantities of marmalade onto the remaining toasts and washing down the loaded triangles with hot coffee. Coffee, extra bacon, jelly, cigarettes, alcohol—it's funny how, when the pressure's on, healthy habits fly out the window.

"So what happened with our little escapade?" asked Ephraim. "You said the Russians didn't call you back?"

"No."

"Call them now."

I got up and took from my wallet the scrap of paper the Russian had given me. I dialed the number and waited.

"Hello?" came a heavy Russian-accented voice.

"I was waiting for your call."

"Is this Victor?"

"Yes. Do you have anything for me?"

"I'm sorry, but we will not be talking to you anymore. I'm sorry." And he hung up. He couldn't know how happy he made me feel.

"Well?" Ephraim was craning his head in my direction as though he could catch what I had to say faster if he was closer. He also helped himself to a piece of my toast.

"They don't want me."

"Yes!" He got up, punching a fist at an imaginary opponent. "Yes! We got the bastard."

"Who did you get?"

"I told you it couldn't be from operations. We got a request from the prime minister's office for information on several people that were let go from the Mossad in the last year. We sent up four files; yours was one. I had someone from Prudot [technical], using some half-assed story, set it up so that we could see which of the files were handled and by whom. The result was as I'd expected. Only yours was opened. It was ordered by the man in charge of security for the prime minister's office, a guy by the name of Levinson."

"Is he from Shaback?"

"No, he's office security, documentation, telephones, that sort of thing. They couldn't get someone in a better position if they recruited the head of the Shaback."

"What now?"

"It will take a while, but we will nail him before the end of the year. I passed a warning to my friend in the Shaback. I told him I got it from a liaison, but he can't use it formally because that would burn the source. He knows the situation, but he'll have to catch him on his own."

"So we did it," I exclaimed. "We actually did it, didn't we?"

He nodded. "Yes, it seems we did."

I was happy. After all, it wasn't every day that you nailed a Soviet spy. And it was so easy, thinking back on it now. It was a stroll in the park.

CHAPTER 16

I lit a cigarette and sat on the end of the bed. There were several minutes of silence, except for the dripping sound of a bad faucet.

"Okay. Now for your next assignment," said Ephraim.

"What is it?"

"You'll make a short journey across town and offer our British friends your services."

"The British? They're allies. What the hell do you need from them?"

"Nothing in particular. It's just that we know they're suspicious that we might have had something to do with the attempt to put a bomb on an El Al flight."

"The one that was foiled at Heathrow?"

"That's the one."

"But didn't El Al security prevent that at the last moment?"

"Exactly. There is a rumor running around that we did it to embarrass their security and show off our own, and at the same time to pin the terrorist tail on the Syrians."

"Did we?"

"Quite possibly. I have no idea, but the rumor has to stop."

"So you want me to go in there and tell them we didn't do it?" I was smiling; I found the whole thing amusing.

"No. You will tell them more or less what you have told the Soviets, except you'll tell them you're no longer working for us here." He handed me a manila envelope. "These are some papers you can give them to prove that you worked for the Mossad."

"Why don't we let them just ask their man in the Mossad to check me out?" I was now laughing.

"This is a simple job." He was serious. "I need you to do it as soon as you can. I will be here while you do it and leave after you're done."

"You know, this job doesn't quite jibe with what you've been telling me about the reason we're doing all this."

"And what's that?"

"I thought we were out to put the Mossad in the shit and force a change in the command. Suddenly, we're protecting their reputation?"

"We're killing two birds with one stone. On the one hand, we're cleaning up the reputation of Israel when it comes to this sort of unacceptable act, as well as putting the lid on Syrian diplomatic relations in England. Then, at the same time, we're giving you a good in with the British. If you don't come on as just a man on a vendetta now, you'll have more credibility with them later. We'll use that credibility to embarrass the Office and blow the London station out of the water."

"Will I have to wait long for the next job? I'm losing my patience, killing so much time here. I want to see the end of the tunnel, or at least a facsimile of it."

He smiled. I could see it wasn't easy for him—smiling, that is. He was involved in a world that was changing every moment, and he had to adapt. It was a lifestyle that took a big chunk out of a man's personality.

"Your next job is in the works as we speak. After it's done, you'll get back together with Bella and the kids."

"What's it going to be?" I was anxious.

"Not yet, Victor. First we have this British thing to do."

I wanted to press the point harder and see if I could get more out of him, but he leaned back in his seat. His rounded face seemed slightly amused, as though he were watching a Roadrunner cartoon for the tenth time, knowing the fate of the coyote but still going through the motions. His stare made me feel like the coyote, making a futile effort to catch the stupid bird and knowing full well I'd soon be taking the short way to the bottom of the canyon. I decided to let it go.

It seemed that he felt this was a time for a pep talk, since he now said: "You asked me once why don't we just leak things to the media and bring the Mossad down that way."

I nodded.

"We can't tear down the organization from the outside—it has too much credibility in Israel. No matter what we say, we can't even scratch its Teflon surface. It has to be shown for what it is: an incompetent, lazy, oversized, greedy monster. And that can only be done one step at a time. What we are starting now is an assault on the Mossad from its flanks. We will be hitting it from all directions, cutting the Medusa's heads off one at a time. We are betting our existence against the incompetence of the Mossad."

"How do you mean, 'betting'?"

"If the Office is as incompetent as we think it is, they'll never know what hit them. If they're as good as they want everybody to think, then"—he smiled—"we are toast."

"What about the reputation of the state? Not everybody can distinguish between Israel and its Mossad."

"That is true, but we will be dealing only with intelligence agencies, and they will know the difference. After all, we don't want to destroy the state in the process. We have to be very careful what we do. It is much like a demolition crew that must bring down a high-rise in the middle of a city. One way will destroy the city center; the other way takes a professional. If we're hasty, we could end up causing a breakdown in relations between Israel and every country in the world that the Mossad is screwing. And that would be just about every country in the world that we have a relationship with, plus a few more that we might have one with in the future. Our target is the Office and only the Office as it is now."

I sat and stared at him. I felt exhausted. I had no doubt as to what I was facing, but I was glad he had put the effort into explaining the situation the way he did. I had volunteered for the Mossad for that exact reason: to protect my country—not to protect the Mossad or its bosses. And if the Mossad was a threat to my country, then it was the enemy. I'd volunteered for the navy after I came back from Canada for the same reason. I believed that what you truly love deserves to be defended.

"There is one more thing." His voice was back to normal. There was not a trace of the emotion he'd just shown. He spoke like a teller counting someone else's money. "There is a Kidon team running around New York searching for a man they believe has made contact with the PLO."

I could feel the blood turning to ice in my veins, and my knees were shaking. I raised my hands and shook my head. "What did you say?"

"You heard me." He kept his matter-of-fact composure.

"You're taking this very well, considering it's not your ass the Kidon is after."

"Well, as things stand at the moment, they aren't after yours either."

"Whose, then?"

"Apparently, the PLO man you spoke to was not as smart as you might have thought, or he didn't really give a shit. Anyway, he passed the information on to Tunis and it was picked up by Unit 8200.[1]"

"You want to tell me the jerk actually phoned them about me?"

"Yes."

"Did he identify me?"

"That's what I'm trying to tell you. No, he only gave a description, and that wasn't too good. I believe the team will try and pick him up and see if they can get a better identification from him."

"Did he tell them who I said I was?"

"Yes, they know he reported a so-called Israeli intelligence officer, but they aren't sure. You know that every little fart says he's from the Mossad. I'll bet you half the Israelis living in New York have told that to someone at one time or another. It's the Israeli *Mayflower*; everyone was on it when it hit Plymouth Rock. And yes, they called for a code white.[2]"

He smiled, but I suddenly wasn't in the mood to do so. I knew he was trying to make light of it, but the Kidon team would not give up easily. Their reputation was not that of losers. "What about the Kahane people, the ones that were watching the PLO office? Has the Office gotten to them?"

"Not yet, but you can bet they will. I don't want to scare you, or on the other hand give you a false sense of security, but I really don't think you have too much to worry about. The Kidon team will do their little song and dance and then go home. There are much more important things for them to do than chase the wind."

"If they can get a good description of me, they will not exactly be chasing the wind. What if they ask the Kahane man, the one I left to piss in that peepshow?"

Ephraim smiled. "Him you don't have to worry about. He wouldn't say anything."

"Why not? He got a good look at me, and so did his friend."

"Well, like I said, I don't think he'll be telling that to anyone, not the way it happened anyway. You see, when his friend finally came to

---

1. Unit 8200: A unit in Aman (a Hebrew abbreviation for military intelligence) that is in charge of shooting down communications: telephone, telex, and just about any other open-air transmission.

2. Code white: An Israeli intelligence officer crossing the line; high alert.

get him, he said that he was attacked by a whole group of Palestinians, and he said that you, or the one who entered the PLO office, was a Palestinian leader or something. It made him a hero in his tiny little circle of Judeo-Nazis, and he didn't have to admit it was done to him by one man that he was supposed to be following."

"How do you know that?"

"We have people in there. You don't think we'd let those jerks run around loose, do you?"

It was good to hear, but it didn't really calm me down. In fact, I was starting to get more edgy the more I thought about it. "It appears that someone in the Office is taking it seriously, or they wouldn't have sent the Kidon team to the U.S. That is sensitive terrain. What do they have? I mean, if it was me doing the investigation, I would first try and find out where the hell I, Victor Ostrovsky, was. I'm the last man out of the system, and here, before you can say Jack Robinson, someone answering my description pops up at the offices of the PLO in New York."

"Well, that's probably what they're thinking, but to be able to pin something on you, they have to find you first."

"So I am a fugitive now?"

"No, but watch out. Make your security checks and don't slip into some euphoria just because you're on American soil. I know that Mousa from security is trying to get ahold of you; he had someone call your wife asking her to pass a message on to you that he wants you to call him. But for some reason or other, I guess she hasn't passed it on to you."

"No, I didn't get the message. It's possible she thinks he wants me back in the system and she prefers I stay out. I have no idea."

"Just make sure you don't ask her. They're listening to her line. If you know something that she didn't tell you, they will realize you're still connected, and you'll blow the whole thing."

"Will you be informed about what the Kidon team are doing, or will you just find out after the fact?"

"I'm in the loop, if that's what you mean. I'll have some knowledge beforehand and, yes, I will warn you if things get hot."

It turned out that this little game with the British was no less dangerous than the Soviet exercise. In fact, it was considerably more difficult. We were facing a very sophisticated agency that had good if not excellent connections with the Mossad. The fact that there was growing concern in that agency regarding the Mossad's dirty tricks was not something we could latch on to right away. It would be necessary to dig a little first.

I had to have a reason for coming to them, and had to be able to prove that I was Mossad. Ephraim gave me several documents that I could use to convince them that I was who I said I was. One was a photocopy of a British passport that I had used in an operation in Europe almost a year earlier. Ephraim handed it to me, with a backgrounder form for the passport.

I was also to use the contact I had made with the British representative to the Middle East who was in charge of the British cemeteries in this particular corner of the now defunct Empire. In the Office, it was believed that he was working for British intelligence and was gathering tactical data in the area. Posing as a Canadian filmmaker, I had contacted him during an exercise and had tried to milk him for information. Ephraim had no doubt that if the gentleman was indeed working for British intelligence, as we thought, he would have reported that incident and would be able to identify me.

We decided that I would play the man who has two reasons for coming to them. One would be money, the other revenge. I would also say that I was worried that Mossad activities in the United Kingdom could bring about a wave of anti-Semitism if things got out of hand and a British version of a Pollard case exploded, exposing British Jews in the service of the Mossad.

There was no doubt that such an event would lead to the revival of the controversy over if not the belief in the *Protocols of the Elders of Zion*.[3] Having the local authorities aware and ready could possibly prevent a wave of anti-Semitism that would result from a high-profile exposure of Jewish assistance to Mossad in Britain.

There was no way that the British intelligence would use such information to launch an anti-Jewish campaign. But since Aaron Sherf was the new head of the Tsafririm[4] department, and he was known in the system as a militant who believed that using the Jewish Diaspora was Israel's God-given right, he would push the activity in that field to the limit and cause something to break somewhere.

"So what do I tell them if they want to know more about this subject? I mean, there's no way we'll hand them *sayanim* on a platter."

---

3. *Protocols of the Elders of Zion*: An anti-Semitic publication that originated in nineteenth-century Russia and spoke of a plan created by the secret Jewish "government" (the so-called elders of Zion) to overthrow Christian society.

4. Tsafririm: The word translates as "morning breeze" and is the code name for the department in charge of actively supporting, helping, and activating the Jewish Diaspora.

"No, but we'll show them how to find them if they look. It's far better that they warn people than catch them. Suppose they caught a Jew working in their military industry and passing on information to Israel against the best interests of his country, or firm, for that matter. Such a case, working its way through the court system with the media coverage it would receive, would put every Jew in the Western world under suspicion. No doubt, in the trial information would come out that would prove he wasn't the only one. Then only God could help us, and the way we've been behaving the last thirty years, I doubt very much if we could count on Him."

It was about two in the afternoon when I got out of the cab about two blocks from the British embassy. The light blue glass building was set slightly back from the road. I came across a pay phone, found the number of the embassy in a phone book, and dialed. In less than two minutes, I managed to get through to the man in charge of security.

The chances were negligible that the phone was bugged. "I have been fired from the Mossad and I want to talk to someone in British intelligence. I have some information that I think might interest you."

The man on the other end didn't hesitate. "Are you in Washington?"

"Yes, in fact, I'm not that far from the embassy right now."

"Would you care to come down here?"

"Sure."

"How long would it take you to get here?"

"About ten minutes." I wanted to see if there would be any activity outside the embassy before I walked in. I had checked myself before, and I knew that I was clean. So if there was someone after me later, I would know where I picked up the surveillance.

I gave the man a description of what I was wearing and told him my first name. He said he would wait for me in the main entrance and that I should have some ID handy.

I was there in just over ten minutes, having grabbed a hot dog from a stand near the phone booth. This sort of activity made me hungry. I would usually lose my appetite once real danger was involved, but as things were, I felt fine. I was wearing a pinstripe suit and a pair of black shoes, a tan raincoat, and a yellow tie with small black symmetrical dots on it—the standard yuppie tie of the time. Paisley would have been my second choice; it appeared to have been the first choice of the gentleman who was waiting for me. Other than that, we were dressed almost the same. He must have been scratching his head when I gave him my description on the phone. No doubt he even had a similar raincoat hanging somewhere in the large building. He smiled as I approached, waiting for me inside the reception area while I went through the security section. There he greeted me with an even larger smile and an outstretched hand, introducing himself as Edward. After the initial niceties, he led me toward a second set of doors where he had to bend down to run his tag through a slot. It seemed that the thin chain that hung around his neck was too short.

We took the elevator to his office, and there was the raincoat, just as I'd thought. He had a set of planters on the window, just as we used to have in the Mossad building. There is apparently something about the game of espionage that makes you want to grow things.

"I haven't had a chance to talk to anyone about you, but I will take the initial information from you, and based on that, we will decide what the next step will be. Does that sound fair?" He was in his late thirties, a very British-looking chap, his smooth blond hair combed neatly to one side, where it kept falling slightly over his forehead. Occasionally, he'd push it back into place. His shirt collar was somewhat larger than his neck, which could have been the result of a diet he was on that was working faster than he had expected, or perhaps someone else was doing his shopping for him. He turned out to be very pleasant.

"Would you care for a cup of tea or something?"

"I'd love a coffee."

Edward popped his head out the door and spoke to someone on the other side, conveying the request. He then came back and took a block of paper out of his desk drawer, opened the passport I'd handed him, and copied my name and all other details onto the top of the form. I was itching to crack a few jokes about writing regulations and strict code demands that we'd usually say in the Mossad on such occasions, but I held back. I had no idea who this man was or what he was like. The fact that he was at the front end of some intelligence agency suggested that he wasn't part of the offensive but rather the defensive team and, in comparison to a Mossad case officer, a second or third stringer. Such a man could indeed be frustrated and not open to some types of humor. In fact, he might take it as a personal insult.

The tea and coffee arrived.

"So, Mr. Ostrovsky, what is it you'd like to talk to me about?"

I lit a cigarette, tossed the smoldering match into the ashtray, leaned back, and said, "Like I said on the phone, I was a member of the Mossad until a few weeks ago, when for various reasons I was sacked."

He was busy writing on his pad, not looking at me. "Why did you leave?"

"I was let go because of a series of fuckups and because of my big mouth."

"Meaning?"

"I voiced my political opinions, which are hardly fitting for a member of an organization with very right-wing leanings." Ephraim had made it clear to me, and I already knew it myself, that we were dealing with a sophisticated intelligence agency. There was going to be some sort of psychological analysis of the information I'd be providing, so all the personal information about me and my opinions would have to be accurate. My cover story, after all, was my real story, and I had to remember that.

The man did not react at all, which made the interview very strenuous. All he did was write and ask questions. At times, he would raise his hand, asking me to slow down so that he could catch up with the writing. I hated when people did that. In the modern world, with the advancement of technology and the availability of recording equipment, I found his way of working archaic and very inefficient. But this was his office, and he represented a group of people I wanted to talk to, so I was not about to complain.

The interview lasted almost three hours. I presented him with a single Mossad document, the false passport cover page that Ephraim had brought me. It was an eight-and-a-half-inch by eleven-inch sheet of paper with a photocopy of the first page of a British passport. The original passport was false, and the top part of the document gave a short rundown of who I was under that cover. On the back was a map identifying my exact address on a section of a London map. Attached was a color photo of my house and imaginary family, with a few words about each of them. The document was what we would call a tutorial cover. This would normally come with or before your false passport to the safe house where you would go over the last details of the cover story before going out on an operation. This was regarded as a thin cover, not what you needed if you were going to cross a border or be placed under more severe scrutiny. Nevertheless, this document was extremely professional, and anyone in the business who saw it would definitely be convinced that the bearer was not an amateur.

"I want to thank you very much, Mr. Ostrovsky, for what you have told me up to this point. I will surely pass this information on to the people that need to know. I'll be back in touch with you once I know what they want to do."

I knew this would be the procedure and therefore did not tell him anything beyond personal and peripheral information that was meant to establish who I was. The inquisition would come later.

"What now?"

"Where can I reach you?"

"I'll call you. When would you like me to do that?"

He thought for a minute. "How about Monday, at about the same time?"

I got up. "Monday, then."

CHAPTER 17

SUNDAY, MAY 4, 1986

Ephraim was not in his room first thing in the morning, but had left me a message with the front desk saying he'd had to leave very early but would be back for a late breakfast. The message was signed "David," the code name Ephraim and I had agreed on for a message that was legitimate. Had he left a message from "Mark," I'd know there was trouble.

I decided to stay in my room and wait for his call, which came at about ten-thirty. He was waiting for me in the dining room downstairs. It turned out that he hadn't had a minute's sleep; a mission in the Far East had been bungled, and he'd been called to take care of it. Having dealt with the Sri Lankans before, he made contact with their security service and was trying to recover the body of a Mossad case officer who'd been in Sri Lanka assisting the local government in rounding up the leadership of the Tamil Tigers, a resistance group fighting for a self-governed area in the north of the tear-shaped island. (At various times, the Mossad supported both sides in this conflict, providing weapons to each for a handsome profit.) The case officer had been shot in his hotel room in Colombo at the same time as a bomb exploded in a Lanka Air jumbo jet on the runway.

The main problem was not that the man had been killed, but rather that the Mossad was supposedly there under the auspices of the CIA station and the American delegation, yet was carrying out this activity without the knowledge of its American hosts.

By the time we were seated for breakfast, Ephraim had managed to get things under control. The body (said to be an apparent casualty of a car accident) was on a chartered plane on its way to Australia, from where the friendly local security service would help ship it back to Israel. He lit a cigarette and said, "Did you ask them for money?"

"Ask who?"

"The British."

I stared at him for a long minute. "No, it never came up."

"Well, next time you mustn't forget to bring up the money right at the beginning."

"Why? We know that no one actually pays until the information is evaluated. I'm supposed to be a professional and know these things."

"Still, you have to bring it up so that they don't think you're some conscientious volunteer. They need to think they have a hook in you so they can ask the questions they want to ask, and not just sit there and listen to you. You see, if they think you're only ideological, how would they know if you have an agenda or not? You need to make them think it's the money, so they understand the reason for your coming to them."

"I could probably get much more from the Syrians. Wouldn't that come up in their minds when they hear I only want money?"

"There would be several reasons why you would not go to the Syrians."

Our discussion took us into the afternoon, and I was starting to get tired. However, the nagging doubts that I'd had before had almost completely dissipated. Ephraim had armed me with some more documents for the meeting tomorrow. After dinner, he retired to his room, which this time was on the same floor as mine.

Ephraim wanted to be present the next day when I called the embassy, just in case there was something we'd overlooked.

I made the call and was asked to come to the embassy as soon as I could; two men had been sent over to talk to me.

Ephraim was satisfied. "We're going to kill several birds with one stone," he said.

"What will the birds be?"

"First, we'll let them know that we did not orchestrate the incident at the airport and that it was really an attempted act of terror that we prevented. Then, by causing the London station to screw up, we get rid of the station head. If we can stifle the London station, then we might just tarnish that clique enough to have an outsider sent in to clean house."

"Are you sure about that?"

"We'll be using the same technique the right-wingers used to get rid of Kimche in '82: tossing garbage into the wind. You're from the navy; you know what happens when you do that." He was grinning, stuffing his mouth with the end of a Coffee Crisp chocolate bar.

I wanted to see Bella and the girls; I was starting to grow more and more impatient in that regard. The urge would come upon me suddenly when I least expected it. I had big problems with the TV commercial for the AT&T phone company. They would show sentimental pictures of families together and then apart, reaching out for one another, under the slogan "Reach out and touch someone." I felt so lonely when that ad appeared that I preferred not to turn the set on when I was alone.

When I arrived at the British embassy, I was greeted by the same chap who'd interviewed me before. He was wearing the tie that I'd had on the previous day, and I wore the paisley that he'd worn then. Other than that, we kept to the "uniform."

"Nice to see you again," he said, bending to get the door open.

"Won't they give you a longer chain?" I asked.

"No, they like to keep our chains rather short." He chuckled and swung the glass door open, allowing me to enter ahead of him. He led the way to the elevator, but today we went to a different side of the building. He let me into an office very similar to his own, except that there were no planters and no papers on the large, somewhat scruffy-looking desk. The man seated behind the desk got up as we walked in and stretched out his hand, smiling. "I'm Steve. Nice of you to come back at such short notice."

I took his hand. "I'm Dave. Nice to be called back." I was smiling too.

"Dave? But I was under the impression that your name was Victor?" He looked down at the paper on the desk in front of him.

"Just kidding," I said, sitting down. "Dave was my 'Steve,' you see."

"Aha." His smile broadened. "So it *is* Victor?"

"Yes."

"Is there anything we can get you?" He sat behind his desk.

"I'd love a coffee," I said, not departing from the script. I took out my cigarette pack and placed it on the table, only to notice I was down to my last cigarette. "Would you happen to have a cigarette machine somewhere in the building?"

"I will see what I can round up," said the young man, and left.

"I understood that there would be more than one man here today."

"Yes. My colleague might come in a little later; he has a certain thing he wants to show you and get your opinion on."

"Will you be handling this case?"

"We'll be doing it together. Why do you ask?"

"There is the matter of the money. We need to discuss that before we go any further."

"I can assure you that we'll be more than grateful for your help. The money will depend totally on the value of what you have to say to us."

"Could you be more specific?"

"I'm afraid not. You see, we're not the ones who make that decision. After all, we don't normally gather information about Israel since it's an ally."

I lit the cigarette, speaking to him through a puff of smoke. "Why don't we cut the bullshit right off the top," I said. "We're here for a reason. You want something that you know very well I have. You want to verify first that I am who I am. Then you want to know what you can get out of me."

"I would prefer to think of it as an exchange. . . ."

"Come on, we both know that if you could get me on a rack and beat the information out of me, you would. And apart from money, there is nothing I want from you. If you paid me now, I would leave and let you keep that neutrality you're talking about. So, where would you like to start?"

"From the beginning, I suppose. What was your rank and position in the Mossad?'

"My rank was colonel, but that was because I carried my rank over from the military, where I was a lieutenant colonel. At the time I left the Mossad, I was working on the Danish desk and occasionally doing jobs for other desks."

"Is there a British desk?"

"Is the Pope Catholic?"

"Did you work on that desk?"

"From time to time."

"Is there a clandestine station in London?"

"Yes. In the embassy."

"How many officers?"

"Five, as of about two months ago. I can't be sure at the moment, but no more than six."

"Who is the head of the station?"

"I'm really bad with names, you know," I said, smiling.

"Would you be able to recognize him from a photo?"

"Sure, do you have one?"

"We have photos of most of the diplomats. It's fairly standard for them to give us a photo when they come to get their diplomatic credentials."

"Let's make life simple. You show me photos, I'll identify the men. What next?"

"Why are you coming to us? Why not the Americans or the French? And if it's money you want, why not some Arab country? I mean, they'd probably pay you a bundle."

"I don't like to deal with people when I'm on their soil; they have too much control. Besides, you're an ally, so in effect I'm not really betraying my country, I'm only selling you information I think you deserve to know. Like they say Pollard did."

The young man came back with coffee and a new pack of cigarettes. He apologized for not having American cigarettes, but these were all they had in the canteen.

After he'd left, Steve and I established a more relaxed dialog. A few minutes later, Steve's partner stuck his head around the door, smiling, and entered the room. He was roughly the same height as Steve, about six feet, well built, and very tanned. It was as if he'd just returned from a trip to the Caribbean—either that, I thought, or he has some odd skin disease. His blond hair had almost completely turned silver. It was combed the same way as Edward's hair, only it seemed to be more used to the position, since it hardly moved.

Steve brought him up to speed, and we went on with the conversation. Robert, the newcomer, opened a large folder and pulled out several cardboard sheets with passport photos on them. "Would you mind looking at these and telling me if you can recognize anyone?"

I glanced at them and then put them back on the desk. "Yes, I do."

"Well, would you be so kind as to point them out to us?"

"Why don't you tell me who you think the head of the station is, and I'll take it from there."

"But," said Steve, obviously taken aback and staring at Robert, "that would be very unusual."

"You mean you get Mossad case officers waltzing into your offices every day, and that is why you flew all night from England to talk to me?"

"Why should we tell you anything?" Robert asked.

"That way we will get over the credibility part. If I can prove to you that I know what I'm talking about, we will have a much easier time."

"This one." Robert pointed to a photo.

"You can do better than that," I said. "I never saw this man in my life. He must be foreign office or something, you can see that by his tie."

"His tie? You mean Mossad people have a special tie?" He was chuckling at the thought.

"No, but back at headquarters we don't go to work with a tie. So when they take a photo for a passport or something, we wear the ties in the photo studio, and they have only about three ties there. So once you know what the ties look like, you'll have no problem in picking out the Mossad people."

The two Brits were smiling as though they had just discovered America.

"Okay," Robert mumbled, pointing at another photo. "We believe it's him."

"And you're right, this is Yair." From my shirt pocket, I pulled out a photo that Ephraim had given me just before I left for the embassy. I laid it next to the photo he was pointing at. "Here, you see?" It was the same photo, only mine was a slightly bigger print.

Credibility was established right then and there.

"Where did you get this?"

"That's not the question now, is it?"

"We'd very much like to see more of the same." His tone was extremely polite.

"That's not possible at the moment. I have no intention of handing you the station on a platter."

"What, then?"

"I'll tell you how you can get the information yourself. That way, when you do, it will be solid."

"Okay." Robert nodded. "Let's get this on the road properly. There are several things we'd like to ask you first, and then we'll take it from there."

I nodded and put out my cigarette.

"First." He opened a second file he'd taken out of the drawer. "There were rumors in the field that Mossad does not keep third-party agreements.[1]"

"Well, what we do is modify the information and then sell it. It is never passed on as is."

"I thought you were not working for them anymore."

"I'm not."

"Then why do you refer to them as 'we'?"

---

1. Third-party agreements: Friendly intelligence agencies subscribe to a gentlemen's agreement that information given by one friendly agency to another will not be given to a third.

"Habit. I haven't been out of there very long. It is possible that even in my own mind I haven't really accepted it, and that is why I'm playing these games with you."

"Do you still have friends there?"

"Yes, I think so."

"Are you in contact with any of them?"

"Not at the moment, but I guess I could make contact if I wanted to."

"What do you know about the attempt by the Palestinians to smuggle a bomb aboard an El Al plane in Heathrow?"

"The security caught it, didn't they?"

"El Al security did, not the airport."

"Well, what do you expect? El Al security is the best, isn't it?"

"Is it at all possible that they could have staged this thing to make us look bad? I mean, would the Mossad do that?"

"And bring a real bomb that close to a plane? Never in a thousand years. Besides, why would they want to do that?"

"We have to look at things from all angles. So you're quite sure they wouldn't?"

"I can't stand them, as you might have noticed, and believe me, I'd be the first one to tell you if they'd done such a thing. But unfortunately, they didn't. The security is just good, that's all there is to it. They don't rely too much on electronics."

"But they do have all the most sophisticated devices."

"I didn't say they don't use technology, I said they don't rely on it. After the technology does its thing, they go over it again manually. Looking the passenger in the eye, so to speak." This was a strange situation; here I was, supposedly selling out my country's most precious secrets and at the same time taking pride in the achievements of its security apparatus. The two stared at me with some apprehension.

The questioning went on for several hours. We went in detail into the way the Mossad activates, maintains, and recruits its more than three thousand Jewish helpers, called *sayanim*, in Great Britain, how it maintains over a hundred safe houses in the Greater London area and services the recruitment needs of other smaller stations in Europe.

The safe house situation was one that seemed to bother them, since it was causing noise in their antiterror system. Neither did they like the fact that such heavy clandestine recruiting activity by the Mossad was taking place under their noses. I could detect something of an injury in their tone, and a determination to do something about this.

"If we wanted to clean up, where would you say we should start?"

"First you have to get your politicians to realize that moving against the Mossad is not a move against the state of Israel, that the Mossad is a loose cannon, and that it is extremely damaging to whoever comes into contact with it."

"I believe we have already established that. What we're asking about is the operational information. What is the flaw in the system? Every system has one, however hard they try to cover it up. What's the flaw in the Mossad that will allow us to sit back and watch what they are doing—and stop them whenever we want to?"

"What aspect of their work would you want to stop?"

"It's not acceptable to us that they're using British subjects in their operations. And targeting an entire minority such as the Jewish community is despicable. Second, we cannot sit idly by as they recruit diplomats who are under our protection and put our relationships with those countries in jeopardy."

"Well, you need to catch them in the act."

Robert had a cynical look on his face. "I should think that was obvious."

"What you need to do is watch the safe houses."

"I would tend to agree with you. But how do we find them?"

"You follow the *bodel*."

"What's a *bodel*?"

"The word *bodel* comes from the word *lehavdil*, which means 'to separate.' The *bodel* is a separator, your so-called flaw in the system. He is the one who takes packages and things from the Mossad station in the embassy to the safe houses and back. He is the secret gofer. Usually, if not always, fresh out of an elite military unit, he is a young Israeli who has received special antisurveillance training and is the best there is in that field. He makes most of the trips to the safe houses during the day and most of the pickups during the night. He rarely uses embassy vehicles and does not have any specific pattern of work."

"So go and chase the wind, is what you are telling us. And you call this a flaw?"

"That is what the man is *supposed* to do; that is not always what he does. The safe houses are also manned by Israeli students who make sure the houses are well stocked with food and other essentials, so that when they are activated, they are ready. They live in some of the houses and visit the others to collect the mail, turn the lights on and off, and make phone calls, so the place is in use and does not raise suspicions when it is used by the case officers. They are usually the same age as the *bodel* and will meet with him socially. What I'm telling you is that several places that he will go to in his free time, and he will do that from his home, are in fact safe houses. Place them under surveillance, and if he comes there during the day, you have your safe house. There is always the possibility of following him with a very big team, never letting him see the same person or car twice. But I don't know if you guys are up to it."

The room was silent for several seconds while they digested all this.

"This is a very sensitive area." Robert was scratching his head. I was the only one in the room smoking, but the air was heavy with smoke. It was easy to see that the two of them were very uncomfortable.

"What do you mean?" I leaned back in my chair, a thin grin on my lips. I was very satisfied with myself; I knew I had accomplished what I'd been sent to do, and I'd had a good time doing it. Until now, that is: It wasn't over yet.

"So, if we follow the man and uncover the safe houses, what will we find? I mean, can you imagine the scandal if we uncover several Pollard-style cases?"

"We will be branded anti-Semitic on the spot," Steve remarked, a serious expression on his face.

"That will not happen," I returned.

"Why not?" Steve stared straight at me, clearly in disagreement. "I mean, when you go fishing, you can't be sure what it is you'll pull out of the water."

"The station will not use the safe houses for their *sayanim*. They meet them in their own houses and under regular everyday circumstances. Rarely will they meet clandestinely, unless of course the *sayan* is in the process of bringing in vital information from his place of work. The safe houses are used purely for debriefing or field planning sessions with case officers who do not enter the embassy. On rare occasions, they'll be used to interrogate an agent, but in that case they will almost always be discarded right after that. The safe houses, I mean."

It was getting dark outside, and we all realized that there was little more we could say at that time. Information had to be analyzed, and more questions would come up after that. It was time to call it a day.

"What now?"

Robert pulled a white envelope from his pocket and put it on the table in front of me. "This is a small token of our appreciation for the time you have given us. We would like to talk to you again in the near future and ask some more questions, and of course pay for the ones you have answered."

"Could you be more specific when you say 'again'? When exactly do you mean?"

"Several days, perhaps."

"I can't be sure that I'll be here that long. I'll call you before I leave and give you my forwarding address."

"What is your address now?"

"I'm here and there. I'll call you tomorrow and give you an address, how's that?"

"Well, we will not be here tomorrow, but you can give it to our friend. He'll pass it on to us. In fact, he could be our *bodel.*" We all laughed.

I counted the money in the envelope outside the embassy building and realized how cheap the British were. Although eight hundred dollars was much more than I had at the moment, I knew I had handed them a golden pickax with which to dig the Mossad's claws out of their soil. At one point, Robert had said that they would pay me in the millions for a list of the *sayanim,* but he was laughing, joking that it was hardly likely that the Mossad would let me back into headquarters to pick up such a list.

But it certainly made me appreciate the batch of photographs of just about all the Mossad case officers that I had stashed away in my hotel room. This was something that even Ephraim didn't know. And he wasn't about to find out.

I knew that I had single-handedly managed to destroy the Mossad's capability in England for some time now. They would start to run into problems in the near future, and if I read the Brits right, they would not let the Mossad know where the problems were coming from. This was fulfilling my duty and tasting the sweet taste of revenge at the same time. I scared myself realizing how much I hated them. I hated the people who'd taken me away from the streets of Tel Aviv and a life I was happy in, with all its small everyday problems. I hated them for shaking my belief in the Zionist dream that had been placed in their hands to protect.

Ephraim was half-asleep on the bed, the television was muted, and the lights were off. He'd probably fallen asleep several hours ago; there was no smoke in the air.

CHAPTER 18

W hat are you doing?" Ephraim asked when I picked up the receiver. He sounded groggy.

"Ordering some coffee. The Brits don't have a clue how to make it right."

"So you trust the Americans with that?" he said, chuckling.

"Would you like something to eat? I'm ordering a hamburger. I'm starved."

"Sure, order me one of those club sandwiches. So how did it go?"

I placed the order and told him everything. I was starting to get impatient with the need to go over things this way. It didn't seem the same as it was when I was still in the Mossad. There it was more organized; first there was the written report, then you'd go over it, answering questions. This was more like merely satisfying the man's curiosity. My feelings toward him were swinging from respect to dislike and back to appreciation.

"What did they say when you handed them the picture?" he asked.

"I think I did it well. I let them show me his picture first, then I pulled out the one I had. I think that closed all the gaps, if there were any left by then."

"Did they bring up the El Al thing?"

"Just like you said, they believe the Mossad is capable of this kind of trick."

"They're right."

"You mean we did do it?" I was taken aback.

"I didn't say that. I said we are capable of it, and we've done similar things in the past."

Ephraim was asking me questions, his mouth full of club sandwich. Ephraim might have been an educated man, but table manners he didn't have. I was taking my time answering since I wanted to enjoy the food. By the time I finished and he was satisfied, he knew about everything that had taken place at the embassy, the remaining coffee was cold, and I was out of cigarettes again.

"Go get some cigarettes, and then we'll talk about the big job I was telling you about," said Ephraim.

I walked to the door. He called after me, "You did a great job, Vic. Even though you enjoyed it, which you shouldn't have, you did a great job."

So he did notice the fact that I liked what I had done, and I thought I had him fooled. I got two packs of cigarettes and hurried back up. This was going to be "it," the final job, the one that would end this state of oblivion I was in, as a gofer for the rebels.

I stopped myself before I entered that cesspool of doubt again. It wasn't that I had no doubts anymore, it was just that I really didn't have too many options at the moment. Should Ephraim want to nail me, he could do so now, in spades, after my latest escapades.

When I reentered the room, Ephraim seemed different, worried, uncertain. It was the first time I had seen him like this.

"What's with you? Losing your cool?" I was trying to make light of it. This was no time for him to go sour on me.

"I'm just thinking about the next stage. There are so many unanswered questions. I think we might just have to put it off for a while."

"What are you talking about? What does that mean to my timetable?"

"A short delay; a week, maybe ten days." There was a note of doubt in his voice. It was very possible the man was testing me to see what I would do, hoping that I would be so anxious to get this thing over with that I would take on any danger, no matter what, just to end it. Later, he would be able to say that he had wanted to postpone it and that it was I who'd wanted to go ahead. After all, we had gotten our training in the same school, and even though I was a rookie in comparison to him, we did think alike.

"No." I was determined. I could play the same game as he did, if indeed this was a game. "You decide now. We go for it, whatever it is, or I'm out."

"Look, Vic." He had a serious expression. "It's not as simple as that. What we have to do is only part of the bigger picture. If you go out and start to solve a problem that doesn't exist yet, you'll be suspected of double dealing when it turns up. And where you're going, this is not something you want to happen."

"You'd better be more specific, Ephraim, or you're going to be talking to the wall in a very short time."

"We have done that for thousands of years." He smiled.

"And a lot of good it did us," I said, smirking.

"Let's go for a walk."

His offer surprised me. He'd never before wanted to be seen with me outside—for good reason. But I wasn't about to question him; he was the senior, and it was dark outside by now.

"Where are we going?"

"Just for a walk. You go first. I'll catch up to you." Several minutes later, he was walking beside me. We passed the subway station and stopped at a small greasy spoon, taking a booth at the end, well-hidden by an overloaded and smelly coatrack.

"Shabtai and his Metsada team managed to kill the Jordanian peace initiative and render Peres helpless. The man was made to look like a fool; nobody else will touch this thing for a long time."

"I could figure as much from listening to the news."

"Up to that point, you could still call this a fair game. Some people believe we should have peace with the Palestinians and some think we should just kick their butts, but what it comes down to is, What are our right-wingers willing to do to get what they want? As you well know, the people who do want peace are made to look like traitors, while the other side is made out to be the patriots."

"Well, you have enough friends in the media. If you have an image problem, why don't you just use them?"

"We do, but it isn't enough, not for what they are planning now." A waitress in a stained white apron took our order, chewing on a huge piece of gum. We waited for her to finish pouring the coffee and serve the large slices of apple pie we'd ordered. She was conversing with someone in the back as she did so; before leaving, she forced a smile at us.

I lit a cigarette and stared at Ephraim. He was keeping his voice down, causing me to lean forward slightly.

"They want to force the 'Jordan is Palestine' thing.[1] They have political support for this and an alliance with some right-wing radicals

---

1. Many right-wing Israeli politicians realize that the Palestinian problem will not go away just because they want it to. They also realize that the Palestinians are in fact a nation with aspirations for a land they can call their own. These politicians have no problem with those aspirations becoming a reality—in fact, they believe that if that were to happen, all the problems of the region would be solved. But since they don't want to give up land to achieve that purpose, they propose another solution: Since Jordan's population is almost 75 percent Palestinian, Jordan should be, and in fact is, Palestine. Thus, they neatly shove the problem onto someone else's back.

that would guarantee massive support from the Diaspora, especially in America."

"But that idea has been around for some time now. I mean, it was shouted from the Knesset podium many times. What's the big deal? Where do we fit into this?"

"As long as it was political, it was fine, but now the Mossad is plunging headlong into this shit. They've decided that it's time to destabilize Jordan to the point of civil anarchy."

"Destabilize? How?"

"A high influx of counterfeit currency, causing distrust in the market; arming religious fundamentalist elements similar to the Hamas and the Muslim Brotherhood; and assassinating leading figures who are symbols of stability, causing riots in the universities and forcing the government to respond with harsh measures and lose popularity. You know what I'm talking about; everything you learned about and more. "

"So what do you want me to do?"

"I want you to tell the Jordanians about it so that they can stop it before it's out of control. I know that the Office is planning to do the same with Egypt to prove that a peace accord with an Arab country is not really worth the paper it's written on, but I'm involved in that one, and we still have time before the plan is implemented."

"I heard about that. Wasn't the Mossad running weapons to the Egyptian fundamentalists through Afghanistan or something?"

"That's right."

"So you still didn't explain how the hell I'm going to tell the Jordanians this and have them believe me. Why don't you tell them? You have channels to the Jordanians."

"That isn't good enough. This has to be an ongoing thing. Every time they manage to stop one thing, our people will come up with another. You will have to get them to recruit you. This time, it's not just a short exercise; this is for real."

I was speechless. This was far more serious than I had imagined: I was setting myself up for a hanging. No matter what might go wrong or whoever might catch me, the result would be the same.

"Is this your idea? Did you think this up yourself, or have you discussed it with someone?"

"I have, and we are in a consensus that this is the only way to go. I haven't told them who I will designate to do this, so as not to compromise you."

"What other options do you have?"

"You're not the only one doing what you're doing."

That was a revelation to me; until that point, I'd been positive that I was the only one on this trip.

"How many are we?"

"Enough to get the job done. This time, we have to go all the way, and time is not on our side. On the one hand, you can't really do much until you know specifically what it is you have to stop, but at the same time, there is only a short time for you to get in there and have a really good chance of not getting detected."

"What do you want me to do?" I had made up my mind to stop piling problems in his way and do what he asked.

What he told me was not music to my ears. I was to totally sever all ties to everything. I would start a fast descent into the gutter, from where I would appear to be much more appealing and believable to my new "masters."

Ephraim was sending me out on the street without a cent. "You make contact when you're hungry, and after you've gotten the link, call this number and we'll meet."

After making the call, I was to wait one day and then come to the Four Seasons Hotel in downtown Washington, D.C. I had the name of the guest I was to ask for. Ephraim would wait for me there. There was to be no other contact with him. I was to make a new group of friends on the street, so in the event of an accident of some sort, there would be someone who knew me and would call my family. I was still under my real identity, and I was to keep a loose contact with Bella. That was the only point that I found difficult. I couldn't tell her anything on the phone, because no doubt her phone was being listened to. She was not to know what was taking place. I couldn't even tell her this was coming closer to an end.

I was going to start this whole charade the next day, so I decided to have one last night out on the town before I moved to scum alley.

I went down to Rumors, a well-known watering hole in downtown Washington, D.C., and plunged into a bottle of tequila and some tall glasses of Coke. I was hurting all over from fear; I was scared of what I was getting into and at the same time ashamed of being scared. I wanted out; I wondered what would happen if I just walked over to the bus terminal and got on the first bus out of there, getting off at the last stop, wherever it was. It would probably be the best solution for everybody. My family needed me like they needed a hole in the head; I'd been nothing but trouble for them as far back as I could remember. I could feel self-pity taking over, which made things even worse.

Suddenly, through my alcohol-induced haze I noticed a woman. She asked me if the seat next to me was taken. What happened next is a blur. All I can remember is getting a positive response. In the cab on the way to my hotel, some time later, alarm bells were going off in my mind. This is too easy, it's a setup, I thought. She is here to kidnap me, take me back to Israel. There was no way such a beautiful lady would just fall for a drunk like me, leaving behind the girlfriend she'd ventured out with and going halfway across town to his hotel. Unless something I'd said that I couldn't remember had made a big impression on her. I decided to take the risk. If she was working for the Mossad, it was only a matter of time before they got me anyway, so I might as well take the easy route and go with her.

As it turned out, she wasn't working for the Mossad. She was as hungry for sympathy as I was, and took just as much out of that night as she put into it. I vaguely remember taking her downstairs and getting her a cab back to the city. By morning, the encounter was molded into my dreams; I could hardly tell what had really happened and what I only dreamed after she'd left.

This was going to be my last breakfast before I hit the street. I was on my own, pointing at a target that I had no idea how to hit. I'd packed all my clothes in the suitcases and was wearing my pinstripe suit. I would roll in the gutter with it, and after several days, I'd look like a man who'd lost it all.

It was then that I realized I was going about this the wrong way. Ephraim had given me a task and had told me how to carry it out. The method he'd suggested might work for him but not for me. Had this been a regular operation in the Mossad, we would have discussed it, and after several hours of brainstorming, would have come up with the best method for me to carry out the task. That hadn't happened, and I was not ready to do things his way. If I was destined to be a street person, it would be out of despair, and that would show. If I tried to play the part, it just wouldn't work.

I was going to take the head-on approach that I knew I could handle. I put my Israeli passport in my pocket and headed for the subway. I got off by the shopping center about one block away from the embassy. I was going to have a cup of coffee and then make my move. Twenty minutes later, I was getting out of a cab at the gate of the Jordanian embassy, less than one hundred yards from the Israeli embassy. I was questioned by the guard inside the main entrance as to who I was and what my business was there. I said I had to talk to the person in charge of security. The guard insisted on knowing the purpose of my visit.

"I need to talk to someone from security," I repeated, pulling out my Israeli passport and showing it to the guard.

He reached out to take it, but I put it back in my pocket. "Only to the man in charge of security."

He hesitated for a moment, then picked up the phone and spoke in rapid Arabic for several seconds. Then he turned to me. "Just one minute, please. The person you wanted is on his way. Would you please walk through the gate?" He pointed to a metal detector gate, like those used in airports, situated in the center of the hall, just by the four stairs leading up to a second level. After going through that, I was checked by a second uniformed guard with a hand-held detector. A tall, thin man in a dark blue suit stepped into the hall. He stopped several feet from me. "What can we do for you?"

I took out my Israeli passport again and handed it to him. "It's more like what can I do for you."

He opened the passport and leafed through it, looking at the photo and again at me. A smile appeared on his face, hesitant at first but gradually broadening into a grin. "Would you care to follow me, please?"

"I'd love to."

He walked up the few steps and led me to what seemed to be the quiet office section of the embassy. We entered a small room with a desk and several chairs around it. The curtains on the large window were shut, but the room was well lit. On the wall behind the desk was a large photo portrait of King Hussein in his military uniform, smiling at the camera.

The place was as foreign to me as a place could get. I had felt more at home in the Soviet embassy. The tall, elegant man sat under the king's portrait and pointed to the seat opposite him. He was far too elegant for this office. "Would you care for something to drink, or perhaps a snack?"

I began to wonder if there was some universal law of interrogation that stipulated subjects always be offered food and drink first. "A coffee would be great," I replied.

He spoke to the guard who'd escorted us to the room and sent him on his way. He then put my passport on the desk in front of me. "What brings you to us"—he glanced at the passport again—"Mr. Os. . . rovvasky?"

"Ostrovsky," I corrected him. "You could say that greed brought me here, also a good dose of wanting revenge."

"Would you be willing to go to Amman and see someone there?"

"Amman?" The question came at me like a locomotive. Amman, the capital of Jordan, so close to Israel, yet so far away. How the hell would I get there, and would I ever come back? Was there a way to get out of this? Could I say no and still pull it off? The general could see I was hesitant. "Think about it. I will be here all day tomorrow, and you can call and tell me what you have decided."

"If I say yes, when will I be going?"

"I didn't say you will, I just wanted to know if you would agree. I have to talk to the right people about this."

"Will you be using the phone line to talk about me?"

"No. I will use the embassy's coded system."

"Don't—that is, if you don't want to kill me. Your code was broken a long time ago, and all your 'secure' lines are anything but."

"So what do you recommend?"

"Use your diplomatic pouch or send a messenger."

"That will take longer."

I got up. "I'll call you tomorrow with my answer. I don't really see any problems. I might just need some guarantees."

"Okay. Until tomorrow, then."

"One more thing. Would you see what you can do to take care of my greed, should things work out?"

"Don't worry. We will not leave you hanging, if you will pardon the expression." He and the others smiled, but I couldn't get myself to do so. "What will you call yourself when you call?" the general asked.

I thought for a moment. "Isa. I'll say it's Isa."

"See you soon then, Isa." The general smiled and walked out of the room. The younger man escorted me to the front door. "Should I call you a cab?"

Getting into a cab outside the Jordanian embassy, right across from the Israeli embassy, was definitely not a good idea. "Could you give me a ride instead?"

We went to his car around the back, and he drove me to the nearest subway station. I gave him the address of the hotel and my room number in case they needed to get in touch with me in a hurry. Then I got out of the car as fast as I could and entered the station. The ball was rolling; I'd hit it halfway across the court, and now I would wait and see what would become of it.

CHAPTER 19

phraim was supposed to have delivered money to me, but for some reason, he hadn't done so. Had this been a normal Mossad operation, he could have gotten as much money as he wanted from a bank *sayan*—a Jewish banker who is regarded as trustworthy and will open the bank for you at any time and provide as much money as needed. He would be reimbursed the following day, once the station got the money from headquarters. Bank *sayans* were used only in emergency situations. But this was not a normal operation, and so I'd have to wait for Ephraim to arrange things, or use whatever I could get from the people I was supposedly working for.

I couldn't help finding the situation somewhat ludicrous; here I was, interacting with the top brass of intelligence agencies of several countries simultaneously, and I didn't have enough money for a proper meal. Things would have to start to move fast, or I'd end up on the street before I knew it. According to my estimation, I could stretch my stay at the hotel for a few more days and then that was it.

I forced myself into a joyous mood and called Bella. She wanted to know what was going on, what I was doing, and what she was supposed to do for money. Ephraim had promised to arrange a check for her that would look as if it had been sent from me. I was to tell her that it was an advance for the security advising job I was doing for some company. There was no reason for her to suffer a lack of funds. If I'd been working for the Mossad, she would have been well taken care of, and if I hadn't been, I would get a job and do it myself. But in this situation of limbo, Ephraim had to do it. As it turned out, Ephraim never got around to it, but at the time, I was still under the impression he would. I was constantly worried about how Bella was making ends meet. I knew that her father would help her, but I also knew that things would have to get pretty bad before she would ask him for help. But there was very little I could do about it except lose sleep.

At three A.M., I decided to find out if the Jordanians had placed someone to check me out. I got dressed and walked out of the hotel. The streets were deserted, and no one came after me. If they had put a tail on me, he was either blind or asleep.

I made a call to the British embassy the next day and asked for an appointment with the gofer. I wanted to meet him somewhere outside the embassy and give him some information. He asked me to call back in an hour or so. When I did, he told me he would not be able to come out and meet me but that he'd be waiting for me at the embassy whenever I'd like to come. I realized that they regarded me as dangerous and suspected that I could in fact be teaming up with someone who might harm them. I couldn't risk entering another embassy just then, so I said I would give him the information over the phone.

This was a snippet that Ephraim had left me just before he went back to Israel. Since terrorism was on the increase in Europe at the time, there was a great demand for information regarding terrorist activity, and the Mossad was more creative in that field than most. Since the Mossad regarded Israeli targets as sacred, they were willing to deal with just about anyone to get advance warning about attacks on such targets.

It was a standing order for field personnel at the time to make contact, under false flag,[1] with whatever terrorist organizations they could. The only restriction was that the meeting be held in a secure environment, meaning that the case officer would have to get clearance from the Mossad European center in Brussels as to the danger level of the said terrorist, and the officer in charge of field security would have to arrange the security for the meeting.

Once the contact was established, case officers were authorized to make any exchange for information that would lead to the prevention of an attack on an Israeli target. Although it was the Mossad's policy to let it be understood that they regarded Jewish targets as having the same level of urgency as Israeli targets had, that was not the case. In fact, officers were on numerous occasions made to understand that it was not part of the job to protect Jews; that was the job of the locals. Under no circumstances was anyone allowed to burn a source who could one day bring in a warning about an Israeli target, in order to save a Jewish one.

---

1. False flag: Intelligence jargon meaning a deliberate misrepresentation of one's nationality.

In some cases, there would be an extra restriction, when it was believed that the terrorists might have an alliance with other terrorists who'd be willing to hit Israeli targets. That restriction was that they were not to be given demolition materials. In those cases, the only thing that could be exchanged for the information would have to be in the logistical sphere, mainly documentation.

None of this was new to me; it was the same as I'd been instructed, and for which I had approved requests many times when on the desks. As part of that drive, a deal was struck with a French group called Action Directe for a series of blank, first-grade British passports, in exchange for information about possible attacks on Israeli targets. Action Directe was led to believe it was dealing with a South American group that wanted to exchange the information for arms from Israel.

A dead letter box[2] in a phone booth in West Germany was planned as the means to get the passports to Action Directe. By using me as an information conduit, Ephraim was leaving it up to the Brits to get the Germans to make the arrest when the French terrorists tried to pick up the passports. The Germans would probably tail the Mossad drop man, then take the Action Directe men into custody when they arrived at the pickup point. Ephraim didn't want the Action Directe to think they'd been tricked by their South American connection, though. If they did think that, they might try to kill the messenger, who was in fact a Mossad officer. Ephraim was therefore going to have the Action Directe people warned, so that they wouldn't think it was a trap and then take revenge on the Israelis for setting them up.

Ephraim was hoping (and so was I) that an incident, even if it didn't come home to haunt the Mossad, would at least put them in some very hot water. We knew, however, that to break the Mossad's hold on the government would not be a short process. Even the passport drop was planned about a month ahead; it was explained to the terrorists that it would take time to prepare, and that would give the terrorists time to get the information that would be regarded as payment for the papers.

The British gofer was out of breath by the time I was finished. "Do you want our people to contact you or anything?" he asked.

"I'll call back in a few days. If they have a question, tell them to

---

2. Dead letter box: A designated place where intelligence information or other material can be dropped off to be picked up later. The Mossad will only deliver to a dead letter box, never pick up from one.

leave it with you so you can ask me. If I can, I'll tell you ahead of time when I'm coming, although I doubt that very much." There was a silence on the line. I realized he didn't exactly know what he was supposed to do. I hung up and called the Jordanians. "Can I talk to Zuhir, please? This is Isa."

"Just one minute please, Mr. Isa." I could tell from the woman's voice that she knew this was important. Seconds later, a second woman came on the line. "Mr. Isa? I'm Lorraine. The general will talk to you in a minute." Things were going much better than I could have imagined. I knew that if Mousa, my field activity instructor and now head of security in Europe, could see me, he would be extremely proud of how I was working. But I prayed that he wouldn't, because if he did, I would be stretched out on a slab in the morgue, with a twenty-two-caliber bullet planted deep in my skull.

"Hello, Isa. How are you today?"

"Very well, and yourself?"

"Fine. I'm getting ready for Ramadan. You know this?"

"Sure. I hope you have an easy fast."

"Thank you. What did you decide?"

"What can I tell you? I was always a sucker for a nice trip."

"Does that mean yes?"

"Yes, it does."

"Great. Now I'll tell my people, and we will get back to you. Will you be at the same place as before?"

"Yes, only I'm running out of money. If I don't make some very soon, I'll have to leave."

"Where will you go?" That was one question I didn't want to hear. What it meant was that there was a possibility it would take longer than a few days. At that moment, I was perplexed; I couldn't understand the laxity with which I was being handled. Maybe I was used to an extremely aggressive agency that would grab at almost any opportunity; the man doing the grabbing could probably see an opportunity for personal advancement in every move. The general wasn't part of this mechanism. He was a true soldier, doing what he thought was right, but not making decisions for others who were not under his command.

I was frustrated and it showed, all the more so since I was not making any effort to hide it. I realized then what Ephraim wanted to achieve by placing me in this situation without any means of support; he wanted me to rely on the success of my mission. I hated him for that.

"I have no idea at the moment, but I will try to solve my financial problems as fast as I can." I could see that he didn't really understand what I meant. "I need to make some money to live on, and I can't work in the U.S., so I'll have to go to Canada and find something there."

"Will you tell me where I can find you there, in case the answer we are waiting for is delayed?"

"If you don't have one before I go, then just forget it." I could feel my insides starting to heat up. I was getting more and more restless, and I realized that I had to start watching my back more than ever.

When I'd walked into the embassy, I was so hyped up on what I had been sent to do that I hadn't given that much thought to the implications. I'd expected them to grab me with two hands and get me working right on the spot. It hadn't happened that way, and things were starting to get sticky.

The process was now irreversible; the information was on its way to Amman and the Jordanian intelligence offices there. Since this was no doubt high-priority information, it would be handled by the top-ranking officers in that service, and if the Mossad was worth its weight in salt, it would hear about it, either from an officer who was recruited or from one of the assistants working for him. Even if neither of those conduits to the Mossad existed, the opportunity of having an Israeli spy working for Jordanian intelligence would most likely be brought before the king. And among the king's retinue, for sure, the Mossad would have an ear of some sort. Knowing what I knew and could give away, it would become a prime directive to stop me. A team could be preparing to grab me or eliminate me as we spoke.

"Call me when you hear something. I hope I'll still be there."

"Will you call before you leave?"

"Okay." I hung up, feeling as though someone had let all the air out of my balloon.

The call came at eight-thirty in the morning. It was Zuhir. "Are you ready to go?"

"When?"

"How about tomorrow afternoon?"

"That's fine with me." I had made it a condition that he would go with me. I sensed that he was an honorable man, and the promise of safe passage was something that I needed. In the short time I'd known him, I realized that he was someone who would readily die rather than go back on his word or lose his honor.

"I'll pick you up at your hotel at twelve."

"For how long are we going?"

"A week. Is that okay?"

"Sure, see you tomorrow." I hung up the phone and sat there for several minutes, trying to digest what had just happened. I was about to go to a country I'd always regarded as an enemy and be a guest of the intelligence agency on the other side. I was going to the other side: That was what I was about to do. If there had been a way to explain everything that I had done up to this point, what I was about to do was unexplainable. At the moment, I figured the Mossad didn't know about me. On the other hand, if they *did* know about me, they couldn't say much since it would expose a source. But then what I could give away was much more than any source could provide, so they couldn't afford to let me go over. They might have tolerated my activity to this point, but there was no way they would allow me to land in Amman.

I was now stepping into an abyss from which the climb back might not be at all possible. I had twenty-four hours in which to prepare for the trip, and there was really nothing I could do to cover myself.

I took a shower and quickly got dressed. I had to get to a phone and call Ephraim. It was a Saturday, and I hoped he would be there. The phone rang several times, but there was no answer. I couldn't make a call from the hotel, nor could I tell Bella what was going on. I decided to try again later. I walked back to the hotel and waited in the room. Time stood still. What if I can't get him? What if they're waiting for me, and this is all a trap just to get me there so someone can hand me over? I wasn't thinking straight. I was too excited and scared. It was like walking on the rim of a volcano with your eyes closed. I could feel the danger, but I couldn't see it.

By six in the afternoon, I got Ephraim. I was exhausted from the tension.

"What's up?" He sounded cheerful; something had apparently gone right for him.

"I'm on my way tomorrow."

He didn't say a word for several seconds, then in a slow and low voice, "Do you mean what I think you do?"

"You bet. I was called this morning. I'm leaving some time around noon tomorrow."

"I'll be damned. We don't know anything about this, not even a hint. Do you know that, even if you don't go, it's already the biggest farce in this organization's history?"

I knew exactly what he was talking about—the myth that the Mossad knows exactly what is going on in Arab countries (in this case

Jordan) was just that: a myth. This was supposed to ring every alarm bell in the bloody Mossad, yet no one had heard of it. I took a deep breath; I couldn't express my relief. "But you do want me to go?"

"Yes. That is, if you think you're up to it."

"And you want me to proceed according to plan?"

"Yes, just like we planned it. That is, if they'll let you."

"So I'll call you when I come out."

"I'll wait for you. How long?"

"The man said one week."

"Just remember that there are other people there, and if they put you in a hotel, stay out of sight. We might not have anyone in their system, but we sure have people in Palestinian circles, and they're all over the place. I still can't believe we didn't hear about this." He was laughing. "What a bunch of bullshitters. I wonder now how many of the so-called agents we have are bogus."

I hung up and went back to the hotel.

It was eleven forty-five. I was waiting in the hotel lobby. I'd made arrangements for the hotel to hold my room, and they'd prepared a bill. At twelve sharp, a limousine pulled up out front, and Zuhir's assistant, the tall slim man, walked in and greeted me.

"Are you ready?"

"Yes, but there is the matter of the hotel."

"What is it?"

"I have no money, and I have to hold the room until I return. I spoke to the general about that."

He went back to the limo and then returned to me with the general's credit card. "The general said to put it all on his card."

"They'll want him to sign."

"I'll sign for him. You go ahead to the car."

I did. Zuhir was seated in the far corner. I could barely see into the car, but his smile was shining through. "*Ahalan w' sahalan,* my friend," he said, stretching out his hand to greet me.

"How are you?" I said, smiling. There was just no way of not liking this man.

"We'll be flying to New York first, and from there we're going to Amman. I have made all the arrangements. We'll be picked up at the airport. All will be well."

"Do you know the people who will be picking us up at the airport?"

"They are all my friends, people you can trust. And here." He handed me a set of tickets: They were in a red folder with the Jordanian crown printed in gold and the word "Alia" in English and Arabic. This was not the sort of thing I wanted to flash around in an airport—either at Washington National or Kennedy.

"Would you mind keeping this for me?" I handed him the folder, slipping the tickets inside my coat pocket. He smiled. "You spies have to think of everything."

"Well, that is if we don't want to hang."

"Don't you worry, my friend, you are with me. No one will touch you."

I smiled back. "Would you drop me off at the entrance to the Sheraton? The one by the airport?"

"Sure." There was a tinge of wariness on his round face. He was puzzled, trying to figure out what I was up to.

"I just want to take a cab from there to Washington National. After all, we don't know who we might meet there, and I don't want to be seen with the most senior Jordanian military man in the U.S., boarding a plane. You'll agree with me that that would not be a good idea."

"I should have thought of it myself, but of course you're one hundred percent right. What about Kennedy? What will we do there?"

"We're traveling first class?" I took out my tickets and looked at them.

"Yes, of course." Zuhir smiled.

"So we will meet in the Alia lounge. Where is it?"

"Alia doesn't really have a lounge, but we do use the Air France one. There is no Air France flight, so we'll be there alone—I mean only people flying to Amman."

"So I'll see you there." I looked out the window. Zuhir instructed the driver to stop first at the Sheraton. His assistant then said something to Zuhir in Arabic, and Zuhir turned to me. "Do you know where the Air France lounge is?"

"No, I'm afraid I don't."

"Do you know where the El Al counters are?"

"Yes." There was a slight hesitation in my voice.

"Well, the Air France counters are on the one side and the lounge is on the other. So when we go to the flight, we will pass by the El Al counters." He gave his assistant a worried look, then said to me, "What do you propose to do?"

"Nothing. I'll meet you in the lounge, and when the time comes, we'll go for the flight. What else can we do?"

The car came to a stop under the large concrete canopy of the Sheraton, and I got out. The chauffeur took my suitcase out of the trunk. Not looking back at the car, I walked into the lobby. I waited there for several minutes, then walked back out again and hailed the first cab that was waiting at the end of the ramp. There was no chance that my friends from the Mossad could have arranged for that cab to be there; there was no time. If someone was following me, and at this point I doubted that very much, the stop at the hotel would have confused them completely. It sometimes sounds childish, all these games of cat-and-mouse, but when it's your life that's at stake, the games stop being fun. Every move that you can make to throw off whoever is after you (if they are there or not) is a blessing and might just buy you enough time to stay alive. There had been times when I was with the Office when I was positive I was clean and went about my business, still keeping an eye open, only to realize that I'd picked up a tail I hadn't identified.

The cab ride took only five minutes, but it turned out to be a smart move. As I handed my ticket and passport to the security man at the airport, I felt a tap on my shoulder. I was sure it was Zuhir or his assistant wanting to tell me something. I didn't want to turn and see them, as this would have worked against all the evasive moves we'd taken.

"Vic." A voice now accompanied the tapping. I knew the voice; it was someone from another world, another life. I turned my head, putting a broad grin on my face. Was this coincidence or something else? "Rolly! How are you?" I put my suitcase on the ground and took his outstretched hand. He shook my hand vigorously. He had once been a good friend; we'd spent much time together talking about things at the top of the world. I never worked with Rolly; he was liaison and I was a case officer. But we'd run into each other quite often when we worked at headquarters. He was doing liaison with the Scandinavians when I was working the Danish desk.

"I heard about your bad luck. I'm sorry." He was genuinely concerned.

"That's life. How are things with you?" He was the Mossad liaison to the CIA, and I knew he wasn't about to spill his guts to me, but I asked anyway. What else could I say? Here I was, on my way to Jordan with a Royal Jordanian Airline ticket in my pocket, and whom do I meet?

"Nothing new, just the usual."

I thought back to the brigadier general who'd been selling arms to the Iranians. I did feel somewhat guilty about him, since it was I who had made the call for Ephraim to the FBI. "What is going on with Bar-Am?"

"Who?" Rolly, a six-foot-one stringbean, leaned forward as if he wanted to hear better. His voice got low as though he wanted mine to do the same.

"Avraham Bar-Am, the general, the one who was arrested for arms dealing with Iran or something."

"What about him?"

"Aren't you guys going to help him out? After all, he did work for us."

"I thought you were out of this game?" He smiled, squinting his eyes as if thinking that maybe all was not as he'd heard it.

"I *am* out, but that doesn't mean that I can forget it all overnight, you know. I did a lot of work for him in headquarters, way back when. I thought that if you put someone in shit, it would be half-decent to be there to get him out."

"As of when does the game work that way? I never saw Bar-Am being forced into this thing with a gun to his head. He went in to make a profit and cash in on his connections. It didn't work out the way he wanted to, that's his tough luck."

"How did they get him?"

"I have no idea. One day, they were doing great; the next day, out of the blue, came the FBI, and it was all over. I have a hunch it was someone from the inside who wanted the deal off. It was getting in the way of Blue Pipeline.³"

"That would be stupid. It would surely make the Americans think that one hand doesn't know what the other is doing." I was hoping he would confirm this. After all, that had been the main reason behind our little exercise.

"You bet that is what they think." I could see by his face that he realized he'd talked too much already, and to an ex who might not be.

"Hey, Rolly, it's me, Victor! What are you worried about? You think I will take what you just told me and fly with it to Amman or something?"

We both started to laugh.

There was more to Blue Pipeline than just sending ammunition to the Iranians: At that point, the Mossad was training Iranian pilots in Germany. The contact was made by the German BND, their secret service. It was not made through the upper echelons but through the

---

3. Blue Pipeline: The nickname given to the Israeli arms sales to the Iranians that had once been mistakenly delivered in a light blue Zim (Israeli shipping line) container. Danish ships were used in the shipping of the products.

working level of department heads. That was the way the Mossad liked to work; it would give the intermediates the ability to bring in good information and help their careers, and keep the top brass out, their so-called political conscience clean.

The Iranian air force consisted mainly of American-made fighter jets such as the Phantom, which until some years earlier had been the leading fighter in the Israeli arsenal too. It was imperative for the Iranians to be able to train their pilots in a safe environment and also receive parts for their crumbling air force. Israel was happy to oblige, using the Germans as intermediaries so that the Iranians would not have to admit to themselves that they were getting help from the Zionist devil himself. In the scenic state of Schleswig Holstein, Israeli pilots were training Iranian pilots in several locations. At two airfields, they were getting flight training in specially modified Cessnas, and at the third they were training in five simulators brought specially from Israel.

At the same time, parts for the decimated Iranian planes were making their way overland from ports in Italy, all the way across Germany and into Denmark, where they were loaded on Danish ships. Other parts and weaponry were transferred directly from Israeli-leased ships to Danish ones in the Danish port.

The local police authorities in the northern German state were well aware of the activity but had no qualms about it, as long as there were no terrorist activities in the area and the operation was pumping money into their personal pockets.

Rolly nodded his head. "Look over there."

"Where?" I asked, turning my head slowly so as not to attract attention. Rolly was never good at field activity. He didn't really need to be: He was liaison.

"Over there in the corner, standing with that tall man."

"Yes?"

"That is Zuhir, the Jordanian military attaché. I wonder where he's off to?"

"You want me to make contact and find out for you?"

"You would, wouldn't you? You are one crazy son of a bitch." He grinned. "Stay away from him. We don't need some international incident, about which I will have to write endless reports."

I knew he would have to write a report about meeting me, where he thought I was going, and, almost to the word, what we'd said. The fact that he'd recognized Zuhir and would try and find out where he was heading was not very promising for me. I was going to make light of it. "Give my regards to Mousa."

"I don't work with Mousa."

"He's head of security in Europe now, and you'll mention me in your report, so send him my regards. Trust me, he'll get it. By the way, are you coming or going?"

"Neither. I'm here to pick up my wife. She's coming back from a trip to Israel."

It was my turn at the ticket counter. I was glad to hear him say, "There she is. I'll be seeing you."

I shook his hand and gave my ticket to the attendant behind the counter. After getting my boarding pass and walking through security, I stood at the gate waiting to board. Zuhir didn't acknowledge me, just as we'd decided, but I could see by his face that he was more than curious about whom I'd met.

It was dark by the time I walked across the long hall in Kennedy Airport after the short flight from Washington National and entered the Air France lounge on the second floor. The El Al waiting area was full, and I was praying that no one in the large crowd would know me. All I could hope for was that the El Al flight would leave before the Alia one, so that I would not have to walk along the aisle with all the people going to Jordan, in front of some three hundred Israelis, one of whom was bound to recognize me.

Zuhir was anxious to hear about my encounter back at Washington National and found what I had told him very amusing. "Of all the places and all the times to meet a friend." He started to laugh. "Fate, that's what it is. And there is nothing we can do about it. We are in the hands of Allah, to do with as He wishes."

"I sure hope He is in a good mood today; I'm still not out of the woods, as they say."

"They don't say that where I come from." He laughed again, clearly in a happy frame of mind. He was after all going home with a trophy, an Israeli secret service agent. I could imagine what it was like by thinking the other way, as if I were bringing him. I'd probably be walking on the clouds.

We stayed in the lounge for more than an hour. At last, it was time to board the plane.

"Do you know?" I turned to him, speaking in a low voice. "Did the El Al flight leave already?"

"No. They'll leave almost an hour after we do." He knew what I was thinking. "Would you like to put on some special clothing or something?"

"Do you have a spare kafia?"

He opened his attaché case and took out the red and white head-gear. He handed it to me. "Will this do?"

I wrapped it over my head, making it hard to see my face from the side. It made me feel much better. "Thanks, it will indeed."

When we walked past the Israeli airline waiting area, almost all the passengers for the El Al flight were staring. It wasn't every day they got to see the enemy this close. I recognized a friend from Holon in the crowd, and I was sure he recognized me. But it didn't matter: As long as he wasn't working for Mossad or Shaback, he would not have anyone to tell it to. Besides, he knew I worked in some secret place, and he would think this was part of my job. I knew that he'd wait for the day when he'd meet me on the street in Holon and tell me how he saw me boarding a flight to Jordan and how smart he was for not making a move that would probably have blown my cover.

We were finally ushered into what was in fact an Alitalia airplane chartered by Alia with a Jordanian crew. When the plane actually took off and was in the air, I realized that there was really no way back. Next stop, Amman.

CHAPTER 20

TUESDAY, MAY 20, 1986

It was getting dark at the end of a long flight. I could see land as the plane banked slightly to the right. We were now heading east. I felt a twitch in my stomach when the plane crossed the shoreline. The pilot made an announcement telling us where we were at that point. I already knew exactly where we were: That gray land below, dotted with the sun's last rays, was Syria.

The concept was hard for me to comprehend; here I was, an Israeli, seated in the first-class cabin of the Royal Jordanian Airline, over Syria, accompanied by the Jordanian military attaché to the United States. At that point in time, there were many who would have haggled over who would hang me if they found out what I was really up to.

Several minutes later, the wide-bodied plane made a second turn and was now heading south, beginning the descent into Amman, Jordan. We had in effect flown around Israel. From my window, I could see Israel passing by as the sun set on the other side of the Moab mountains. I was so close to Bella, I could almost touch her, yet I was further from her and my children than I had ever been. It was then that the proverbial mountains of darkness took on a whole new meaning.

By the time the plane had touched down in Queen Alia International Airport south of Amman, it was dark. Once the plane came to a complete stop, the stewardess who had served us diligently all the way from Kennedy Airport in New York stood behind us blocking one aisle while the purser blocked the other, curtaining off the rest of the passengers from us.

"They will make sure that no one gets off the plane before we clear the terminal," Zuhir said to me, pointing in the direction of the open door. We headed out of the plane alone. Zuhir shook the hand of the pilot, who by then was standing at the door smiling as though he were about to meet the king himself. At the other end of the gangway, we were met by several officers in full parade uniform who stiffened like a steel spring and saluted as soon as they caught sight of my escort. He gestured back and was quick to shake their hands. It was clear that the officers were responding to more than just the man's rank: There was admiration present. We were ushered swiftly through the small terminal. My passport was in Zuhir's hands and was not stamped—quite a standard procedure in this business.

At that point, we were shown into a large VIP room where we were greeted—or, rather, Zuhir was greeted—by a group of uniformed officers; several of them were generals, and most of the others were colonels. While Zuhir was mingling among his peers, I stayed somewhat in the background. A tall, slim, dark-haired gentleman with a neat black mustache and a large smile walked up to me. "It is an honor to meet you, Isa. You must call me Albert."

I smiled back at the man and shook his outstretched hand, nodding to him. "Pleased to meet you, Albert."

"Do you speak Arabic at all, my friend?"

"I'm afraid I don't."

"In that case, I hope you will forgive my English and allow me to ask the meaning of words I don't understand."

"No problem," I said. "From what I can hear, your English is nothing you need apologize for."

"You are too kind." He smiled.

I was not about to start the game of names with this man in this strange place, not until I got to know some of the ground rules a little better. A smile could be deceiving, hiding something very cynical behind it. I was keeping one eye on Zuhir. It was his personal guarantee for my safety and the trust I had in him as a man of honor that had convinced me to make the trip. I didn't want to lose sight of my security blanket. I trusted Zuhir mainly because he was a military man and not part of the intelligence apparatus. I had no doubt that, if he lost sight of me, things might happen that would be beyond his ability to change, and then the system would provide him with a story to calm his conscience. I was not going to let that happen.

Once I caught Zuhir's eye, I gestured to Albert as if to ask Zuhir if he thought I could trust the man. Zuhir nodded to me, smiling, then he left the group of officers and walked over to me. "This man will take you to the hotel and will take care of you. I know him and hold him personally responsible for your well-being." He put an arm around my shoulder. "Welcome to Jordan." He then turned and walked back to his comrades.

Albert led me out of the terminal into a warm night. There were several parked cars and about ten men in civilian clothes standing by the cars, waiting. When we came closer, they noticed us, and one man opened the door of the second car in the row for us. Then his companions all got into the other cars. The small convoy made its way for almost twenty minutes on what reminded me of the roads in the Negev desert. The cars stopped in front of the Regency Palace Hotel in Amman. I didn't get to see much of the city as we drove in, but as far as I could tell, there wasn't much to see. It wasn't a city in the American sense of the word, with high-rise buildings and neon lights, but rather what looked to me at first glance like a very big village. Albert explained that, since it was Ramadan, there was very little activity at all—not that it was a hopping place at any other particular time.

Much to my surprise and somewhat to my dismay, I was registered under my real name, even though I'd been "Isa" all along. I was handed a key to a room on the eighth floor. Albert walked me to the elevator and said he'd be back in about an hour with some people who'd like to talk to me. He suggested that I get some rest; if I wanted, I could order food from room service. "I think you should stay in your room until we get everything sorted out."

"How come I'm under my real name?"

"I don't know, I didn't make the arrangements. The man who did will be coming with me later. You can ask him." The fact that they might have just made a blunder that would cost me my life didn't seem to bother Albert much. "What is your rank?" I threw at him just as he was about to leave.

He turned to me, puzzled. "Why do you want to know?"

"Since we both carry a rank, it would be nice to know where one stands." It was utter bullshit, but for people in military organizations, things like that matter. I was shooting in the dark.

"I'm a captain. What are, or should I say were, you?" There was a faint irony in his tone.

"Colonel." His eyes opened slightly. I knew it had worked; a small hierarchy was established. "One more thing."

"Yes?"

"I need a phone number or something in case of an emergency."

"Sorry. But of course." He took out a small pad and a pen and scribbled something on it. "Here, this is the number of the security police headquarters. I should be there in about ten minutes. You can ask for Albert. But, as I said, I'll be back in an hour."

The room was almost identical to the one I'd left behind in Washington except for the selection on the television. I was hoping to get Israeli television, but it wasn't available. On the radio, however, I could hear the Voice of Israel and almost all the other stations, including Aibi Natan's Voice of Peace.[1] There was a basket of fruit in the room and the windows offered a beautiful view of the desert night. The air was warm and had a sweet taste to it. I took a shower and ordered a dinner that consisted of humus and kufta, which I knew better as kabob. I was seated at the small table the waiter had rolled in when there was a knock on the door.

It was slightly more than one hour from the time Albert had left me at the elevator. I got up and walked to the door. Through the peephole, I could see Albert and another man. I unlocked the door and stepped back into the room. Albert and three other men walked in; apparently, two had been standing to one side, out of sight of the peephole. They shook my hand, nodding and smiling, then walked in and sat around a small coffee table by the French window. After the introductions, they all insisted I finish my dinner. I offered to order some food for them. They said they would eat after their friend Fadllal had joined us.

They asked if they could smoke, and within minutes the room was filled with the familiar cigarette smoke. It appeared they were all smoking Marlboros. I stuck to my Camels. One of the newcomers was a young chap of about twenty-five; he was apparently the assistant of a heavyset man in a black suit whose smile seemed to have been tattooed onto his face. The third looked like Albert's older brother, with silver hair and gold-rimmed glasses. By observing their posture and manners, I could easily see that they were officers. I politely pushed away what was left of my food, explaining that I'd in fact eaten on the plane and wasn't that hungry. The truth was that I was very hungry, but I'd decided to get this thing off on a good footing and eat later, when they did.

"So, Isa." The heavyset man turned to me, patting his mustache with one hand. At this point, I realized that we all had mustaches, all of which were very much alike except for the one belonging to the man who looked like Albert, which was a longer, British-style mustache with what seemed to be waxed sharp ends pointing up.

"I read the report Zuhir sent in," continued the man, "and I find that we have so much to talk about, I just don't know where to begin. What would you recommend we do first?"

---

1. Voice of Peace: Pirate radio station anchored outside Israeli territorial waters.

"Well." I took a cigarette out of my pack and tapped it on the table. "What I would recommend is to see what it is I can't do for you, so that you don't have expectations that I can't meet."

"Sounds logical," the one with the sharp mustache said, looking at the older man. "What, for example, do you think that we would like to know and you cannot help us with?"

I could see where this was going. It was a very good technique. One of the biggest dangers in questioning is letting the person being questioned in on what you do and don't know. They handled this technique well, not revealing anything about themselves.

"First, I assume you would like to know if the Mossad has agents in your midst and who they are."

"That would be a fair assumption," the youngest one said.

"Well, I can tell you that according to the reports, there are many agents in your system, mainly in the field command. Because of the way the Mossad is constructed, I couldn't know who they are unless I worked directly with them, in other words, unless they were my agents. I can tell you I was never in that position, so I can't help you there. I can, however, put your mind at ease in one regard, and that is that intelligence officers are not good targets and are rarely sought by the Mossad."

"And why is that?" the heavyset man muttered.

"Well, they are usually suspicious and on the lookout, they are well aware of the techniques used, and once they have been recruited, they don't have that much information that is vital to the big picture. They usually know more about you than about their own country. So, in other words, the results are not worth the hassle."

There was a knock at the door. All eyes turned to it, and I wanted to get up and open it, but Albert stood up instead. "I'll get it. It's probably Fadllal."

"So, you were saying," the young man said, as though he wanted to keep the conversation going. I turned to face him. "What I said was that I can't really help you much in the way of names."

I could hear the door open and a short conversation at the door in what sounded to me like an angry voice that Albert was trying to calm down. I saw astonishment in the faces of the people facing me. Before I could turn my head around to see what was going on, I felt something hard press against my head, almost at the top. A strong hand grabbed the back of my collar. The man said something in Arabic that sounded like an order of some kind. The voice was harsh. I could feel all the blood rush out of the top half of my body and the cold sweat everywhere.

"What the fuck is going on?" I called out, making sure not to move my hands. It seemed to me that the gun was of small caliber, but even a twenty-two at this range was more than enough to scramble my brains. I had no idea what was going on, and I forced myself not to try to figure it out. I had no doubt that I would be told in a very short time, or I would be shot, in which case it really didn't matter much.

Albert translated, trying in vain to imitate the harshness of the man's voice. "He says you are a Mossad agent and that you are here to trick us."

"It's not a secret that I come from Mossad." I was trying to keep a tremble out of my voice; I could feel my bottom lip getting stiff with fear. "I mean, if I wasn't, would we all be here?"

"He says you are here to trick us; he says he has it from a good source."

This was it, as far as I was concerned. Either the man was bluffing or else he had something. If he did, there was nothing I could do. It wasn't as though I was on a legitimate job for the Mossad, in which case some political safety net could be thrown in to save me. If the Mossad got their hands on me, they would probably do the same thing to me that the Jordanians would, and no one would say a word. I put the cigarette I'd just taken from the pack into my mouth; I hadn't yet had a chance to light it. Moving only my eyes, I looked at Albert, and with the best smile I could muster, I said, "Tell your man to shoot me or light my cigarette, whichever, but please do it fast. I need a smoke."

Everybody in the room began to laugh, the gorilla with the gun too. He put the gun back in his belt and moved to stand in front of me. His hand was outstretched, and he was grinning. "It is my job to try and catch you, see?" he said in English. "No hard feelings, I hope?"

I took his hand and shook it hard. "None at all. You do your job, and I'll do mine." He took a lighter out of his pocket and lit my cigarette.

"Can we get something to eat around here?" Fadllal said in a loud voice. "Why don't you just order a table," he said to Albert. "We are going to be here for some time."

When Albert went to the phone to make the order, Fadllal turned back to me. "Tomorrow we will see if we can really trust you. The two of us will go on a day trip, and then we will know for sure."

"Where are we going?"

"That you will see tomorrow. Now we will eat, and"—he opened the small bar in the room—"have a drink. What will you have?"

"I'll have a tequila, if there is one."

There was more than one, and we all had a drink except the heavyset man and his assistant, who declined on religious grounds.

"So, Isa, what can we do about the Mossad agents that we have in our midst?"

"You can find them." Ephraim had gone over this with me several times; we were not giving them anything that they couldn't arrive at on their own. It was standard procedure, and there was no way around it. But coming from me, it was like hearing it from the burning bush. If they did follow the procedure I was recommending, agents would be falling out of the few trees they had in this piece of desert, something that would more than likely force a reevaluation of the Mossad leadership.

"Well," asked Albert, sipping his brandy, "how do you propose we do that?"

"First you have to identify the group they belong to. What I mean is, there are several types of agent. One is the basic type, working in a menial job at a hospital or a fire department. He could pass on what is called tactical information. For example, if a hospital gets ready to take in casualties by expanding the number of beds it has, or the fire department calls in the reserves, we can see the first stages of a country going on a war alert. To find these people, you'd have to spend the next five years interviewing and pounding the sidewalks. The results will be negligible, especially since most of them don't realize what it is they're doing."

They were looking at me and nodding; up to this point, I wasn't teaching them anything new. "Then there is the second level of recruits. They're from the civil service, the foreign office, that is—diplomats, etc. Again, they'd be difficult to detect. At the top of the hierarchy, we find the military officers who've been recruited and are working at the moment. They're the most important group and the most vulnerable to detection."

"So how is that done?" the heavy man asked, leaning forward, his face taking on a pinkish color. The man was hooked, I could feel it. I was about to tell him exactly how it could be done, but then I remembered what Ephraim had repeated again and again: You are there to make money, don't lose sight of that. "Well, I would really like to oblige you, but I seem to have a slight problem."

"What is that?" Albert quickly asked, seemingly ready to tackle whatever it was.

"What will I get out of this? I came here in good faith, and I want to know what it is you are willing to pay me."

Fadllal was smiling. He put his hand back on his gun. "The first thing you already got was your life, my friend."

"That is a lot of bull, and you know it. I came here under the protection of Zuhir's honor, and unless you can prove that I am not what I say I am, it's as if this conversation is taking place in Washington. You don't have the advantage here, my friend. So back to my question." I paused and looked around the room. "What will you pay me?"

"What do you want?" It was the man who looked like Albert's brother.

"I want a lump sum and then a salary for one year, after which we will renegotiate."

"What is the lump sum?" the young man asked.

"Twenty thousand U.S. Sort of pocket money." I knew I could ask for ten times that much, but I wanted to make things easy on them. "Then five thousand a month."

"Will you stay here in Jordan?"

"No, I'll go back in about a week, like we agreed before I came here, and I will do whatever we decide should be done."

"If we agree, what will you do in return for all that money?" Albert wanted me to get it; I could see it in his eyes. He was going to be my case officer, and this assignment was going to propel him to the top of his organization. He wanted me and was going to make sure he got me.

"That will depend on what you want. I can help you install a system that will prevent anyone from recruiting your people and help you catch those who have been recruited already, almost guaranteeing that any you don't catch will quit on their own. That will be stage one."

"So there's more?" It was Fadllal, wiping some humus,[2] looking at me with his small black eyes as if he wanted to see right through me. The man didn't trust me and wanted above all to be the one to nail me. From the way he was staring at me, I was almost certain he had a way to do that. Maybe he was going to the following day.

"Yes, there'll be more. Once you've secured your rear, you have to go on the offensive; what I mean is, actively recruit Israelis. First you'll need a good basic level of military expertise, and then from there the sky is the limit."

---

2. Wiping humus: A term used in the Middle East for eating the humus dip. You scoop the humus off your plate with a piece of pita bread and bring it to your mouth.

"What about recruiting Palestinians?" It was the young man again.

"What about it?"

"What if we want to recruit Palestinians? Could you help us there?"

All eyes were on the young man. He instantly realized he'd made a mistake. I felt sorry for the guy; he'd revealed to me a problem they had, which was more than they'd wanted to do. I wanted to get him out of it and calm the atmosphere. "Very funny. What is this, a trick question? Me recruit Palestinians, like you need my help? What do you take me for?"

The young man could feel the soft landing. He smiled. "You can never be too careful, now can you?"

I changed the subject. "Okay, what do you say? Do we have a deal, or do you people have to go and talk it over with your bosses?" I could see I hit a raw nerve there with the heavy man, who was probably a top-ranking officer, if not the top man in the Jordanian service. Even though I'd worked on the Jordanian desk for a short while during my time in research, I didn't know much, if anything at all, about the Jordanian service. I was sorry about that now.

"Twelve and a half thousand walking money," the heavy man said, his face frozen in a blank expression. The tattooed smile was gone. "Three thousand five hundred a month for six months, then we renegotiate. Take it or leave it. We will talk again tomorrow night if you are still here." He got up, signaling to his assistant. "Meantime, my friend Isa, enjoy your stay in Jordan, and if you decide not to take the deal, have a nice trip home."

I shook his hand, and he headed for the door. The young man made a mock salute as he trailed him. The one who looked like Albert left almost immediately after them, and Fadllal stood up, smiling. "I will pick you up tomorrow at six-thirty in the morning. Dress casually." He lit a cigarette and dropped the almost full pack on the table. "I see you're almost out of cigarettes. Allow me to offer you mine."

"Thanks. I can use them." He walked straight for the door, where he stopped. "Don't go out of the hotel on your own, and lock the door."

"Will do," I said, but he didn't stick around to listen. What was the SOB preparing for me for tomorrow? Albert was now seated on the larger chair where the heavy man had sat before. "We need to talk," he said, sounding worried.

I sank into a chair opposite him and opened another of the small tequila bottles from the mini-bar. "What's on your mind?" In fact, I was quite satisfied with myself at the moment, thinking that under the circumstances I'd handled things pretty well.

"I've been assigned to you. What I mean is that from here on I will be your . . ." He hesitated, searching for the right word.

"Case officer, handler, operator?"

"Yes, exactly." He seemed relieved that I knew what it was all about. "I know you come from an agency that is very sophisticated, but now you are working with me. We'll be doing things my way and at my pace. We're working together, not against each other. So work with me, okay?"

"Look, Albert, I like you, and it's true that I come from a more sophisticated agency, but you're not my boss, and I won't do things your way. I didn't leave the Mossad to be bossed around. There are things that I can do for you, and others that I will not. If you want something, all you have to do is ask." I raised my glass. "Here's to the king."

"That"—his face was grim—"is not a joke here."

"I didn't mean it as one. So, Albert, what is it that worries you so much?"

"I'm worried about Fadllal. He doesn't trust you, and I don't want him to harm you. The man is a little crazy; he sees a spy under every bed."

"So what do you suggest I do?"

"Just be careful, that's all. I don't want something to happen to you and then have Zuhir after me." The psychological game they were playing was not bad—a little crude, but not bad at all. Albert was the good cop, and Fadllal was the bad cop. In telling me to be careful, Albert was making the bad cop even worse. Then, to make things worse still, and knowing that I got my self-confidence from having come there under the auspices of Zuhir, he showed me that despite that, something could happen. I knew it was a game, yet it really was effective, especially on top of several tequilas and a very urgent need for sleep.

"I'll be careful. I mean, I do have a vested interest."

"I'll be in the next room if you need anything." Albert got up. "Do you want me to help you get the things out of the room?" He pointed to the rolling table loaded with leftovers.

"Forget it. I'll handle it in the morning. Can you arrange for a wake-up call for me, say at five-thirty?"

"Sure." He headed for the door.

"Where do you think we'll be going so early?"

"I haven't a clue, but wherever it is, you watch out for him. He is full of surprises. I know the man, and he'd be happy to trip you up even if he knows you're okay."

"So what are you telling me?"

"Just be careful."

"Do you think Zuhir knows what we're going to do tomorrow?"

"I don't think so. Fadllal doesn't answer to anyone but head of security. All I'm saying is, be careful." On that ominous note, he left the room. I was so tired, my eyelids hurt, but still I couldn't fall asleep. I was so close to Bella, I could almost smell her, yet there was no way for me to tell her where I was. What if something went wrong tomorrow and I wound up a John Doe on a slab in the Amman city morgue or whatever it was they had here? As far as she was concerned, I would have run out on her and the kids.

I was starting to go out of my mind with worry and grief. Here I was already moaning and feeling sorry for myself, and I hadn't even begun to do what I had come there to do. I knew that if I didn't do something now to alleviate the stress, I wouldn't be able to function by morning. I grabbed the phone. The hotel operator was on the line almost instantly. "Can I help you?" she said after saying something I didn't understand in Arabic.

"I want to make a call to the United States."

I gave her the number of the Holiday Inn in Silver Spring, where I still had a room. I was surprised how fast they connected me.

"Holiday Inn, Silver Spring."

"This is Victor Ostrovsky from room 805."

"Yes sir. What can I do for you?"

"I'm expecting a call from my wife sometime today. Will you please give her a message for me?"

"Sure, Mr. Ostrovsky."

"Will you tell her that I'm in a place where I can't call her from, and that I will call her the moment I get back, which will be in about a week."

"And what is her name?"

"Bella."

"Okay, Mr. Ostrovsky, will do."

I hung up and dropped on the bed. By the time my head hit the pillow, I was asleep, but almost as fast, it seemed, I heard the phone ring. They won't let me sleep here, I thought. It was my wake-up call. At first, I almost lay back to grab just a few more minutes of sleep. But I knew that the moment I did, I would be unable to get up until much later. I didn't want to keep Fadllal waiting. I dragged myself sluggishly to the shower and was dressed and ready to go with time to spare. I ordered coffee and toast from room service and was finished when I heard a knock on the door. I looked through the peephole and saw the person I expected. Fadllal was especially cheerful this morning and was happy to see I was all ready to go. I offered him coffee, but he turned me down, saying we had no time and that we would have coffee on the way, or in Jericho.

I wasn't sure I'd heard him right, and even if I had, I assumed he was talking about some coffee place in Amman named after the king's favorite winter house in Jericho.

"Here." He handed me a passport, a British passport.

"What is that for?"

"For you. You can't use your Canadian one—it was issued in Israel."

"Where are we going that I need a passport?"

"I told you. We're going for a coffee in Jericho."

My blood was turning to ice. If this man meant what he said, then we were about to go to the West Bank. There couldn't be a more dangerous place for me on earth. I was going to have to enter and exit Israel with a false British passport, escorted by a Jordanian intelligence officer. This was just too much. "No way, my friend, will you get me to go to the West Bank. I'm a dead man there. I told you the Mossad wanted me to go to the south of Lebanon so that they could eliminate me. Now you want me to cross and reenter Israel so that you can play some little game? You're crazy."

"I don't believe a word you're saying. I think that you were sent by the Mossad to mislead us and that you'll cause havoc in our midst, sending us on a wild goose chase after traitors we don't have. If you're who you say you are, then you have nothing to fear; the passport is good, and you'll have no problem crossing. I'm the one who should be afraid; if you're working for the Mossad, it's me who may not be coming back."

"What if you're a traitor yourself and you are taking me and escaping back to Israel?"

He said something in Arabic, and two armed soldiers entered the room. "We are going. If, on the other hand, you don't want to, I will tell them to shoot you, and we'll say it was an accident of some sort. You have a choice: Come with me on a trip or die."

"I'm coming, but it still doesn't make any sense. What the hell do you think you'll be gaining? I mean, if I *am* working for the Mossad, all I have to do is go with you on the trip and then when we come back I'll have a clean bill of health."

He didn't say a word but walked out of the room. The soldiers waited for me to follow and then closed the door behind me. We got into a cab outside the hotel and were driven to a bus station in the downtown area. The city was still very much asleep, and except for vegetable merchants preparing their colorful displays, hardly anybody was around. From the smell in the air, it was clear that the bakeries were already working at full steam, making some of the most phenomenal pita bread to be found anywhere.

The bus was almost full, and I seemed to be the only foreigner on it. I still couldn't believe what was happening: This was my worst nightmare. I was hoping that I would wake up in the hotel in Amman, or better yet in Washington. I would then call Ephraim and tell him to shove it. I didn't want to spend the rest of my life in some rat-infested jail cell somewhere in the Negev, kept secretly alive like some zombie. I knew that was the fate awaiting me if things didn't go right.

I tried to remember my name, the one on the passport I'd stuck in my shirt pocket. I couldn't. I had to take it out and look at it again. Steven Emmens. How the hell was I going to remember that name? I tried repeating it to myself over and over. I would use an address that I remembered from another cover I had once had. All this was relevant if he wasn't setting me up. It was very possible that all he wanted was to get me across the border before I showed them how to clean house because he was really an agent for the Mossad. Things were not looking good.

King Hussein Bridge, the driver announced, and the bus came to a stop. I knew it as the Allenby Bridge; I'd served some time ago on the other side when I was an officer in the military police. The thought caused me to break out in a cold sweat again. What if one of the reserve military policemen on the bridge recognizes me? What if the man from the Shaback station on the bridge recognizes me? What if one of the Mossad people here to meet an agent sees me?

Calm down, I said to myself. Go over your cover story before it's too late. The one thing you don't want to do in front of a border policeman or a soldier who's checking your papers is stutter. The story that had been given to me went like this: I was on a day trip and was meeting some merchant whose card I had in my pocket. He had religious artifacts for sale, and I was in that line of business. I'd been referred to him by his brother in Amman.

I wasn't the only one on the bus who was uneasy. For the first time, I looked at the people around me, who'd been talking quite cheerfully until a few minutes ago. I hadn't paid much attention to them until this point, absorbed as I was in my own problems. The silence that overcame all the chatter was suddenly very tense. I could almost feel the heartbeat of the passengers. We were approaching a place that somehow seemed dark, frightening. Up to this moment, entering Israel had always been something that I associated with security and strength, never with fear. Yet now I was surrounded by that exact feeling. You could see it in every pair of staring eyes. I'd always thought that the stare was hate, because I never thought that there was a reason to fear me. When I was a soldier, I didn't want to harm anyone; all I wanted was to do my job. Only if someone had ill intentions did he have reason to fear me.

A Jordanian policeman boarded the bus and made a short inspection. Then he directed the bus to the narrow forty-meter-long bridge. We made our way slowly, under the watchful eye of the Israeli military policeman on the other side. I could hear the orders shouted out in Hebrew. "Meshulam, you check the bus. We strip this one."

What I heard was not good news for me. The bus stopped, and all were ordered off. The military policeman was a reserve soldier, there to do his thirty or sixty days. He wasn't looking to earn any medals. He just wanted to get the day over with so that he would be one day closer to going home. I knew the feeling: I'd been there too. He was polite and courteous to me and to the other passengers. A young regular soldier was teasing him. "Why don't you carry their suitcases while you're at it?"

"Why don't you shut up," the older soldier answered. "There is no reason to treat people like your mother treats you."

"Don't talk like that about my mother, you son of a whore."

A sergeant walked over and shouted at them. "Shut up, you two, and get to work. The day has just started, and already you two are at it."

When I showed my passport, the sergeant pointed to a small shack at the end of the long canopy that provided shade for the customs tables. "Over there, please."

I knew he was sending me to the foreign tourists' shack. As I started to walk, he called me. "You Englishman?"

"What is it?" I turned to him, smiling at the term he used.

"You no have luggage?"

"No, I'm only going to Jericho for a few hours."

"What if bridge close before you come back?"

"Then I will have a problem, won't I. Why? Is the bridge going to close today?"

"You never know."

I turned and walked over to the hut. Fadllal was being body searched, as I could see when I entered the small building. The young soldier inside asked me a few questions, for which I was well pre-pared. I was grateful that he kept using my name all the time; it helped me remember it. I asked him not to stamp the Israeli seal on my pass-port, so he put the seal on a separate piece of paper that he then slipped into the passport. It was a given that people coming across the bridges who wanted to go back the same way wouldn't want the Israeli seal on their passport. That could be a problem later. Had I not asked for that, it would have seemed very strange. "Have a nice visit to Israel," the soldier said.

"I didn't know the West Bank was considered Israel," I heard myself say.

"I'm an Israeli soldier; you're crossing the border I protect. Where the hell do you think you are?" He laughed scornfully.

"When we were here this wasn't regarded as England."

"You see?" He smiled at me with what looked like pity. "If it was regarded that way, you might still be here, right?"

I walked out the other side and to the waiting taxis. The taxi filled up, and then we were on our way to Jericho. Fadllal was the last pas-senger to enter. From the time we'd boarded the bus, almost three hours earlier, we'd not exchanged a word. It was about nine-thirty now, and we were at the entrance to Jericho. The cab was hot, and the traffic was slow. We were driving behind a long military convoy laden with tanks and half-trucks on trailer trucks. They were covered, but it was hard to mistake a Merkava tank for anything else. They were probably returning from an exercise up north.

Fadllal started a casual conversation with me. One thing led to another; we arranged to have lunch in a restaurant he recommended. Then he said he'd take me to the store I wanted. The conversation was to benefit anyone in the cab who might be an informant or just a curi-ous person with some connection to the authorities, who—I found it hard to comprehend—were hostile to me. I had a constant pain in my stomach; I knew it was fear. Fadllal led me to a restaurant filled with Israeli soldiers. The convoy had stopped for a break, and most of the soldiers were seated around the large open marble balcony, shaded only by a vine weaving its way through a wire pergola.

"What will you have?" Fadllal asked as the waiter approached us.

"Whatever you have, I will try." Fadllal didn't argue and ordered in Arabic.

"So what now, my friend?" I asked, feeling it was time to run some sweat down his forehead. There was no way that this man was a Mossad agent or he would have handed me over already. He was as calm as if he were still in downtown Amman and not in the Occupied

Territories surrounded by well-armed enemy soldiers and seated across from a man he didn't trust.

"We eat. Then I take you to the store you are to see, then we go for a walk in Jerusalem, and then back home."

"And what did you achieve by that?"

"A good meal, a nice trip, and a new friend."

"What makes you so sure now that I am what I say I am? That is, if we get back."

"I am head of a department in the Jordanian secret service. I'm too big a fish to pass up." He was not even keeping his voice down. I was getting worried one of the soldiers might overhear us. The food, when it came, smelled great, but I could barely eat. All I could think of was that small cell I'd seen on several occasions. The overpowering smell of disinfectant and urine etched an everlasting impression on my mind, always returning when I felt in some danger of losing my freedom—something that was happening very frequently lately. There was a phone on the counter at the restaurant. I felt like using it to call home; the urge was almost uncontrollable. Then I thought I could call Ephraim; what if Fadllal was right about being a prize worth having? I tossed that thought out of my mind; the Mossad as it was today was far more dangerous to the state of Israel than the Jordanians could ever be.

We walked over to the jewelry store I was supposed to visit to reinforce my cover. I was starting to relax; there was no reason at the moment to feel any apprehension. That would come later, when we would have to go back and over the bridge again. I couldn't help thinking of what would happen if we were fingered. I had a plan all set up in my mind: I would have to make it to the southern city of Elat and from there cross to the Jordanian side. That was the only way to get out if something went wrong.

We talked to the merchant, who believed I was who I said I was, especially since I'd been sent to him by his brother. He showed me several items he thought would interest me and then gave me some photos of the items I'd showed interest in, as well as a small gold brooch as a gift in the hope of good deals to come. He wouldn't let us go without first drinking hot sweet tea and eating homemade sweets. When we left the store, Fadllal led me to a small garage not far down the road. Everything in Jericho is not far down the road. A young man was waiting for us, next to a white Peugeot 404 with Ramallah license plates. "My friend here will give us a ride."

Within a few minutes, we were out of Jericho on the road leading

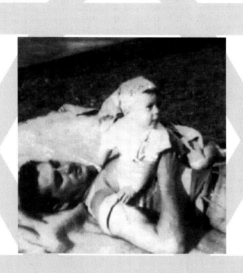

Curiosity is a trait I would
exhibit from infancy to adulthood.
It wasn't until forty years after this photo
was taken that my father and I would regain
the closeness we had in 1950, shortly before
my parents' separation.

My wife, Bella, as
she looked the day
she entered the
Israeli Army.

At my wedding, surrounded by fellow
officers from the military police.

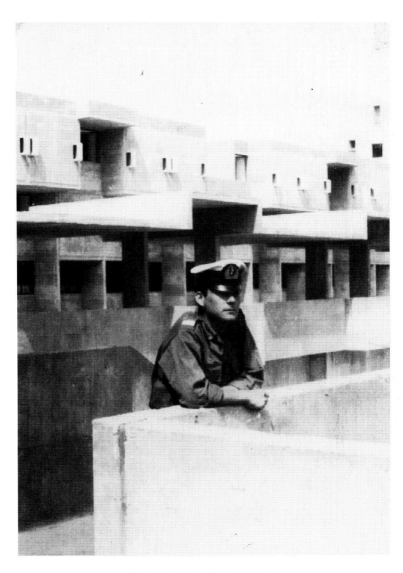

Outside the officers' school
in Mitspeh Ramon, 1968.
I'd just turned eighteen and
looked forward to a long
military career.

פיקוד הדרכה • בסיס הדרכה מס' 1 • בית ספר לקצינים

תעודת גמר

מס' אישי 2035913 דרגה סר"ש שם אוסטרובסקי ויקטור חיל חמ"צ

השתתף בקורס קצינים בסיסי מחזור מרץ 68

מתאריך 18 מרץ 68 עד תאריך 27 יוני 68

וסיים אותו בהצלחה

27.6.68

מפקד בית הספר   תאריך

מופס 2520/4
(2/60)

OPPOSITE PAGE: My certificate
of graduation from the Israeli
Army Officers course.

While with the military
police in 1969, I was part of
a special unit that regularly
trained to protect VIPs
who traveled through the
occupied territories.
That's me at the top.

Eventually I tranferred from
the Army to the Navy. Here
Rear Admiral Zeeve Almog
congratulates me on my
promotion to major
as Bella looks on.

Standing on an American aircraft carrier docked in the port of
Haifa, 1981. Because I could speak English fluently, I often
served as a liaison to American ships.

Stopping to load
a camera while
in the midst of a
Mossad photog-
raphy exerrcise.

On my second trip to Amman, I again met with Jordanian Intelligence and advised them on how to set up a spy network. Shown here is my ticket for the Royal Jordanian Airlines flight.

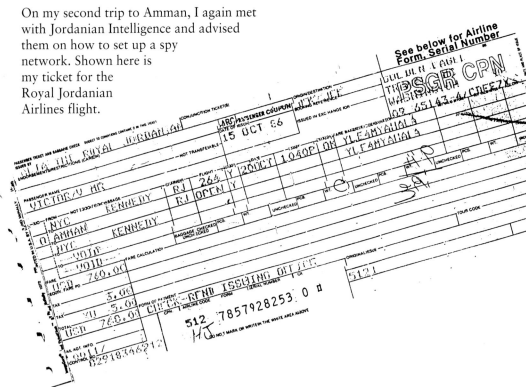

Had I known, before I boarded the EgyptAir flight, that I would be incarcerated upon landing in Cairo, I'm sure I wouldn't have gotten on the plane. As it was, I eventually succeeded in gaining the confidence of Egyptian Intelligence and helped avert several operations launched by Mossad extremists.

northwest to Ramallah; I'd taken it countless times when I'd served in the Jordan Beka'a, many years ago. The road was now in much better condition, but the view was the same.

We drove for about twenty minutes, during which time Fadllal explained to me that this for him was still Jordan, and he didn't really feel he was in a foreign land. "We have many friends here who are as loyal to the king today as they were before '67," he said. "Actually, they are probably more so today, since they had to put their lives on the line for His Majesty and did so, and are still doing so." Fadllal tapped the driver on the shoulder and pointed to a fork in the road, then said something to the man in Arabic. He turned to me. "We'll stop there for a coffee and then head back. I've seen enough; you could have sold me out ten times, and you didn't. I trust you. I need to see one of my people here and give him some money. I make this trip almost once a month, you know." The man was clearly proud of his ability and courage, entering enemy territory in such a nonchalant manner. I felt a sense of relief; I only had to get back to Amman in one piece, and my mission was almost guaranteed success. In a short time, I had reached a higher stratum in the Jordanian intelligence than had any other Israeli up to that point.

The car came to a stop in front of a two-story building in the village of Dir Jarir. Children were playing soccer in the dusty field at the end of a short row of houses, right next to what looked like an abandoned mosque. Several old men were seated across the "street" in the shade of a green pergola at the entrance of what was probably the local grocery. They were unimpressed with the visitors and kept on sipping at their tiny cups of coffee.

It seemed as if I was walking through a dream. There was something surrealistic about it all. Fadllal knocked on the metal door and was almost instantly greeted by our host, who wore a long white galabia and a smile from ear to ear. After an extended series of greetings, we were ushered into a large living room. The furnishings were extremely loud and ornate. It could have been a showroom for Italian velvet furniture. Within minutes, coffee and sweets were brought into the room by the host's wife, who set the treats on the dark wooden coffee table. Smiling at us, she backed out of the room.

Fadllal was not one to waste time. The moment the woman was out of sight, he took a large bundle of American dollars from his pocket and handed it to the host. He then said something to the man in Arabic and signaled me to drink, saying, "We will be leaving in a minute, so drink your coffee and have a sweet. We will go back to

Jericho and spend the rest of the day there and go back to Amman in the evening, after the shift change of the guards at the bridge."

I nodded and sipped the hot coffee. Suddenly, a loud crashing sound came from the front door. Fadllal's eyes opened wide. The host's face was horrified. Something was wrong. Within seconds, there were several Israeli soldiers in the room, pointing their weapons at us and shouting in Hebrew to others outside. "We got them," the officer shouted. "Search the rest of the house, go, go, go." Soldiers were all over the place. We could hear the women's cries and the sounds of breaking dishes.

One of the soldiers was quickly tying our hands behind our backs with plastic disposable handcuffs. "What the hell is going on?" I shouted in English. "I protest. I'm a British citizen, and I demand to know what is going on."

"You will be quiet," said the officer, pointing his automatic weapon at me. "Bring him in," he said to someone behind him in the hall. One of the old men I'd seen sitting on the other side of the street was brought in. He stood there for a second, hesitant. The officer shouted at him in Arabic. The old man pointed to Fadllal and said something.

What I had dreaded had happened; nothing could be worse than what was taking place. There was no way out of this. My only hope was to stick to my story and bluff it out as a British subject. The soldiers were speaking Hebrew between them. "He's a Jordanian officer," they said. "The others are probably his men. We'll get more out of them in Ramallah." I knew that I had to do something. I considered jumping out the window and risking being shot, which would be better than what awaited me in the interrogation rooms of the Shaback in Ramallah.

"Take him downstairs," said the officer, pointing at Fadllal. "And him." He pointed at the host. They left the driver and me on the floor, guarded by two soldiers. Once the others were out of sight, the driver started crying to the soldiers, talking in Arabic. One said to the other in Hebrew, "He says he's a stinker.[3] He wants us to call the boss." The soldier who spoke Arabic walked over to the driver and picked him up by the collar, placing the rifle at the back of his head and pushing him toward the door. Suddenly he slipped, and at the same instant his weapon discharged. The sound was deafening, and the wall around the door was at once covered with blood. The driver's head was half-

---

3. Stinker: Slang for informer.

missing. The soldier let go of the man, who slumped to the floor like a sack of potatoes. The soldier started shouting at his friend, "You're crazy! Look what you did! You're crazy!"

"It was an accident," the soldier shouted back. "A fucking accident." He ran to me, grabbed me by the collar, and shouted at me in Hebrew, "Accident, right? Accident!" I couldn't say a word, only nodded. The other soldier shouted in Hebrew, "Shoot him, you have to shoot him. He's a witness, and he'll tell. Shoot him, you idiot, or I will." He lowered his gun and came at me. I could hear the sound of running up the stairs. The officer was at the door, but he just stopped and stood there. I could see the soldier's finger tightening on the trigger. I hoped it would be over fast. I felt calm; there was nothing I could do. I said to myself, Bella, I love you, I'm sorry for everything. The soldier pulled the trigger. I heard the knock of the hammer on the empty chamber.

There was a moment of silence. I had my eyes shut tight, expecting the final blow. Then I heard the loud laughter of Fadllal. In a single instant, it became clear to me that this was all a test. But how the hell did he get the soldiers to play along?

Fadllal walked over to me and helped me up. He then gently removed the cuffs from my hands and ushered me out of the place and into the car. There was a new driver behind the wheel, and we drove off. Fadllal explained it all on the way. The soldiers were Palestinians from a special unit of the Jordanian intelligence; they'd been working in the West Bank almost from 1968. They had several storage locations with Israeli uniforms and arms and would assist in all kinds of reconnaissance jobs. They worked all over the country, and all of them spoke excellent Hebrew. At first, they were to be an asset in case of war, like the Germans had behind American lines in World War II, but when the Jordanians started to work in the Territories, it was decided to use them all the time. They monitored exercises and brought in ample tactical information regarding the front line.

The driver was a real traitor and had been under suspicion for some time now. Fadllal had decided to use the elimination of the traitor to test me. He had no doubt now that I was not working for the Mossad.

Crossing back into Jordan was as much of a strain on me as was the crossing into the West Bank. The guards were different, but they were just as thorough, and the clearance seemed to take forever. Once on the other side, we took a taxi to a place called Tel Nimrim, where a light blue air-conditioned limo was waiting for us at the side of the road. I slept the rest of the way to Amman. Fadllal woke me up when we got there and said that we would all have dinner in the main dining room in about an hour, so I should change and come down then.

They were all there: Zuhir, Albert, Fadllal, and the heavyset man and his young assistant. My head was still aching, and the sound of the shot in the house in the West Bank that had literally wiped the expression off the driver's face was still fresh in my mind. I wasn't in shock; endless training in the Mossad had taken care of that, but it was still something I couldn't just shrug off. Not to mention the Jordanian unit that I'd seen, like Israeli soldiers in every way. I suddenly had a new respect for the people seated around the table. Gone was that sense of arrogance that had been part of my whole attitude until early that morning. I was seated with a very capable, and very dangerous, group of people.

Nothing was said about my little trip that day, unless it was hinted at from time to time in a smile or a wink. After dinner, everybody left except Albert, who walked with me to the bar on the main floor of the hotel. We sat in large wicker chairs by copper tray tables. I ordered a beer and Albert had another coffee: no drinking in public for him.

"I heard about your day," he said finally, after the coffee and beer were served.

"Not a trip I'd like to repeat," I said, lighting a cigarette.

He then leaned forward and nodded his head toward the other side of the bar. Several people were seated around a small table, seemingly in deep conversation. "Do you know who that man over there is?"

"I can't say I do, although the big one with the big mustache seems familiar. Who is he?"

"Habash, George Habash.[4] Would you like me to introduce you?"

My first reaction was to jump at the opportunity, then almost against my own instinct, I said, "No thanks, I'd prefer if we got out of here now."

"Why?"

"If he's here, there is a good chance someone from the Mossad may be watching. I have seen endless photos of PLO and other Palestinian leaders in just about every location. I don't want someone to identify me in such a photo taken in Amman." Without waiting for his reaction, I got up and walked out of the bar. He caught up with me at the elevators, and we agreed to meet again the following morning. "I'll come for you at, say, eight?"

---

4. George Habash: Leader of the Popular Front for the Liberation of Palestine, known as the PFLP.

"No, I'll call you. I find it hard to fall asleep here, and I need to rest. I'll call you when I wake up."

He nodded and walked back to the bar. I went to my room and called the hotel in Washington. They'd given the message to Bella when she called—at least, that's what they said. I undressed and walked into the shower. I stood under the hot running water for the longest time. I was tired and couldn't get the sight of the soldier shooting the man in the back of the head out of my mind. I wanted to cry, but I couldn't. I just stood there thinking of everything and nothing. All I wanted was for this whole thing to be over and a memory, nothing more than a memory.

Over the next two days, we put together a security mechanism similar to the one used in the Mossad to prevent moles. The Jordanians were going to start running lie detector tests on a regular basis, and also doing sporadic checks in the military units, mainly in the lower command echelons. Then they were going to start a systematic check of all personnel who had served in Jordanian embassies around the world, especially Europe, since just about all the agents recruited by the Mossad are people serving in embassies and students studying abroad, mainly military people. Since the Mossad has no time to develop talent in the hope that people will get into a position where they can provide information, but rather want people already in that situation, the targets are fairly easy to identify.

I had no doubt that once they implemented the system, they would almost instantly identify all agents working for the Mossad. However, implementation of such a system would take some months and could not be kept secret during that time, giving the Mossad ample opportunity to pull its agents out to safety. The Jordanians would not make public the fact that they had identified such agents for some time; meanwhile, they would try to turn as many of the agents as possible, and through them feed the Mossad false information. Those who were neither saved by the Mossad nor turned by the Jordanians would end up wearing the hangman's noose.

Though none of my countrymen was likely to be included in that latter group, the thought did cause me considerable discomfort. It could not be denied that a real consequence of attempting to bring down the corrupt Mossad leadership was that decent people would suffer. I could only hope that many more would be helped by what I was doing.

I was quite sure, as was Ephraim, that the Jordanians would share most of the newfound information with their Syrian and Iraqi counterparts, who would then start their own housecleaning. The Syrians had a lot of work in front of them, but the Iraqis would be chasing the wind, because Mossad had hardly any agents there. Since Iraq was considered a hard intelligence target, it was at the bottom of the Mossad's priority list.

My last two days in Amman were spent putting forward a plan to recruit Israelis who would supply the Jordanians with as much tactical and technological information as possible. They wanted to have all the military base locations and to know what was done in each. They also wanted to find out all they could about the stages of the reserve calls in case of an emergency and the deployment of special forces in reconnaissance activities as they crossed their borders, especially regarding the placement of TRS's.[5]

It was decided that I would return to the United States and then settle in Canada, as had been my original plan. Albert would run his part of the operation in Mexico, and we would use several of Fadllal's special soldiers in the operation. I named it Operation Joshua, because we were sending spies to tour the land from the same location and direction Joshua did, and I had no doubt that the result would be the same. The spies would return to tell of a land that eats its own inhabitants; it seems that nothing changes.

On my last night there, I heard on Israeli radio that British prime minister Margaret Thatcher was visiting Israel and that Ronald Reagan had vetoed Congress's block on arm sales to Saudi Arabia, mainly the sale of fighter jets.

By now, I knew that what Ephraim was after was working: We were inoculating Jordan from the dangers of the Mossad. Even if we were not able in the long run to make changes in the Mossad itself, we'd taken a large step forward in removing its fangs.

---

5. TRS: Temporary relay station. Special relay units that are planted or thrown from airplanes. They act as relay stations for special listening devices that have a shorter range than is required to be received in the deciphering unit in Israel.

CHAPTER 21

The flight back to the United States went without a hitch. We arrived in New York's Kennedy Airport some time after seven in the evening. The first thing I did was call Bella from the courtesy phone in the VIP room at the terminal, where I was waiting with Zuhir for our flight back to Washington.

The conversation was brief. She told me that she was coming out to the States the next day and that nothing in the world could stop her. The girls, Sharon and Leeorah, were sixteen and twelve and could manage with no problem, especially since Bella's father was close by. I for one was not even going to try. The mere thought of seeing her again was more than I had hoped for. I didn't want to get too emotional on the phone, especially not in front of Zuhir, who was watching me. I had to make the call short. All I could say to her was that I was in New York, that I was on my way to Washington, and that I'd call her once I got back to the hotel. After I hung up, I could feel a surge of joy run through my whole body. I could have jumped up and kissed everyone present in the room, including Zuhir.

By the time we reached Washington, it was after ten and I was famished. Zuhir had arranged to meet me the following day to bring me the money we'd agreed on, but it turned out I'd have to wait one more day, since it was Memorial Day and all the banks were closed. It didn't matter to me that much; I had some money left from what Ephraim had finally sent me. Even so, I made an issue out of it to Zuhir, so that he wouldn't think that suddenly I had money when before I'd put on a show of being someone who didn't. I told Zuhir that I'd be changing hotels the next morning, and that I'd call him the day after to tell him where I was so that he could have the money sent to me. We said goodbye on the plane, not wanting to walk out of the terminal together.

I reached the hotel just before eleven and managed to buy a McDLT and a shake to go. I was so hungry I could have eaten the burger in the wrapping. After eating and taking a shower, I called Bella again. She told me that she was arriving in Washington the day after tomorrow.

I told her that I was going to change hotels and that I would pick her up from the airport. She was going to call me the next day before leaving for the airport, and I agreed not to leave this hotel until she did. I started to count the minutes. After I'd hung up, I tried sleeping, only to realize that I was too tired even to do that. When Bella called again at four A.M., I was still watching television. She was leaving for the airport, and Arik was going to take her there. That was a surprise to me, since contact between ex-Mossad members and active workers was prohibited. You weren't expected to ignore the person if you met him on the street, but neither were you to create a contact, not with the person or with members of his immediate family. There had to be something to the fact that Arik was driving Bella to the airport. The phone, however, was not the proper tool on which to do the asking.

I had a bad feeling that someone might be trying to play a dirty trick. There was only one man to whom I could turn to see if things were as they appeared to be: Uri, my friend from Al. If there was any operation planned for the United States, at any time, he'd be the one to know about it, and I was sure that I could get him to give me a warning. He was a man who'd seen it all. The only problem was making contact with him. It wasn't as if he had a number I could call or an address he could be reached at. The man was a *katsa* at work. All I knew was that he was in the United States. There was one other thing I knew about him, though: He had a lady friend in Chevy Chase, Maryland, which wasn't that far from my hotel. Reaching him through her had a double significance: First, she was working in a sensitive position in the Pentagon and was Jewish, which made his personal relationship with her something of a no-no; second, her husband was prominent in Washington circles. Even so, I found the address in the phone book and headed out to the house. There was no point in trying to do it over the phone; I knew I'd get nowhere because the woman would have been told in her training not to respond to anyone on the phone except Uri. I had the cab wait about a block away; I walked up to the large, red-brick, mansionlike residence.

The quiet neighborhood was clearly home to the more affluent members of society. I rang the bell and waited in the cathedral-like entranceway. The heavy wooden door opened; a glass door still separated me from the very elegant blond woman who was now staring at me with a faint smile. "Yes?"

She was about five foot five and small-figured. Her brown eyes were large and shiny, and she appeared to be very cheerful.

"I would like to ask you to please give a message to Uri, if you could."

Her smile faded instantly. She wanted to know who I was and what my connection was to Uri. A tall, slim man came to the door as we spoke; it was her husband. She told him that I was a friend of Uri's. He seemed to know who that was and asked if I'd like to come in.

I had gained his instant respect just for being Uri's friend. I agreed to come in, saying that it would have to be only for a moment since I had to be on my way. The woman was clearly uncomfortable, not sure whether I knew she was having a fling with Uri. The husband was obviously not in tune with what was going on, and from the way he spoke, it sounded as if he wouldn't notice if he was present when it did. He left us in the round vestibule to answer the phone. I could see part of a tastefully decorated living room through a large arched doorway. On a small table by the wall, beneath a large gilded mirror, was a photograph of the couple standing on either side of President Ronald Reagan, in what seemed to be a black-tie state function.

I declined a drink and a cool invitation to dinner from the woman. My declining seemed to make her very happy. I jotted my phone number on a piece of paper and handed it to her. "I would very much appreciate it if you could pass that on to Uri."

The husband was not in the room when she said that she had no idea when she would see him.

"Use the emergency phone," I said and headed back to the door. I was relieved to be out of there; the awkwardness of the situation did not at all amuse me. I could understand what Uri saw in her, and after meeting her husband, I realized how easy it must have been for Uri to win her over.

I knew she could get hold of him since she had to have an emergency call setup; after all, she was a *sayan*. I'd never intended to use this contact, but I was worried that the office was up to something and that Bella and the girls might get caught in the middle. I had to make a move.

The first time I'd met Uri was when I was still in the military police, in 1968–69. I was serving in the Jordan Valley in a base called Giftlick, later renamed Arik after Colonel Arik Regev, who was killed by a Palestinian guerrilla in a chase. The colonel was killed with another officer, with whom I'd had a run-in on my first day in the valley, by the name of Gady Manella. Gady was very much what is called today a hotdogger, doing things by the seat of his pants, the ultimate Israeli warrior. During that time, Uri was the intelligence officer for the paratrooper battalion stationed in the Giftlick, and I was the commander of the military police post on the base.

At the time, chasing Palestinians who infiltrated the border to carry out acts of sabotage was almost a daily occurrence. Most of the time, the infiltrators would be killed during the chase or in short skirmishes in the parched desert. There were cases, however, in which the terrorists would be captured alive; nevertheless, most of the time, even if they were taken alive, they'd be announced as dead over the radio so no one would await their return.

That was where I would come in as a military police officer; my job was to take the prisoners to a holding facility in Nes Ziyyona, a small town south of Tel Aviv. I'd always assumed that it was an interrogation facility for the Shaback. We all knew that a prisoner brought there would probably never get out alive, but the brainwashing we'd gone through in our short lifetimes had convinced us it was them or us; there was no gray area.

It was Uri who enlightened me regarding the Nes Ziyyona facility. It was, he said, an ABC warfare laboratory—ABC standing for atomic, bacteriological, and chemical. It was where our top epidemiological scientists were developing various doomsday machines. Because we were so vulnerable and would not have a second chance should there be an all-out war in which this type of weapon would be needed, there was no room for error. The Palestinian infiltrators came in handy in this regard. As human guinea pigs, they could make sure the weapons the scientists were developing worked properly and could verify how fast they worked and make them even more efficient. What scares me today, looking back at that revelation, is not the fact that it was taking place but rather the calmness and understanding with which I accepted it.

Years later, I met Uri again. This time he was in the Mossad, a veteran *katsa* in the Al department, and I was a rookie. He had come back from an assignment in South Africa. I was then a temporary desk man in the Dardasim department in liaison, helping him prepare for a large shipment of medication to South Africa to accompany several Israeli doctors who were headed for some humanitarian work in Soweto, a black township outside Johannesburg. The doctors were to assist in treating patients at an outpatient clinic for the Baragwanath hospital in Soweto, a few blocks away from the houses of Winnie

Mandela and Bishop Desmond Tutu. The hospital and the clinic were supported by a hospital in Baltimore, which served as a cut-out[1] for the Mossad. Uri was on a cooling-off period from the United States.

"What is the Mossad doing giving humanitarian assistance to blacks in Soweto?" I remember asking him. There was no logic to it; no short-term political gain (which was the way the Mossad operated) or any visible monetary advantage.

"Do you remember Nes Ziyyona?" His question sent shivers up my spine. I nodded.

"This is very much the same. We're testing both new infectious diseases and new medication that can't be tested on humans in Israel, for several of the Israeli medicine manufacturers. This will tell them whether they're on the right track, saving them millions in research."

"What do you think about all this?" I had to ask.

"It's not my job to think about it."

Even though he didn't say it, I knew his heart was not in it—at least I hoped not. The fact that he was barred from the States by the Mossad for this cooling-off period after the Pollard affair was not doing his career much good. He was the one who'd brought Pollard into the fold in 1982.

When they first met, Jonathan Pollard was an American Jew who believed wholeheartedly that there was a holy alliance between the United States of America and the state of Israel. He did not see a conflict between total loyalty to the United States and total loyalty to the state of Israel; to him it was one and the same. This ideology did not spring out of itself; it was a result of a long process of indoctrination many Jewish youths are put through with the generous help of the state of Israel in the form of *shlichim*, or, as they are known, messengers of Alia. These are people who work within the Jewish community to instill a love of Israel in the hearts of the Jewish youth. In Jonathan Pollard's case, they were extremely successful.

The young man had volunteered in 1982 to the American Israel Public Affairs Committee, a pro-Israeli lobby group, another link in the chain of organizations manacling the Jewish community to Israel in general and to the Israeli right wing in particular. Pollard, already a member of the American intelligence community, had volunteered his services for the benefit of the state of Israel. As is the procedure, his name was passed to the security section in the Israeli embassy in

---

1. Cut-out: A person or group used to conceal contact, creating an information buffer.

Washington and from there on to the Mossad as a potential *sayan*. After thorough checking, including using the Mossad's connection in the Anti-Defamation League, the Mossad decided that he was a good candidate and would fit in well, since he was both a Zionist zealot and well placed in the American intelligence research community, with ample access to vital information about the Middle East and Africa. And since he was Jewish, there was no thought of making him a paid spy. In fact, he was perfect for Operation Reindeer, which was meant to reestablish the ties between the American intelligence establishment and that of South Africa. Not that the two didn't have a link of their own, but this one would be monitored by the Mossad and would be much more secure and lucrative.

There was no hesitation on Pollard's part once Uri made contact with him, bringing in a reference from a friend Pollard had in Israel. The AIPAC was notified that the Mossad was not interested in Pollard, and Pollard was instructed not to contact the Jewish organizations again. He was now a *sayan* for the Mossad or, as he was told, for the security organization of Israel.

At the time, Pollard was not getting any money for the work he was doing, since it is a clear Mossad policy not to pay Jewish helpers. That way it could never be said that what they're doing is for any reason other than love and concern for Israel.

Uri had supplied the South Africans with photos (which the Mossad had received from the Danish intelligence) of the SSC-3 Soviet weapons system that the Americans were eager to get at the time. This was all part of Operation Reindeer, in which the South African intelligence was endeared to the Americans using Pollard's school contacts. (Apparently, someone with whom Pollard had gone to school and remained friends with afterward had subsequently become a senior South African intelligence officer.)

For some time, Uri went on using Pollard for obtaining various pieces of information, never overstraining the relationship to the point where the man might be placed under suspicion. In his reports, Uri constantly warned—just for the record—that he was not sure if Pollard was telling him all of the truth all of the time. Uri thought that Pollard might be getting himself into trouble, trying to get information he wasn't asked to get. If he was, Uri couldn't help him, because Uri wouldn't be aware of the danger.

Sometime in 1984, Uri had decided with the agreement of his bosses that Pollard was too volatile to handle, since he was always trying to do more than he was asked, taking unnecessary risks, and generally becoming more of a liability than an asset. Therefore, he was put on the dormant list as a sleeper. Pollard was informed that he'd been of great help to Israel and that for his own safety, the Israeli intelligence had decided he needed a cooling-off period. Should they decide at a later date that it was again safe for him to work, they'd contact him and revive the activity.

Pollard was not thrilled at the prospect, but according to Uri, he didn't make a fuss. It must be remembered that up to that point, he hadn't been paid one red cent and was doing it all because of sheer ideology.

Not long after the file was rendered dormant, Rafi Eitan got his hands on it. Even though he was no longer a Mossad officer at the time, as the saying goes, once a Mossad always a Mossad. He had access to Mossad files, both because of his past in the Mossad and because he was the adviser on terrorism to the prime minister and also the head of the LAKAM.

For him, finding the dormant Pollard file was like striking gold. Not bound by Mossad rules of conduct regarding Jewish helpers, he activated Pollard through his reviving code word and arranged to create a so-called natural setting for him to meet his new operator, Avian Sellah. Sellah, a decorated Israeli pilot who'd taken part in the bombing of the Iraqi nuclear plant in Osirak, was a natural for the job. He wanted to study in the United States and would be working for the LAKAM at the same time. He didn't have to recruit Pollard, only activate him, and the meeting between the two was set up by Eitan to look like a coincidence brought about by a third party, a relative of Pollard's who had attended a speech by Sellah. Sellah was chosen to be the operator because he was an expert in targeting and could talk shop with Pollard, who was an intelligence analysis expert. The fact that Sellah was not a trained intelligence man also contributed to the fall of Pollard, who, in this new phase, was now getting paid and was in fact almost running himself.

The Mossad had heard from sources in the CIA that they were closing in on Pollard, but the Mossad preferred to stay out of the picture, hoping the affair would be settled quietly, behind closed doors, putting the LAKAM out of the game. To buy time once things started to go haywire, the Israeli ambassador to the United States was sent on a lecture tour to France, and the running of the embassy was left in the hands of a lower-ranking diplomat, Eliyakim Rubinstein, who couldn't make a policy decision on his own. Once all the LAKAM people had fled the United States, Pollard was left behind to fend for himself. He fled to the Israeli embassy in Washington. Once he was inside, the security people turned for instructions to Rubinstein, who then turned to the Shaback representative to see what he had to say. That man turned to the Mossad representative, who, without checking back with headquarters and assuming things hadn't changed, told the Shaback man that Pollard was not Mossad and therefore was none of his business. The Shaback man then said that his people had no claim over Pollard, and since all the LAKAM people had left the country and were not to be found, it was up to Rubinstein. He also mentioned the fact that the embassy was surrounded by the FBI.

Rubinstein was not able to contact Israel on the secure channels that were controlled by the Mossad liaison, who said they were down. So Rubinstein decided to take the initiative. He had Pollard and his wife sent out of the embassy into the hands of the stunned FBI. Much later, I learned from FBI people involved in the Pollard investigation and capture that they were almost as surprised as he was that he was sent out; at that point, they'd been ready to negotiate some sort of compromise with Israel. It was also learned later that a large portion of the information that Pollard had handed over to Israel made its way to the Eastern Bloc in exchange for the release of Jews from those countries. That knowledge, and the fact that admitting it would verify the information that was now in the hands of the Soviets, was the reason Caspar Weinberger, the American secretary of defense, asked for the maximum sentence for Pollard and was not able to explain why publicly.

Uri was forced to leave the United States then, since the Mossad was worried that Pollard, to get a shorter sentence, would expose the Mossad connection. But Pollard, because he knew that doing so would open up a whole new can of worms that would make his situation worse, kept quiet about it. This was why the Justice Department did not feel obligated to fulfill its side of the plea bargain with Pollard, in which he was promised a reduced sentence and no jail time for his wife, who was sentenced as his accomplice, in exchange for a full disclosure of all the relevant facts.

Now the affair had quieted down, and Uri was back in the States, actively running large numbers of more reliable and more discreet sayanim.

At ten A.M., I was packed and ready to go when the phone rang. It was Uri, and he was furious. How dare I call his operative? He said I'd scared the shit out of her and that she was thinking about quitting. I tried to calm him down for a while. Then, as if someone had waved a magic wand, he changed his tone. It was as though the man had shot out all his anger and then was overcome by serenity.

"So, Victor, what's new?"

"Apart from being out of the Office and on my own, searching for the meaning of life, not much."

"So what brings you here?"

"The never-ending search." I was joking, and he knew it.

"What can I do for you? And what's the damage in it?"

"No damage, really. I need to know if there is something planned for Washington in the next twenty-four hours."

"In what way?"

"You know what I mean. Anything out of the usual, something they'd warn you to stay away from."

There was a short silence on the line. "What are you up to, man?"

"You didn't answer my question!"

"Nothing that I know of." His speech was slow, as if he was thinking. "Where are you now?"

"In my hotel. You just called me, remember?"

"I called, but I don't know where this Holiday Inn is. Can we meet somewhere?"

"How about the lobby of the Four Seasons downtown?"

"That's fine with me. When?"

"How about two this afternoon?"

"See you there." He hung up.

I settled the bill and left the hotel. I took a cab to the Sheraton overlooking the airport, got a room there, and headed back downtown. At two, I entered the Four Seasons. Uri was waiting for me and led me into the dining room at the far end. Uri was in his late forties, five foot nine, and stocky. He had shining silver hair and a high forehead; in his gray suit and his horn-rimmed glasses, he was very distinguished-looking. We were led to a table, but Uri had a preference for a corner one. Once we were alone, he got to it: "What can you tell me about Ephraim?"

I stared at him for a moment. "What can *you* tell me?"

"If I tell you that I'm in his group, will that mean anything to you?"

"Are you?"

"Yes. Are you the loose property he's talking about?"

"I could be, but then I believe I wouldn't be the only one." I leaned forward. "What can you tell me about Kuti?" I asked, referring to the general who had been killed before taking over leadership of the Mossad.

"You *are* the property," he said, smiling. "I would never have guessed. Yes, I believe the man was murdered by our people."

"Let's not tell Ephraim about this conversation," I said. "I would prefer to have someone in the group that he doesn't know I know."

"I don't have a problem with that. Don't you trust him?"

"I do today. But, as you well know, things change."

Very little else was said on the subject after that. We decided that the woman would be our contact point and that he would tell her this was just a way to make sure she was safe. He would call to see if I had left messages for him, and I could do the same. At last I had a second lifeline, someone I could trust and who would eventually keep me alive.

CHAPTER 22

As I was waiting for Bella to arrive, a man stood next to me in the terminal leafing through a book. It was the latest novel by John le Carré. I found the title somewhat ironic, given my situation: *A Perfect Spy*. I remembered how much I used to enjoy that kind of book, before I joined the Mossad and learned how different the real world of espionage was from the fantasy of the so-called spy novel. Reality was far more dangerous and unpredictable than any fiction could be. I remember thinking how it would be almost impossible to describe the complexity of the tangled web of intelligence.

A crowd of passengers who had arrived on a flight from New York emerged, and a few minutes later Bella appeared. She was breathtaking. Her smile was the light I'd been seeking at the end of the tunnel. I was happier than I could remember ever being before. At some point in this bizarre journey, I'd lost hope of seeing her again, and here she was. I held on to her and was going to keep holding her that way for as long as I could.

We both knew that we'd made a leap across a vast abyss to be with each other. She didn't know the depth of the chasm that had separated us, but she could sense its vastness. We hardly said a thing until we reached the hotel, and there we sat facing each other. She wanted to know where I'd been and what was going on. I couldn't tell her. I had to keep her out of it, and so I told her that I'd visited Zaire and was a security adviser to some people from there. I told her I was going to get some money the following day, and then we'd leave for Canada.

The next morning, I went downstairs to meet with Zuhir and get the money from him. I then went up the block and bought a car, paying cash. It was a 1985 Pontiac 6000, metallic gray. After arranging for insurance and temporary plates, I returned to the hotel. The following day, we headed up to Canada. I was extremely anxious to leave Washington, D.C. The memories I had of the place were not altogether pleasant.

It was like a second honeymoon, although we'd never really had a first one. We couldn't seem to get enough of each other. After a three-day drive, we arrived in Ottawa, the beautiful capital of Canada. It was a city that Bella had once seen in a television program and had always wanted to live in. Since it didn't matter what exact location we chose, Ottawa it was.

We spent the first few days in the downtown Holiday Inn on Queen Street. Then we found a three-bedroom apartment, also in the downtown area, in a modern apartment building called Kent Towers.

As far as Bella was concerned, I would have to travel from time to time in my advisory capacity, but otherwise would be able to devote my free time to what I'd always wanted to do on a full-time basis, and that was sketch and paint. Eventually, after Leeorah came over and Bella went back to Israel to pack everything, coming back with Sharon, we were all living in the apartment on Kent Street. The girls were not very enthusiastic about the change, but such was life, and they accepted it.

From time to time, I'd call Ephraim from the pay phone across the street to see if all was going well and to receive instructions about my next step. At the time, not much was happening. He wanted me to make contact with the Egyptians, but I kept putting that off. I wasn't comfortable about working with two Arab countries at the same time. We had no idea what the relationship was between them; as far as we knew, they were in full cooperation. From the little we saw of any Jordanian activity, we realized how little we knew.

But since we were not yet ready to set up the Israeli spy ring for the Jordanians as I'd promised, I couldn't put Ephraim off much longer. He felt that there was a need to inoculate Egyptian intelligence against the Mossad. That had to be done before some incident occurred that would expose the Mossad's assistance (mainly logistical) to the Muslim fundamentalists through contacts in Afghanistan.

The peace with Egypt was pressing hard on the Israeli right wing. In itself, the peace, so vigilantly kept by the Egyptians, was living proof that the Arabs are a people with whom peace is possible, and that they're not at all what the Mossad and other elements of the right have portrayed them to be. Egypt has kept its peace with Israel, even though Israel became the aggressor in Lebanon in 1982 and despite the Mossad's warnings that the Egyptians were in fact in the middle of a ten-year military buildup that would bring about a war with Israel in 1986–87 (a war that never materialized).

The Mossad realized that it had to come up with a new threat to the region, a threat of such magnitude that it would justify whatever action the Mossad might see fit to take.

The right-wing elements in the Mossad (and in the whole country, for that matter) had what they regarded as a sound philosophy: They believed (correctly, as it happened) that Israel was the strongest military presence in the Middle East. In fact, they believed that the military might of what had become known as "fortress Israel" was greater than that of all of the Arab armies combined, and was responsible for whatever security Israel possessed. The right wing believed then—and they *still* believe—that this strength arises from the need to answer the constant threat of war.

The corollary belief was that peace overtures would inevitably start a process of corrosion that would weaken the military and eventually bring about the demise of the state of Israel, since, the philosophy goes, its Arab neighbors are untrustworthy, and no treaty signed by them is worth the paper it's written on.

Supporting the radical elements of Muslim fundamentalism sat well with the Mossad's general plan for the region. An Arab world run by fundamentalists would not be a party to any negotiations with the West, thus leaving Israel again as the only democratic, rational country in the region. And if the Mossad could arrange for the Hamas (Palestinian fundamentalists) to take over the Palestinian streets from the PLO, then the picture would be complete.

Mossad activity in Egypt was extensive. Now that there was an Israeli embassy in Cairo, the walk-in traffic was heavy. Egypt was being used both as a source of information and as a jumping-off point to the rest of the Arab world. It would be much easier and much less suspicious to have an Egyptian who was recruited under a false flag in Cairo and had never set foot outside the Middle East carry out intelligence gathering in other Arab countries than Arabs who had been to Europe and therefore might be suspected.

That in itself was a "legitimate" part of the game, but once the Mossad began trying to undermine the fiber of Egyptian society by supporting the fundamentalists, also under false flags, it was something completely different. It was more like cutting off the branch on which you're sitting.

SUNDAY, JUNE 29

Bella had gone to Israel for a week to get the rest of our things together and bring them back to Canada. When she'd left Israel, it had been in haste, and all she had wanted to do was find me, having been almost totally cut off from me when I was in Jordan. She was due back in Canada the following week. At about noon, I received a telephone call at my house.

"Vic?" I recognized the voice instantly. But I was surprised that Ephraim was calling me at home.

"What?"

"How about we have lunch?"

"Where are you?" I could feel my body turn on to an alert state.

"I think that if you look out your window, you will see me. I'm in a phone booth across from a store called Canadian Tire."

I looked down at the street, and there he was, in a light blue pinstripe suit.

"Where did you find the suit?" I asked, chuckling.

"Are you coming down, or should I come up there and drag you down?"

"Do you realize how close we are to the Israeli embassy?" I asked.

"Sure, it's about a block down the street. But the man in charge of security is now on a shooting range in New York state with most of his men, and our liaison is in Washington. The coast is clear. We can eat anywhere you want to."

I was down in a few minutes. It was a beautiful day. We ended up on the mezzanine level at the Westin Hotel, where we had a light lunch. After giving me the Office gossip, Ephraim came to the point, namely the reason for his visit. "You have to make the move to Egypt now. We can't wait any longer."

I had in fact already made contacts in the Egyptian embassy in Washington and had been there twice. But at the time, on Ephraim's advice, I'd declined the invitation to go to Cairo. We were involved in more important things just then, such as the Jordanian setup and the meetings with the British, and as Ephraim put it, the time was not right. I had a standing invitation from the then military attaché to come for a visit.

According to Ephraim, the man who'd made that invitation was about to be replaced, and since we didn't know who his replacement would be, but already knew for a fact that the acting attaché was not working for the Mossad, the window of opportunity for a safe entry into Egypt was fast closing.

"You have to get in there and point out the connection with the fundamentalists. I'm getting some bits of information from time to time, and I need a way to let them have that information from a source they will trust."

"Are you going to plant information to make a point?" I had to know; if he was planning to use me as a tool for spreading disinformation, he could count me out. I had no special feelings for the Egyptians; it was just that I didn't believe in the Mossad's way of doing things. I didn't think that what was bad for the goose was okay for the gander.

He assured me that this was not the case; the information that he had would lead to the arrest of several fundamentalists and the exposure of the armaments supply line from the Mujahideen in Afghanistan to the Muslim Brotherhood in Egypt.

"That is a long way to carry arms," I noted.

As it turned out, it was a complex pipeline, since a large portion of the Mujahideen's weapons were American-made and were supplied to the Muslim Brotherhood directly from Israel, using as carriers the Bedouin nomads who roamed the demilitarized zones in the Sinai.

The Mossad could of course also supply Soviet-made equipment from the spoils of the PLO stores seized in the 1982 war on the PLO in Lebanon. Once it was on Egyptian territory, the matériel was passed to an intermediary who would make the final delivery. As payment for the armaments, the Mossad would contract targets to be hit inside Egypt.

"Destabilize, destabilize, destabilize," Ephraim said. "That is all they're doing, all the time. No matter what anyone says, all they can think about is creating a shambles. They don't understand that this jungle they're creating will one day swallow them too."

"Bella is due back on the first. I'll take her and the kids on a small trip to Washington and pick up my visa there. That is, if my contact is still working."

"Don't delay. I hear you've been talking to Uri."

His statement caught me totally by surprise. I wasn't quite sure what to say, if anything. "Do you have a slow ignition or something? That was a long time ago."

"Not that long. Have you been in contact with him since?"

"Ask him."

He didn't say another word about it. At the end of the day, he had me drive him to the airport, and off he went. He was going to give me some information about the armaments transfer after I got back from Washington and had a firm date to travel.

*　　*　　*

We took our little trip to Washington on Friday, July 4, entering the United States on a very festive occasion. I planned to drive down on the weekend, making it to the Egyptian embassy first thing Monday morning. The drive went without a hitch. I'd told Bella that I was to meet some diplomats from Zaire and arrange for my trip there. At the embassy, things went smoothly. After I handed my passport to the security man at the door, my contact escorted me into a large room fancily decorated in light blue. I was asked to wait under a gold-framed portrait of the smiling President Hosni Mubarak. Several minutes later, the attaché came in and greeted me warmly. He was curious as to whether I was superstitious at all. I assured him I was not. He said that my flight to Cairo was scheduled for July 13, which was but one week away. I felt a slight weakness in my knees, but I wasn't going to let on that I had any problem with that.

My tickets would be waiting for me at the Aer Lingus counter in Kennedy Airport, but I would have to pay for them; they were going to make the reservation only. He handed me an envelope with two thousand dollars in it. I was to come back on July 20, according to him, and would be picked up at the airport and taken to a safe place. He promised me that I had nothing to worry about and that the matter of payment for my services would be discussed by the authorities when I got there. He made it very clear that, because of his diplomatic status and the respect he had for the United States as its guest, he was not able to get involved in this matter beyond the liaison stage.

"As long as your heart is pure when you deal with us," the man said with a smile, "you have absolutely nothing to worry about."

That statement scared me more than any threat I'd ever received. It was a veiled threat if ever I heard one—or was it because I was the thief with his hat on fire that I took it that way?

I was very preoccupied on my way back to Ottawa. I was feeling a strange sense of imminent doom. At last, I'd settled in a place where I felt comfortable and started a new life, and here I was leaving it all behind and embarking on a journey back into the hell I'd so recently left. But I knew that this new life was only make-believe and that I was still a soldier on the most remote outpost of his country's border, a border so distant and murky that it was not clear which side of it you were on. It was the kind of border you needed philosophy to define, and I didn't like it at all.

Sunday, July 13

I arrived in New York in the afternoon and picked up my ticket at the counter, just as planned. I was to go aboard Egypt Air Flight 986, departure time 22:00, so I had some time to kill.

I felt very uncomfortable about what I was going to do. Leaving the safety of the United States was something my whole body rebelled against. I'd been exposed to far too many intelligence agencies in the past few months to feel safe on such a trip. It seemed almost impossible that the Egyptians, who had a very efficient although somewhat obscure intelligence agency, had not heard about at least one of my escapades.

The flight took off on time, and I was trapped in it, heading inevitably for whatever awaited me. I couldn't sleep all the way, feeling guilty about not telling Bella where I was going. But it was more a selfish thought than one of concern: If I'd told Bella at least someone besides Ephraim would know where I was.

We flew into daylight above the sparkling blue Mediterranean. The pilot announced the beginning of our descent into Cairo International, and the stunning yellow landscape of Egypt took over from the cool blue sea. The closer we got, the more hazy the scenery became. By the time we landed, you didn't have to be outside to know how hot it was.

Friday, July 18

The naked lightbulb dangling from the moldy ceiling flickered momentarily, ending my recollection of the past six months. I heard a faint scream somewhere in the bowels of what I had thought to be an empty building. The barely audible shrieks instantly drenched me in cold sweat. I lay on my back, my eyes following a large brown cockroach making its way across the ceiling of my cell.

Then the old man was back with a fresh pitcher of lemonade and a food tray. Lying there, driven to exasperation by the metronomic quality of my existence, fearing that the old man would appear like this at the appointed time for the next thousand days, I realized I had to do something to get someone's attention. When the codger was attending to the shower, I tossed the loaded food tray out the door, barely missing the guard. For an instant, I was sure he was going to use his weapon and cut me down where I stood. Instead, he looked surprised and shouted something to the old man, who hurried out of the cell. I lay back on the bed. The fan abruptly stopped working, and it was too hot to do anything about it. The cockroach on the ceiling was gone.

I thought about my predicament. It was already four days since I'd been thrown into this cell. The possibility that this might be "home" for the rest of my life was terrifying. To escape the horror of such a prospect, I began a fantasy of how things were working out and how I would soon be out of there.

I think it was some time in the early afternoon when the door opened and a large man in a light gray short-sleeve suit entered the room. I'd just stepped out of the shower and was still half-dressed. I was taking a shower every few hours, and I only dressed sufficiently to be decent, in case I had a visitor.

"Mr. Ostrovsky?" the large man said with a friendly smile. His shining bald head was well tanned and so was his face. I could tell from his tan line that he normally wore a T-shirt and not the V collar that he wore now.

I turned my head as if looking for someone behind me. "I guess you must be looking for me?"

His smile broadened. "I must apologize for the delay in coming to greet you."

I stared at the man without a word, still in the dormant mode I'd adopted. This man could depart at any minute and not come back, leaving me to my torment all over again. I decided that I would do anything to get out of that horrible place.

"If you would get dressed, I'll escort you to meet some people who're expecting you."

I nodded and within minutes was following him down the hall into a large conference room. At the end of the long table was a pile of *Bamahaneh*[1] magazines. The room appeared to have been plucked out of a modern office building; it was fresh and clean and seemed quite out of place in this dilapidated old structure. There was a coffeemaker in the corner, and the aroma of American-style brewed coffee hung in the air. The big man offered me a cup and then pointed to the tray with milk and sugar. To the right was a large wall mirror. Someone opened a door behind the mirror, causing the mirror to be transparent for a split second. I saw several people sitting behind it and a camera on a tripod set up in the corner.

---

1. *Bamahaneh:* The word means "in the camp" and refers to the weekly magazine of the Israeli military.

"What are the magazines for?" I asked. The man told me that they were for me, and that I could take them to my room after we were finished today. What he said had an ominous ring to it. I didn't want to go back to my "room"; I wanted out of the whole rotten place, but I had to keep my cool.

Things began to move very fast. The Egyptians handed me a pile of photographs and asked me to identify people from the Mossad. They were not playing games as most of the other agencies had. Each photo had a name under it in both English and Arabic. There were fewer than five photos that I couldn't identify. And I was told that they were serving in Europe, so it was quite likely that I didn't know them. They also had a chart of the Mossad departments and the floor plan of the building on King Saul Boulevard. They wanted me to show them where I used to sit when I worked on the Danish desk.

At that point, it was clear that they'd already spoken to someone who'd worked in the building and were quite up to date on the organization. My host became much more relaxed once he learned that I could not name any Egyptians working for the Mossad. And he was more than happy to get the information about the weapons infiltration for the Muslim Brotherhood.

He then wanted to hear as much as I could tell him about Robert Maxwell, the British newspaper magnate. His reason was that they were aware of the constant Mossad interest in purchasing media so that it could both influence public opinion and use journalism as a cover for inserting agents into countries.

It seemed my host was as eager to show me how much he knew as he was to hear about things he didn't know—not a good trait for an intelligence officer. He identified Maxwell as a Mossad agent and also reminded me of other occasions on which the Mossad had been behind the purchase of newspapers in England. As an example, he gave the *Eastern African*, which was bought with Mossad money by an Israeli businessman. The purchase was made, he said, to assist the South African propaganda machine in making apartheid more palatable in the West.

Suddenly, the sinister nature of what was being done with Maxwell became clear to me. In his zeal to cooperate with Israel, and even though he was not an agent himself (as the British had made clear when I had spoken to them in Washington), Maxwell was a *sayan* on the grand scale. The Mossad was financing many of its operations in Europe from moneys stolen from the man's newspaper pension fund. They got their hands on the pension funds almost as soon as he'd made his purchases (initially with money lent to him by the

Mossad and on expert advice he received from Mossad analyses).
What was sinister about it, aside from the theft, was that anyone in his
news organization, anywhere in the Middle East, was automatically
suspected of working for Israel and was only one rumor away from
the hangman's noose.

I explained to my host, as I had to the British, that in the beginning the Mossad would help Maxwell purchase the newspapers by
lending him money and causing labor disputes and other problems,
making the target purchases more vulnerable. Later, the tactics
changed; they would target in advance a paper that he was to purchase and start it on a collision course with bankruptcy using all available strategies, starting with workforce agitation and ending with pull-
back of funds from the paper through bankers and advertisers sympa-
thetic to the Mossad. Then, once the target was softened, they'd send
Maxwell in for the kill.

That night, my host took me on a drive into the city of Cairo. I
knew the man felt safe with me when he took me in his car, just the
two of us, out in the big city. For the first few minutes, he had me
blindfolded, and I was blindfolded again on the way back. The city
didn't really impress me, nor did the pyramids. I was far too frustrated
and tense to take in much of it. But I enjoyed the open spaces and the
semifree feeling I had. By midnight, I was back in my cell, with my
host's guarantee that he would be back in the morning and that I
would in fact be on board Egypt Air Flight 985 to New York on Sunday.

I lay on my back in the cell, staring at the ceiling, wearing only my
underwear. I had a feeling that the man had not lied to me and that I
would indeed be on that flight, but since things so far had not gone
the way I'd anticipated, there was no guarantee that they'd start now.

I made a pledge to myself that if I got out of this place, I would
not leave Canada again as long as I lived. I'd been a normal human
being when I had entered the Mossad, maybe a bit on the naive side,
placing my trust in just about anyone. The Mossad had changed me; it
had programmed me for survival, which meant I could no longer trust
anyone for anything. It had made me callous, and it had also made me
tenacious. Once I had a goal, nothing but death could stop me from
reaching it. It had tried to brainwash me into agreeing with its twisted
political agenda. As a result of its failure, it had created what it would
later call its worst nightmare: a man with the perseverance of a
Mossad officer who is devoted to the destruction of the Mossad.

I knew there and then, in that small cell, that the only way to kill
the Mossad would be to expose it. By now I knew that it was not the

organization it wanted everyone to think it was. Yes, it was dangerous. Yes, it was vicious, but it was not efficient. Nor was it what it
pretended to be: an intelligence agency dedicated to warning the state
of potential danger.

I was put on the flight to New York as promised. I was given ten
thousand dollars for my help. I had to sign a form saying that I had
come to Egypt of my own free will, had been well treated, and had
received the sum of ten thousand dollars as a gift.

When the plane touched down in New York, I wanted to kiss the
ground. I'd promised the Egyptians that I would come back if they
wanted me to, and go over some things with them if they felt the need.
But I knew when I said it that if I could help it, my foot would not
touch Egyptian soil again.

It was some time later that I learned the reason for the treatment I
had received in Cairo. The Egyptians never gave me any explanation,
except to say it was a misunderstanding.

What really happened was that someone had tipped them off that
I was a Mossad operative still working for the Mossad. I was to disin-
form them and cause havoc inside their organization by pointing the
finger at someone who I would say was a mole working for the
Mossad.

They decided to hold me in isolation and see what they could
extract from the Mossad by devious means. They informed the
embassy that they had found the body of a man answering my description who'd come to Egypt on the same flight as I had and who was a
resident of Canada. They also said that they believed he might be an
Israeli. The message made its way to the Mossad, and because the
Mossad had no one in the area answering the description, it didn't
respond. After four days, the Egyptians were convinced that I was not
with the Mossad, because they believed the Mossad would, by that
time, have at least asked to see the body. All that came back from the
Israeli embassy was that no Israeli answering that description was
missing and that the Canadian authorities would be a much better bet.
Meanwhile, back in headquarters, Ephraim was climbing the walls,
thinking I'd somehow slipped, revealing my true identity, and was not
coming out or, much worse, that—as he later put it—I had sold him
out.

CHAPTER 23

It took me several days to get used to being a free man again. I was never again going to be a puppet on a string, for anyone. I was going to participate only in things that I knew would hurt the Mossad. I knew now that the Mossad was a deadly machine without a purpose, and if Ephraim was not going to work with me the way I wanted, he could go to hell and I would do it on my own. I made it clear that I would not cooperate in any more activities unless they were directly detrimental to the success of the Mossad.

He wanted to know whether I would continue to work with the Egyptians, and I told him I would not unless it was to pass on information to them that could hurt the Mossad. I would, however, continue my activities with the Jordanians, since I thought that it could help bring about a peaceful solution to the conflict between Israel and Jordan. If the Mossad succeeded in bringing down King Hussein, there would never, ever be peace in the region. The fundamentalists would prevail, and that would be the end of that.

I also said that I would be happy to provide information to the British and to make contact with the French. As it turned out, that did not happen for some time.

I contacted the Jordanians and arranged a meeting with Albert in Ottawa. At first, he was reluctant to come, fearing a trap, but he eventually agreed and was supposed to arrive in Ottawa in mid-September. I contacted a local gallery owner, a Mr. Koyman, who had several galleries in Ottawa, Toronto, and Montreal. I brought him some samples of my work. He had them framed and began to sell them through his main gallery in Ottawa, at the Rideau Center. At the same time, I wrote in any official documents that I was a security adviser to foreign countries. That was the truth; I'd started work on an analysis paper of the political situation in the Middle East and the significance of the various political activities in the area, mainly analyzing what was behind the statements of Israeli politicians. This paper would allow the Jordanians thereafter to plot their decision making on a realistic picture of the political arena, and not on what some farfetched, over-paid, and one-sided American media analysts said. If you turned on your television set at any given time, you'd hear them babble on and on about how they saw the picture, while it was clear to anyone with a brain that they were feeding on one another.

Albert came to Ottawa, and I gave him a two-week crash course in how to analyze the analysts. In many Arab capitals, the leaders were delivering a lot of rhetoric for internal consumption but at the same time eating up what the so-called experts were saying about what other Arab leaders were saying. For some reason, they'd stopped relying on their own common sense.

Albert was starting to press me for the Israeli spy ring that I'd promised him, and he also had a request. His people were extremely anxious because of the forthcoming change in government in Israel. Since the Israeli election about two years previously had been com-pletely indecisive, the two major parties (left-leaning Labor and right-leaning Likud) had agreed to a unity government in which their lead-ers would share power in rotation.

It was decided that Shimon Peres, then leader of the Labor Party, would be the prime minister for the first two-year term, and that Yitzhak Shamir, leader of the right-wing Likud Party, would be the foreign minister. Then after two years, Shamir would become prime minister, and Peres would be foreign minister. Yitzhak Rabin, the number two of the Labor Party at the time, was to be minister of defense for the full term. The time was approaching when Shamir would become prime minister. They wanted me to come to Amman and analyze what that would mean to them. They were happy with my written analysis, but for this occasion, they wanted me there.

As far as they were concerned, there was no reason for me not to want to come. They'd treated me well when I was there, and they'd upheld their end of the bargain in every way. I agreed but said that I would need a few days to set the date. After all, what was the point in coming if I didn't have all the information needed for the analysis? I also wanted to get Ephraim to help me set up that spy ring we had talked about, or at least get a list of people and give the Jordanians several operational options.

After Albert left on September 30, Ephraim arrived. We had sev-eral meetings in his hotel room at the Holiday Inn. He said that things were getting a little turbulent back home and that he would have to stay there for some time now, so Eli was going to be my contact man. He'd be arriving in town on Friday, October 3. I knew Eli from the academy; he was an instructor there during my first course, and we'd had a good relationship. I had had no idea that he was part of this, and if I'd had to guess, I'd never have picked him. I'd always regarded him as a hard-line right-winger.

Eli was very happy to be in Canada; he was there as a tourist and was staying in the Holiday Inn on Queen Street (later to become the Radisson Hotel). As far as Bella was concerned, I was meeting with some people on business.

We placed ads in several Jewish papers and one in the Hebrew-language papers in the United States and Canada. We were calling for Israelis with a military combat background to work for a security company named International Combat Services (ICS). We gave a post office box in Ottawa as an address and within days were inundated with letters from Israelis across the continent and from Israel, giving their resumes in Hebrew to a strange company they didn't know. They gave us their names, addresses, and military rank, and many were not shy about putting in their exact military background, names and locations of their military units, and their special training. That in itself was a fountain of knowledge that would normally take a well-trained and well-oiled intelligence apparatus to collect. There was no doubt that some of the information was bogus and some of the writers were boasting connections or experience they didn't have, but from what I knew of the naval command and other units in the military, I could tell that the majority of it was right on the nose.

Eli took most of the letters with him and had them faxed to Ephraim, who was to prepare a list that I could take with me to Amman. It would consist of seven names that I could use. And if this thing actually materialized, and we recruited them, then the Jordanians would have good information, but not information that would endanger the state of Israel.

I was getting ready for the trip. Ephraim had insisted that I leave on October 20. He said that two of the three Kidon teams were on ice after the Vanunu case and the third was on standby. Also, because that was the day Shamir and Peres were to exchange jobs, it would take at least forty-eight hours to get approval for any Kidon activity should something go wrong with me. At the time, he wouldn't expand on the Vanunu case. Only months later, after the Vanunu affair was a matter of public record, did I hear more about it from Uri.

As it turned out, there was quite a rift on the matter between Shamir (then still foreign minister) and Peres (then prime minister).

Mordechai Vanunu was a technician in the Israeli secret nuclear facility in Dimona. He knew Israel was developing nuclear weapons and realized that, even though Israel appeared to be a sane democracy, it would not take much for some extremist leader to lose his cool and plunge the Middle East and the world into nuclear war. Moreover, the game of hide-and-seek that Israel was playing bothered him. As long as the West took Israel's denials at face value and pretended it had no proof that Israel had nuclear weapons, the West would not have to take steps to stop the proliferation.

Vanunu decided to expose the facts and force the world to acknowledge it and therefore act on it. He took some fifty photographs inside the secret facility and, after leaving the country for Australia, contacted the London *Sunday Times*. The paper brought him to London, planning, first, to publish the revelations and, second, to put Vanunu in front of the media to answer questions that would reinforce his credibility. Prime Minister Peres, who'd learned of the affair and realized that there was no way to put the genie back in the bottle, wanted to take advantage of the situation. He would verify to the world, and especially the Arab world, where several countries were busy developing other weapons of mass destruction such as poison gas and bacterial weapons, that Israel did indeed have the capability to annihilate them. He wanted to let the story run but also to get Vanunu back to Israel before he could answer further questions so that there'd still be doubt about the story's credibility. That way, he figured he'd kill two birds with one stone: The world would have good reason to fear Israel, and at the same time, Israel could keep denying it possessed nuclear capability because the man behind the story would not be around to verify it. Shamir advocated a different plan; he wanted Vanunu *and* his story killed.

Peres realized that there was a hesitation on the part of the newspapers to run the story, mainly because they feared being duped. To help ensure that the story *would* run, Peres called the editors of the Israeli papers and asked them to keep the story in low profile, hoping that word of his request would reach the British publisher and prove to him that it was a serious story. After all, no less than the prime minister of Israel wanted it kept quiet! At the same time, Shamir contacted his friend Robert Maxwell, the British media tycoon, and had him run a story in *his* paper that would tarnish Vanunu's credibility and expose him as a charlatan. He also wanted the man's photo in the paper, so that Vanunu, who was not a professional in the spook business, would panic.

The *Sunday Times* ended up publishing the story on October 5, a week after Maxwell's *Daily Mirror* did. The Mossad, who'd sent a Kidon team to London on September 20, lured Vanunu to Italy using a woman named Cindy. From there, they kidnapped him and took him to Israel. Mordechai Vanunu was tried and sentenced to eighteen years in prison, a term he is serving in solitary confinement.

My visit to Jordan this time felt somewhat casual. I flew to New York and then via Alia, the Jordanian airline, to Amman aboard Flight 264 leaving New York at ten-forty P.M. The only problem I had with this trip was that the ticket, which was sent to me from the Jordanian embassy in Washington and purchased from a Golden Eagle travel agent in Washington, did not have a date of return. It was left open, something that after my latest experience in Egypt made me somewhat uneasy, especially in view of the fact that I knew Egypt and Jordan had cooperated on many matters in the past.

The flight was as pleasant as a flight can be. I sat across from an Air Canada captain who was going down to Jordan to arrange an air delivery of a herd of Canadian cows as part of a Canadian agricultural assistance program.

Albert was supposed to meet me at the airport. But he was late, which caused me to feel extremely anxious, mainly because I was traveling on my Canadian passport, which was issued to me in Tel Aviv, as was clearly stated on the first page. If I had to go through the passport check, things would start to get messy. The Amman airport is not a very busy place, and after a few moments of waiting, I was alone in the arrivals section. The terminal police were starting to stare at me in a strange way. In the nick of time, just as one of them was about to come over and start questioning me, Albert showed up. He was pale and extremely apologetic about miscalculating the time of my arrival.

He ran me through passports and customs, waving his ID card. Minutes later, we were on our way to the city and the Regency Palace Hotel. The hotel was full this time around, and it seemed that most of the guests were from Saudi Arabia, in their white tunics with thin gold trim.

The first day was spent in niceties and meeting people I'd met on my previous visit—except that this time we were like old acquaintances. The feeling of anxious anticipation dissipated before the day was over. The next morning, I was taken on a trip to Petra, which is an ancient city carved out of the red mountains. Its colossal palaces and giant columns are all of a piece with the mountain. It is a breathtaking sight and a reminder of how short our visit on this planet is.

For the builders of this wonder in the desert are no more, as if they'd just drifted away into oblivion one day, leaving all this behind.

We ended up in the city of Al-Aqaba, across the Gulf of Aqaba from the Israeli city of Elat, where I'd spent two years of my youth. The two cities are very close to each other. When I lived there, I remember being on the beach one night (the youth of Elat spend most of their time on the beach) during a power failure in Elat. Tourists pointed out Al-Aqaba, only a few kilometers away, and asked why there was light in that neighborhood.

It was again an eerie feeling to sit on the porch of a beautiful white villa on the beach of Al-Aqaba, a cold lemonade in my hand, with friends from the Jordanian intelligence, and to look across the bay at Elat and the navy patrol boats leaving the military portion of the harbor. I could even see the bow of a Saar-class missile boat on the giant dry dock.

In those very comfortable surroundings, we discussed the repercussions that could be expected due to the change in government the day before. What had them worried was that Sharon would be pushing the concept of Jordan as Palestine. He'd been promoting a line of reasoning that said that because some 70 percent of the Jordanian population is of Palestinian descent, Palestinians should overthrow the king, create their own state there, and forget about the West Bank.

I expressed the opinion that Shamir too thought that the Palestinians should forget about the West Bank, but that he didn't really care if Jordan became Palestine or not. If he cared either way, then I supposed he'd prefer things as they were.

We spent two days in Al-Aqaba, and then it was back to Amman. My old friend Fadllal was waiting for me at the hotel. He came straight to the point.

"What about the spy ring you promised us?" His face was smiling, but his eyes were not. I took a sheet of paper out of my attaché case and handed it to him. "This is a list that I have compiled of Israeli officers who are presently in Europe and the United States and who are willing to work in the security field for whoever will pay them the most. What you need to do is get some of your men who can speak Hebrew, preferably with an American accent. You will send them to Mexico, and from there you will contact the men on this list. You will bring the Israeli officers to Mexico, on your account of course, and interrogate them one on one as if it were a job application. Have them stay in a nice hotel and give them some spending money."

"What makes you think they'll talk?"

"If you have them convinced that they're in the presence of Israelis, and from what I have seen you can do that, they'll not stop talking. You must remember, however, not to overdo it. If any of them want to leave at any time, you mustn't stop them. And, most important, you must not let them meet each other. Arrange it so that the interviews are on individual basis."

Fadllal nodded his head. I went on to describe how they would weed out the applicants who could give them more than just knowledge, that is, those having tactical military techniques to pass on. These applicants would then be recruited, meaning they would be sent to a camp in Mexico where they would train "soldiers" in techniques that would be of great interest to the Jordanian intelligence.

We spent the final days in Amman going over this plan. Some time later, Albert, who saw several of the videotapes made during the interrogations in the hotel in Acapulco, told me that his people had said that at last they were starting to understand what Israelis were all about. At first analysis, they appeared to be overgrown children with a lot of self-confidence and hostility, but still very friendly. They also realized that Israelis were extremely prejudiced against everybody who wasn't Israeli, and even then there were internal prejudices.

My somewhat uneventful visit was just about over when I got the scare of my life. On the day before I was to leave, I walked out of my hotel room and encountered a maid emerging from the adjoining room, heading back to her loaded service cart. Out of habit and without realizing, I greeted her in Hebrew, saying *boket tove*, which means "good morning." She hardly paid any attention, but two hotel guests standing by the elevator turned their heads. I walked back into my room so that I would not have to take the elevator with them, but since I was a guest of the local intelligence, I was not too worried. I went down to join Albert at the breakfast table in the wood-paneled dining room on the second floor. The tables were round and were meant to seat eight, but we were just the two of us; Fadllal might join us later.

I made a trip to the circular buffet in the middle of the room and returned with my breakfast. Seconds after sitting down, I froze. I could hear two men seated behind me at the other table whispering to each other in Hebrew. My first instinct was to turn around and see who they were. I stopped myself in the nick of time. I had no intention of telling Albert about it; I was not about to hand over Israelis who were there, for whatever reason. One thing I had no doubt about; they were not there for me. If they had been, they wouldn't have sat behind me and surely wouldn't have spoken in Hebrew. I assumed they were there on official business and that it was not with the Jordanian intelli-gence. It had to be with the foreign office. On my next trip to the buf-fet, I glanced in their direction and got my second shock. This one almost caused me to lose my balance: I was looking directly into the face of a man I knew from the Mossad. I had no doubt that he was in the Mossad; I was sure I used to see him regularly. I thought that he was a much better actor than I could ever be; he didn't even move a muscle. He turned back to the men he was seated with, the same ones who'd whispered in Hebrew, and went on talking to them in English.

"Did you see a ghost?" Albert asked once I got back to the table.

"No, I just think I had too much to drink last night, and it's com-ing back to haunt me. I think I'll excuse myself, if you don't mind, and wait for you in the room."

"Sure. I'll be there in a while," he said with his usual politeness.

I lay on the bed, trying to figure out what I was seeing. It finally hit me. I knew the man, but he didn't know me. It was Amnon P., or, as I knew him by his code name, Hombre. He was the liaison officer in Denmark and Scandinavia, and I had stared at his photograph every day of the week while working on the Danish desk. It was a method of work in the Mossad that photographs of officers in the overseas sta-tions were plastered on the wall over the desks that serviced them, to give the desk officers a face to relate to while they were dealing with the men in the field. I knew his face, but he didn't know mine. I could not figure out what he was doing in Amman, nor could I imagine why the other two Israelis were there. There was no way I could ask with-out running the risk of burning them; they could be in Jordan under cover.

I stayed in the room as much as possible until I left the following day.

CHAPTER 24

WEDNESDAY, OCTOBER 29, 1986

I took a flight back to the United States. I'd received ten thousand dollars as a bonus from the Jordanians, given to me in cash in Canadian currency. I declared it when I entered the United States and even filled out a special form, since I intended to stay in New York overnight. But after calling Bella on the phone, I decided not to stay in New York but to fly straight to Canada that day. I didn't declare that I was taking the money with me out of the country. I did, however, present it upon arrival in Canada.

Several days later, and much to my dismay, there was a knock on my door at my apartment in Ottawa. A man from the Royal Canadian Mounted Police escorted a U.S. customs officer from the American embassy who wanted to ask me a few questions. The RCMP man made it clear to me that I didn't have to cooperate with the American, but if I wanted to, this would be appreciated. I could see my cover blowing right in front of my eyes. If this American wrote some report that ended up in the hands of the Mossad just because he needed some verification, and they realized that I'd been to Jordan, my life expectancy would shrivel right there to a matter of weeks. On the other hand, I decided I had no choice but to cooperate and hope that it wouldn't get back to the Office. In fact, I made a point of explaining to the officials that it was imperative they didn't pass this information on. I told them I was a security adviser, that I'd just come back from helping the Jordanians improve their security (which was true), and also that I'd trained them in the latest techniques in VIP protection (which was also true).

The two seemed to accept my story and they explained that, because of my short stay in the States and the fairly large sum of money I'd brought in but apparently, on paper, had not taken out, they were mainly worried that I was involved in drug dealing or something of that nature. I know today they believed me because I never saw or heard from them again.

Ephraim was very disturbed when he heard about this incident and wanted me to cool it for a while. We had a regular contact with the Jordanians, and there was no need to overstress the situation. Generally, he thought it was a good time to lay low. As he put it (and even though I couldn't see his face over the phone, I could imagine his angry expression), "Shamir has just instructed the liaison department to start a relationship with the KGB. The man actually wants to cooperate with them. He says it will help bring out the Soviet Jews since the contacts with the Romanians are proving fruitless. But we all know this is something he's wanted to do for a long time."

"He doesn't have to look far," I said. "He had a KGB man in his office. All he has to do is have a talk with Levinson. Or was this Levinson's idea to start with?"

But Ephraim didn't appreciate my little joke. "You stay out of things," he said. "It is getting much too hot here, and I can't have things happening all over the place at the same time. I'll need you to reestablish contact with the British and bring them up to date about an operation that's taking place in London. But I still don't have all the information, and I don't want to get one of our people killed."

"Who is running it?" I asked.

"Barda," he said flatly, as if to say that in itself would cause the operation to crumble. The ex–taxi driver turned spy was a flamboyant, self-serving opportunist. He'd been caught several times with his hand in the proverbial cookie jar, but because of his connections, he always got off with a light reprimand.

"But there's not much the Mossad can do at the moment without getting nailed," I said, referring to the fact that after our meeting in Washington, the British most likely had all the Mossad's active safe houses under surveillance.

"They realized that their safe houses were under surveillance. So they've cooled things down, and now Barda will run this operation using two other attack case officers[1] from Brussels."

---

1. Attack case officer: A case officer who has the ability to make fast contact with a target and proceed quickly with recruiting him to work as an agent for the Mossad. Once the person has been recruited, the attack case officer will transfer the everyday running of the agent to a regular case officer and start a new recruiting operation elsewhere. Attack case officers within the Mossad number about five men at most, and are usually stationed in Mossad European headquarters in Brussels.

"So what do want me to do?"

"Like I said, once I have more information, you'll call your English friends and pass the information on to them. For the time being, just do whatever it is you're doing now. Service the Jordanians on a regular basis and wait."

I waited for the next several months and enjoyed life. I started a small T-shirt business, designing and printing shirts for businesses and for the Ottawa tourist trade. I named it after a combination of the names of my two daughters, Sharon and Leeorah. It was named Sharlee Creations and it was doing quite well. It wasn't turning a big profit, but it gave me something to do that I liked, we were living well from the money coming in from the Jordanians, and all my expenses were covered by Ephraim. All this money was entered into my company account; as far as Bella was concerned, it was money I received for shirt designs or for being a security adviser to Zaire and Sri Lanka.

But it wasn't as long as I had hoped it would be before Ephraim was back, and we were on our way to put another dent in the Mossad's Teflon armor.

MONDAY, JANUARY 5, 1987

I had made a call several days before to the British embassy in Washington and told them there was some new information they needed to know.

Ephraim had provided me with a file on Operation Domino, which was supposed to play itself out over a period of a year in England. The plan was for a Mossad team to carry out the assassination of a Palestinian cartoonist who worked for a Kuwaiti newspaper and then lay the blame on the PLO, or, as the buzzword went, "Force 17." This operation was to be a long and elaborate one, involving several elements of the Mossad.

As Ephraim and I were going over this operation plan, we had no doubt that if the British managed to catch the Mossad in the act, it would damage Anglo-Israeli relations for some time. What made the exposure worth it was that there was no way the Mossad leadership would be able to survive such a scandal. This would be the proverbial straw that would break the camel's back.

Ephraim got a room at the Westin Hotel in Ottawa and made me promise that I would come to see him the moment my meeting with the British was over.

At about noon, the Brit arrived at my apartment building. I buzzed him in and went downstairs to meet him. We sat in an area on the mezzanine floor outside the pool. I wanted our first talk to be in a place that I knew and was comfortable in. Later on, we'd move to my apartment or to a hotel room, also at the Westin, that Ephraim had already taken under my name.

I didn't know the man. He introduced himself and said that his people were very thankful for the information that had brought about the passport catch in West Germany. I asked him if they'd done anything with the information I'd given them regarding Maxwell and the large sums of money he was transferring to the Mossad station in London.

The man assured me that although he was not privy to that information, he had no doubt that it was taken care of. He was extremely anxious to hear what I had to say, or, as he put it, the cause for my alarm. This was slightly too hot a subject to handle in our present location, so I suggested that I drive the two of us to a hotel room I had secured for us. I was very surprised at the speed with which he agreed to go with me to the hotel, without taking any precautionary steps.

I drove us over in my car, parked in the underground lot, and went to the front desk to get my key. We got a corner suite, and once we were there we wasted no time. We ordered coffee and sandwiches, and after they arrived we got down to business. I handed him the file that Ephraim had brought me. It detailed several aspects of the operation that was already under way in England.

Most of the players were already in place. Probably as a result of the information I'd given the British in Washington, they'd managed to follow the *bodlim* leaving the Israeli embassy and uncover several safe houses that they were now keeping under close surveillance. That meant they were aware of most of the station's routine activity. However, several weeks earlier, a *bodel* had realized that he was being followed and reported the incident to his station chief, who had a Yarid team[2] come in from Israel and check the security of operations. Mousa, head of European operations, arrived from Brussels to handle the job. The Israelis realized that several safe houses were under surveillance and dropped them. They theorized that one of the case officers must have been neglectful during his routine testing to verify if he was clean and had picked up a tail. Now that the territory was cleaned, they were confident that they could carry on, but to be safe they'd brought in three attack case officers from the Brussels headquarters who'd be working outside the embassy, meaning that they

---

2. Yarid team: A team used to check security procedures and Mossad operations security.

wouldn't be part of the embassy staff as were the case officers at the London station. Several days after the Yarid sweep, the British were back on their trail because they knew who the *bodlim* were, and as long as the station followed security procedures, they were going to be discovered by the British.

Mousa, knowing that the British were watching, had decided to offer the operation to the Mossad heads as a double blind operation,[3] hence the name Domino. No doubt the official operational name was some computer-generated word that would appear on all official documentation, but it was nicknamed Domino.

A new face came on the scene, a PLO officer with very few options who'd been recruited by the Mossad during the war in 1982. The man had been a second lieutenant in the late seventies, had been a member of the Al-Sa'iqa,[4] then graduated from the Fatah military academy and served in the Palestinian armor unit in the Syrian army. In 1978, he was moved, still with his military unit, to Lebanon, where he was recruited by the Mossad. It had him ask for a transfer to Force 17, which he obtained. The man's name was Muhammad Mustafa Abd-al-Rahaman, serial number 13952.

The man's only contact in Britain was a Palestinian named Sawan, who had already been working for the Mossad for some time. Mousa assumed (and was probably right) that Sawan was under some sort of observation because he was in contact with Barda, his case officer, who in turn had used the safe house that was under surveillance. From this point on, Abd-al-Rahaman was going to be portrayed as the villain and the one with the direct tie to the PLO and Force 17.

He was going to bring weapons into England and have Sawan keep them for him in his apartment. This would give the British a false sense of security: They wouldn't act as long as they thought they knew what was going on and might reel in some bigger fish. Moreover, they were confident that they were doing it all without the knowledge of the Mossad. At the right time, both Sawan and Abd-al-Rahaman would leave the country, and a Mossad Kidon team would come in and carry out the assassination of the Palestinian cartoonist, leaving it

---

3. Double blind operation: An operation carried out for a particular purpose, yet, because the opposition is watching, manipulated to give the impression it has some other purpose.

4. Al-Sa'iqa: Pioneers of the Popular War of Liberation, a Palestinian group established by the Syrian Ba'ath party as part of the PLO in 1968. It broke off from the PLO in 1983 and has some 1,200 members.

to be blamed on Abd-al-Rahaman, who would be the stooge. But by then, he'd be resting in a comfortable, unmarked grave in the Gaza Strip.

As good friends should, the Mossad would then provide the British with all the information they needed for the investigation and would deliver the weapons stash into their hands, throwing in Sawan as an agent gone bad, who was meant to bring in the information but didn't.

The Brit was taking all this down, as well as having the tape recorder running all the time. He hurled an endless barrage of questions at me, wanting above all to know where this information came from. As best I could, I answered his technical questions, but when it came to the sources, I had to make it clear to him that it was none of his business.

Instead, I told him I had a new tie pattern for him. I handed him a passport photo with the face cut out.

"What is that for?" he asked, staring at it.

"Give this to the people I met in Washington. Tell them this is a new pattern. They'll know what I'm talking about."

I'd shown the Brits in our meeting in Washington that all the Mossad people whose photos they had were wearing one of three tie patterns. The photo lab where everyone had his photo taken offered generic ties and jackets to throw on, since it's very rare in Israel to come to work with a tie. A new diplomat working in the embassy has to look dignified in a photo handed in to foreign authorities, so he has no choice but to wear one of the ties. That's why the Mossad people can be easily identified by their ties. I knew that this had helped the British identify the new *bodlim*, and now Ephraim had brought me a new photo of himself, wearing a new tie someone had donated to the photo lab.

"How about coming to London for a few days?" the man asked, smiling as if he were awarding me a prize of some sort. "All expenses paid, of course."

"Why? So that I could end up like Vanunu?"

"What are you talking about? We had nothing to do with that." He sounded almost insulted.

"Don't give me that crap. You had the London station under observation at the time, and you watched several of the safe houses. There is no way in the world that you didn't know that the girl he was meeting, Cindy what's-her-name, was not who she claimed to be. You *had* to know; I gave you people enough information for you to realize that she was going in to meet people from the London station after she had meetings with Vanunu. She was being briefed and debriefed in a safe house, and you had to have *him*, at least, under surveillance, so please don't give me this crap about 'We had nothing to do with that.'"

The man kept a straight face, but it was clear from his posture that he was very uncomfortable. He handed me an envelope. "Our friends wanted you to have this, I know it's not much, but we just want to say thanks." The envelope contained eight hundred American dollars. We left the room together, and he said he could find his way from there. I knew he was going to hurry to the British High Commission and send his report as fast as he could get it written. Before we said goodbye, I gave him the name of Operation Domino's target so that they could protect him in case all else failed.

I walked over to the Byward Market in Ottawa, a small but delightful place where I did a quick exercise to see if I was being followed. I was clean, and I headed back to the hotel and Ephraim's room. I gave him a thorough rundown and told him that I hoped they'd manage to stop Operation Domino. I asked if he didn't think that we should call Scotland Yard and inform them that such an operation was taking place.

"That, my boy, will defeat our purpose. They'll stop the operation before it even starts, and then the Mossad will come out of it smelling like a rose again. You mustn't worry; they will handle it right. You gave them more than they need for that. I'm not happy, however, with you blowing your top about Vanunu."

Ephraim left the next day. I wouldn't hear about what happened next until later. It was July 22 that Ali Al Ahmed, a cartoonist for a Kuwaiti newspaper critical of the PLO leadership, was killed, supposedly by Abd-al-Rahaman and a large team of Palestinian assassins. There was uproar in the Palestinian community. The British woke up from their long sleep and kicked the entire Mossad station out of London. I always wondered after that if they would have made such a big show of anger if the fact that Sawan was a Mossad agent hadn't made its way to the press as a result of his open trial in June 1988. One thing is sure, British intelligence is just as responsible as the Mossad is for the death of that cartoonist, because they *could* have prevented it. It reaffirmed what I already knew, that any organization that came into contact with the Mossad was affected in a way that was not to the benefit of the country it served.

After I met the British, I had a strong gut feeling that they were not going to be the source of anybody's deliverance out of the darkness of the Mossad's shadow. The task would eventually fall to those who really cared, individuals who would have to take a stand as good men should and expose the monster for what it was—expose it not to the Mossad's rotating bed partners, but to the public. I had decided, conceited as it may sound, that I would go to the people.

At first, I assumed that the fastest way to do this was to make a movie. Let the public know the truth about the Mossad, and what better way to reach as many people as possible than through a movie?

I did a bit of research, not informing Ephraim of my plans, and eventually I had a meeting with a gentleman in Montreal called Robin Spry, who has a small motion picture company named Telecine. After checking his background, I thought that he was sufficiently far removed from the Jewish community that he could be regarded as relatively safe.

We met in his office in a renovated old building in Montreal. He was very courteous and extremely enthusiastic, but he made it clear from the start that he'd prefer to handle the story as fiction, because he wouldn't be able to take the kind of heat this project might generate. I asked him to make me an offer and a proposal, and decided that if all else failed, I'd take this route.

My next stop was a publisher in Toronto. I arranged a meeting with two representatives of the publishing house in the Prince Hotel.

Having a temporary case of cold feet, I decided at the last minute to present the idea as fiction based on a real story. It was a bad idea, and the publisher turned me down. "Since you have not written anything before, we'd need to see a full manuscript," they said, and they were quite right. I abandoned the effort for the time being and decided that I might just as well bring Ephraim in on my idea and take advantage of his vast wealth of knowledge and his well-placed connections.

Ephraim was not enthusiastic about my book idea and at first tried in every way he could to dissuade me. He told me that the Mossad was not going to take such an act lying down. Never before had anyone struck a blow of such proportions against them and succeeded. We had a long history to draw on, and it was full of examples of men who'd tried to go against the grain. Most of them are well planted six feet under, and others are in little bits littering some godforsaken piece of desert. The only person ever to have written a book on the Mossad and to have lived to tell about it was the ex-head of the Mossad, Isar Harel, who was universally regarded as senile. And the only reason he could tell his story was that he'd sterilized it until it became no more than a song of praise for the Mossad. What I was intending to do was completely unheard of.

"They'll call you a traitor," Ephraim said. "The name Ostrovsky will be synonymous with the name Benedict Arnold in the United States."

"And what if they find out what I've been doing for the last two years, because of some screwup by you or one of the others? What do you think they'll call me then?"

"But that won't happen. You're not at all at risk. Things are going just great at the moment."

I looked at him, and I knew he could see the anger in my face. "Are they really so great? We spent over two years playing games your way, and we've achieved nothing. I think it's time to get the real show on the road. Whatever you decide is okay with me. I just want you to know that no matter what you say, I'm going to attempt to do this. If you stick around, I'll consult you as to what will go into the book and what will be left out, because we have, in the end, the same agenda."

He sat silently for a moment, his cigarette slowly burning in the ashtray. Then he looked at me and smiled. "What the hell, let's kick some butt."

I had not felt that good for a long time. I knew I was back on the high road. Now things were going to come out into the open. The only problems that were still unsolved were small ones.

Or so we thought at first. But the more we considered the task that lay ahead, the larger it seemed. Who would actually do the writing? I was not in a position to do it myself, I wasn't confident enough in my abilities, and I wanted a new man who would be able to tell the story in the simplest way and give it the maximum impact. He couldn't be Jewish, for security reasons, and he'd have to have balls. Then there was the need to find a publisher who'd be willing to take on the Mossad, to keep all of this under wraps while it was being handled, and to refrain from speaking about what we were going to put in the book. There was also the question of how we were going to get people to believe us. At that point, we had no doubt that the Mossad's official reaction would be "Victor Ostrovsky? We've never heard of him, but you might check with the mental health department in the Ministry of Health."

Little did we know what was in store for us.

CHAPTER 25

SUNDAY, APRIL 3, 1988

Ephraim insisted that the book I was about to write be handled by as many of the clique as possible. He also laid down the rule that, since it was going to be my ass in the sling, I had a veto on what was going to go into the book and the last word on how it was going to be handled.

We were sitting in a room at the Four Seasons Hotel. Present were Ephraim; Uri, who made it clear that he couldn't stay more than a few hours so we'd have to listen to him first; Eli, who still thought this was a crazy idea and wanted to be on record as being vehemently against it (so I guess this paragraph would make him extremely happy); and me.

I was somewhat preoccupied. I'd told Bella that I was intending to write a book about the Mossad. I'd assured her that it was going to be fiction, but told her that still it should be kept a secret. When I said that, she stared at me as if I were a man in a straitjacket making a comment about fashion. I knew she didn't believe for one minute that I'd actually be able to get a book published. Now I was going to write one that was not fiction, and I wasn't sure exactly how I was going to tell her and when. I was also worried that once I started to work with someone, it would be harder to keep it from her. And since she was very much in love with the state of Israel, I didn't know how she would take it.

"So what are we going to do here today?" Uri asked.

"I need an outline," I said. "Some sort of rough sketch of what the book is going to be about, in headline form. I'll need more headlines than I'll actually use so that the person I work with can have a say and influence the outcome."

Eli wanted to know the purpose of the book, and Ephraim agreed that that was one of the first things we should be talking about. Then we could find the right stories to achieve that goal. "There are a million stories out there," he said. "But most of them would put anyone to sleep, and many others are repetitive—sort of the same lady in a different coat."

"I want to show what the Mossad is," I said. "Give people who have no idea what an intelligence agency really does a taste of what is going on. I have no doubt that many will find it fascinating and repugnant at the same time. Also, I want to give all the people we haven't been able to reach, in all the intelligence agencies that are working with the Office, a reason to reexamine the relationship they're in. I don't believe the Danes or the Germans would be very proud to know how they are being used. And even if the people of Israel think of me as a traitor, at least they'll have to examine the facts in the book, and that will do the job. I mean, after this kind of exposé, there'll be no way in the world that someone will not go in and clean up the Mossad."

"I have to agree with you," Ephraim said. "I recommend that in the beginning you give some of your own background, and then go into operations. You have to pick the ones that people have heard something about or at least know the end result of, like the Iraqi nuclear reactor."

"I agree," I said, and wrote down "Operation Sphinx" on my yellow pad.

Uri lit a cigarette. "We should have one story from each department so that we get full coverage. Why don't you list the departments, and we'll find one that will be fitting from each?"

Ephraim turned to Uri. "Will you be able to cut short your turn in the States and come back to Tel Aviv?"

"I'm due back in a month, anyway. Why?"

"We'll need a good warning system while he's writing this thing because he's going to involve outsiders. We must be prepared to let him know the moment this becomes known at the Office."

"I thought that you might have that under control?"

"I do, but I don't have a handle on your friend Aaron Sherf from Tsafririm."

"How does he tie in?"

"The information might come back to us from one of the Jewish organizations we're tied in to, like B'nai Brith or the UJA. And then there are all the others that are handled by the *schlichim* [messengers]. I mean, the moment a member of the Jewish community anywhere in North America gets a whiff of this, they will run to their organization and tell them about it. They'll be sure they are doing their Zionist duty. And Sherf is the one telling them what to do."

"I see. That won't be a problem. I'll be there anyway."

After that was put to rest, we made a small chart of the Mossad on a piece of hotel letterhead and taped it to the television screen. We then began to chart the stories that would be told, patterning the structure on the makeup of departments. We also decided that the operations picked should have a large scope and that the description should cover as much of the clandestine component as possible, including the planning and decision-making part, so that the potential reader would understand the degree of corruption that has taken over the Mossad.

"I think," said Ephraim, "that Operation Hannibal and its abrupt closure would do for a nice chapter." He turned to Uri. "The way Ran H. nailed that German politician would make a great story."

I have alluded to some of the aspects of Operation Hannibal earlier. I knew about it from my days on the Danish desk. It was a combined operation that included liaison and clandestine field activity on behalf of Melucha. It involved the cooperation of three countries and their respective intelligence agencies. To be more accurate, it was the intelligence agencies that were cooperating and not their countries.

Operation Hannibal was in itself an arms deal between Israel and Iran, using the German intelligence agency as a cut-out for the operation. Since Iran was in need of parts for their dilapidated air force and since Israel had the spare parts, mainly for the F-4 Phantom, a sale was a natural occurrence. It was natural too that the Mossad would have as a clear goal prolonging the Iran-Iraq war, since there was money to be made. Because Iran and its Ayatollah Khomeini were not especially enthusiastic about dealing directly with Israel, which they vowed morning and night to destroy, the Germans were a natural go-between. The BND, which is the German federal intelligence agency, was the entity the Mossad chose for the job, even though the Mossad was keeping the local police intelligence in both Hamburg and Kiel fully in the picture. The reason for plugging in the locals was that this sort of relationship between the Mossad and the BND was a fairly new thing. The BND was usually kept in the dark regarding Mossad operations in Germany.

Among Mossad personnel, the BND was regarded as untrustworthy for two reasons. First, there was a strong suspicion that the agency had been deeply infiltrated by the Stasi,[1] and second, it enjoyed a close relationship with Helmut Kohl, who was not a big fan of the Mossad.

---

1. Stasi: East German State Security Police.

For this operation, however, the Office recruited a BND liaison—one who also happened to be working on the side running some shady deals through ex-Mossad officer Mike Harari.

In this operation, the jet parts (ranging from electronic elements for on-board radar all the way up to full-sized jet engines and wing assemblies) were shipped overland to ensure delivery and to hide the source of the shipment should it be caught before it reached its destination.

The shipments, which were prepackaged in special containers, were originally loaded on Israeli ships at the Ashdod harbor. The containers were of the kind that could be taken off the ships directly to waiting trucks and become a part of the truck. The ships would arrive at various Italian ports where the Italian secret service (SISMI) would handle the necessary document approval, verifying that the containers were in fact loaded with Italian agricultural products headed for Germany. Signs depicting Italian produce were actually affixed to the trucks. The manpower for the operation and the drivers were supplied by a Mossad Italian ally, the right-wing followers of a man named Licio Gelli and a group, by then outlawed, called Propaganda Duo, and a second group (a NATO offspring like the one in Belgium) named Gladio.

The drivers were to deliver the trucks to a warehouse area in Hamburg where they'd be turned over to a new set of drivers, Israelis this time. The Mossad called these drivers OMI, which is an abbreviation for *oved mekomy*, meaning "local worker." To be a local worker, you must be an actual student who has come on his own to the country in question. A student may apply to the Israeli embassy for work, and if the Mossad needs help, it will have the Shaback run a security check on the applicant. If all is well, the student can be employed to do low-echelon jobs such as driving trucks or inhabiting safe houses.

From Hamburg, the trucks would head for an abandoned airfield some twenty minutes outside of Kiel, where an Iranian who'd studied in the United States and received a degree in aeronautical engineering would come from Kiel and inspect the shipment.

Once the shipment was approved for delivery, half the money for the parts would be paid in cash at the field. The second payment would be made once the shipment had arrived in Iran. The entire operation was carried out with the joint cooperation of mid-level field operatives of the BND and the Mossad liaison in Bonn. Historically, it must be mentioned that Helmut Kohl approved cooperation with the Mossad in combating terrorism, and therefore the top brass of the BND agreed to allow the Mossad to assist their field stations and regarded Mossad's seminars on terrorism (given to the BND people without any charge, as guests of the Israeli intelligence community in Israel) as a great gesture of friendship. What the BND brass didn't know was that these seminars that the Mossad was holding in the friendly environment of the country club were in fact well-oiled recruiting operations that had brought into the Mossad's bank of manpower hundreds if not thousands of law enforcement personnel from the United States, where they were recruited by the B'nai Brith, and from the intelligence agencies of Denmark, Sweden, and many other countries.

In the intelligence field, what really counts for a possible promotion is the ability to prove that you've managed to thwart a terrorist attack. And so with that promise in hand, the Mossad went ahead and manipulated the mid-level of the BND into cooperating, letting them understand that the top brass wanted this to take place but could not sanction the operation officially. Also, the fact that the Mossad had the total cooperation of the local intelligence agencies (each state in West Germany has its own intelligence service usually attached to the state police and is totally separate from its federal counterpart) helped convince the BND mid-level personal that what the Mossad said was true.

The shipments were occurring as scheduled, and there were no problems with them for a long time. From Germany, the trucks would make their way to Denmark, where they'd be loaded onto Danish ships under the watchful eye of the Danish intelligence and their liaison to the Mossad, Paul Hensen Mozeh. From there, they'd be delivered to Iran. Emboldened by the success of these equipment transfers, the Iranians asked their BND connection to see what could be done with regard to training Iranian pilots, preferably outside the war zone. The BND contact then turned to the Mossad contact and asked the same question. At first, there was a proposal in Mossad to carry out the training in South America, in either Chile or Colombia, where the Mossad could obtain both the necessary airfields and the local approval for such an operation. But the proximity to American activity in that hemisphere caused the Mossad to have a change of heart.

After the Mossad and the STT conferred with experts from the Israeli air force and obtained more information from STT about the skill level of STT pilots, they decided that most of the training could be carried out in simulators and therefore could be done in Germany. The same abandoned airfield with the large empty hangars used for checking parts on their way from Israel to Iran could be used to house the five simulators and all the related equipment needed. The Iranians were to purchase the simulators outright and pay for all the installation and other expenses, including the training itself.

A team of at least twenty Israelis would have to be on hand to train the Iranian pilots, and they would live independently in both Kiel and Hamburg while the Iranian pilots (whom the Germans were afraid would draw attention) would stay at the airfield for the duration of the training.

The BND contact man worked directly with the Mossad liaison in Bonn, who in turn passed the information to the Mossad clandestine station, also located in the Bonn embassy. At one point, the Germans suggested that, for security and the smooth running of the operation, the prime minister of Schleswig Holstein be brought in on the secret. This man's name was Uwe Barschel, and he happened to be a close friend of Helmut Kohl's. To guarantee his cooperation, the BND would use its influence to secure a commitment of federal moneys to save a faltering shipping company, which would be a feather in Barschel's cap. Then there was the matter of a large new international airport in the area, which he was promised would be helped. The Germans also made several other promises that were not of any interest to the Mossad or to Ran H., who was now running the operation.

When I left the Mossad, the training of the pilots was in full swing. In addition to the simulators, several specially modified Cessna planes were being used to train the Iranian pilots at a second airfield some forty-five minutes from Kiel. I remember very well that as I was on my way out of the Mossad, Ran was becoming a star. Fluent in German, he'd been in charge of El Al security in Germany and Austria before joining the Office.

At the Four Seasons suite, Ephraim filled me in on what had happened since. According to him (Uri added several details while Eli voiced his dissatisfaction), Ran had realized at some point in mid-1987 that trouble was on the horizon. There was growing dissatisfaction in the Mossad and in the right-wing elements of the Israeli government regarding the behavior of Chancellor Helmut Kohl, who was defying direct Israeli warnings regarding his relationship with the Austrian leader Kurt Waldheim, who'd been branded a Nazi. (The branding was done by a field unit of Al that entered a UN building on Park Avenue South in New York and placed several incriminating documents that had been removed from other files into Waldheim's file—and the files of a few other individuals—for future use. The falsified documents were then "discovered" by Israel's ambassador to the UN, Benjamin Netanyhu, as part of a smear campaign against Waldheim, who was critical of Israeli activities in southern Lebanon.) Kohl had brushed off these Israeli threats as nonsense, causing fury in Israeli intelligence circles, where he was described as a stupid klutz.

Causing the Mossad leadership additional worry was the sudden political crisis in Denmark that had caused the local intelligence to get cold feet and ask that the arms shipments through that country be temporarily halted until they knew what the new political atmosphere would be like.

To keep the arms flowing, the BND asked Uwe Barschel to allow the use of the shipping facilities in his state for the transfer of arms to Iran, something he was opposed to. The Mossad didn't think there was any need to consult Barschel about this, but the BND didn't know that the Mossad had already secured the cooperation of the local intelligence. So they asked Barschel anyway, also telling him more about the shipment than they were supposed to. The BND had miscalculated Barschel's resolve. When he refused, everyone began to panic, realizing that he might be a threat if he should find it necessary to inform Helmut Kohl about what he knew.

It soon became clear that the Mossad needed a new independent political link that could replace the deteriorating hold the BND had on Barschel.

So many birds could be captured in this bush that it was extremely tempting. The Mossad could take the lead in controlling the politician and bring in the BND as a partner, leaving no doubt about who was calling the shots. They would eliminate from the scene a troublemaker, namely Barschel, who was partly cooperating, but not for the right reasons. He wasn't really "bought," as they liked their politicians to be. Instead, he was extracting from the situation what he thought would be the best for his constituents, and at the same time shoring up his political support.

The last, but certainly not least, dividend to be gained from removing Barschel was that it would be a blow to Helmut Kohl.

Ran at that point made contact with the opposition party, getting into a close relationship with one of the leaders of the opposition and feeling him out to see if, in the event he was elected, he'd be willing to cooperate with those who'd helped put him in power and repay them for the favor. It was made clear to the opposition politician that the BND was behind the people who were making the approach and that it was all done in the best interests of Germany. The response Ran received was more than he had expected: The opposition politician, thinking there was no real chance of his party winning the election anyway, was willing to promise anything. With that politician securely in Ran's pocket, at a cost of a new pipe and some fresh tobacco, it was time to get Barschel out of the political arena.

Yoel, a case officer from the Bonn station, was called in for this operation and given the task of passing himself off as a Canadian with a German background who was very wealthy and was about to immigrate back to Germany. Before making the big move, this Canadian wanted to start a new business in Germany and wanted to become acquainted with the political establishment so that he could maneuver his business in the proper manner and take as much advantage of his move as possible. A political apparatchik in Barschel's party, whom Yoel and Ran nicknamed "the Whistler," was their target. Ran supplied Mossad liaison with a list of all the people working around Barschel who had direct contact with him and asked them to run the names through the Hamburg and Kiel police files to see if something damaging could be found on any of the names. The Whistler's name came back with a blotch on it. As it turned out, the man had been accused of assaulting a prostitute in Hamburg, but since someone had managed to pay off the hooker, the file was closed without any formal charges being brought.

Yoel was introduced to the Whistler through a *sayan* who, according to a Mossad file, was acquainted with the Whistler. After a short period of buttering, Yoel told the Whistler that he had to return to Canada and introduced the Whistler to Ran, who was posing as Yoel's business adviser in Germany. If the Whistler needed anything at all, he could turn to Ran in Yoel's absence, and Ran was authorized to help him.

Several days after Yoel supposedly left the country, Ran called the Whistler and arranged to meet him. In the meeting, Ran made it clear that he was not in favor of the Whistler's political affiliation, and in fact he was a supporter of the opposition. Ran then explained that he was obligated to take care of Yoel's best interests, and so he'd carried out a small investigation of his own. He'd found out about the incident between the Whistler and the prostitute, and he knew that should such information get out, his political career was over, and whatever Yoel would have invested would also be lost. He then proposed that the Whistler help get Barschel ousted. Ran was surprised at the enthusiasm with which the Whistler greeted the proposal. The Whistler made it very clear that he was not a fan of Barschel's and would do whatever he could to nail him.

Ran, who already had a plan in place to remove Barschel, went through the motions with the man he'd just recruited to make him feel as though he were part of the planning process, thus giving him a feeling of self-importance and also setting him up to shoulder the blame if things didn't go right. Ran told him that because this process might affect the Whistler's own political future, he would be handsomely taken care of financially. Ran let the Whistler understand that he was part of some Mafia-type organization, and that there was no way he could change his mind or undo what had taken place. Nor would he be able to talk about Ran at all.

All this time, the Mossad was feeding the local intelligence services false information regarding Barschel's supposed secret dealings with arms and other illegal transactions, implicating Barschel's brother in the activities in a way that suggested he was a gofer for Barschel.

The plan was approved by Mousa, who was in charge of operations security in Europe and at that time acting head of the European command.

At this stage, the BND was kept out of the picture. Ran had the Whistler start to leak false but damaging information regarding the opposition leaders in general and the top leader in particular to the local media without revealing the source of the rumors or even letting it be known who the leaker was. As the election drew near, a Mossad team was brought in from Belgium to play private detectives in the employ of the Whistler. They acted flamboyantly, driving expensive flashy cars while on surveillance and gathering information about the opposition leader in an amateurish way that attracted attention to themselves.

It was done in such a manner that only a reporter for the *Braille Times* would not be able to see it for what it was: a smear campaign. At the last minute, when denials by Barschel would be too late to make a difference at the ballot box, the Whistler admitted that he was behind the dirty tricks and that he'd acted on Barschel's orders, thus bringing to an end the career of a politician who wouldn't deal, and putting into office one who would—and getting an opportunity to embarrass Kohl in the process. All Barschel's protests that he was an innocent man were ignored and brushed off as political rhetoric.

"I think this would make a great chapter," I said. "This has all the dirty elements that are so typical of Mossad activity in a friendly country."

"That won't be possible," said Eli. "Ran is still in the field. Including the story in the book would expose him and also Yoel."

"We could alter it a little to make the point, but hide the location and the exact information," Uri suggested.

"Then forget it," I said. "If we can't tell the full story, then we won't tell it at all. We could, however, separate the two parts and tell about the training of the Iranian pilots in Germany."

Ephraim did acknowledge that there was more to the story. He explained that, after Barschel's defeat in the election (a direct result of the campaign that Ran had organized), he contacted his BND connection and threatened to expose all their wrongdoing if they didn't take action to clear his name. The BND upper hierarchy, which was getting information from the local intelligence—the same information that was fed to the locals by the Mossad—thought that Barschel was dirty and called on the Mossad for help.

The BND had to use the Mossad to handle this situation because Barschel's threat against the BND would have affected the mid-level that was keeping in contact with the Mossad against the direct orders of their superiors, so they couldn't go for help to their own people.

The BND contact told the Mossad liaison that some hearings were going to take place in several days, and if Barschel was not satisfied before the hearings, he'd use them to spill the beans. The timetable was too short for the Mossad to wind down the operation in the two airfields and get all the Israeli crews and equipment out of there in time. Barschel had to be stopped before he could testify.

The BND gave the Mossad liaison Barschel's location (he was on vacation in the Canary Islands) and the phone number at which he could be reached. He was staying in a house loaned to him by a friend.

Ran called Barschel on the island. The first call went unanswered, and Ran assumed that Barschel must be out. He called back one hour later and was told that Barschel was not available at the moment. On his third try, Ran made contact with Barschel and told the man that he had information that could help clear his name, and he introduced himself as Robert Oleff.

He insisted that Barschel come to Geneva. He, Oleff, would have him picked up at the airport. Barschel wanted more information before he would commit himself, and so Ran said that some interested Iranians might be involved in the deal. This led Barschel to realize the matter was serious and that the man he was talking to was well informed. He agreed, and the details of the trip were discussed.

The Kidon team was already waiting in Geneva, dispatched directly from Brussels. After examining the field files regarding Geneva, they'd decided that the Hotel Beau-Rivage would be their best bet for the activity they had in mind. Two couples took rooms at the hotel, one on the fourth floor close to an exit to the roof. The second couple came in the same day Barschel did and took a room on the third floor, adjacent to the room Ran had reserved for Barschel.

The rest of the team scouted the area and located themselves in the vicinity, ready to play out their separate roles as they were called upon. Ran met Barschel in his room on the afternoon of October 10. After ordering a bottle of wine to go with the cheese he'd brought with him, he made a gentle pitch to Barschel in which he tried to convince him to take the fall. Ran would guarantee him a very lucrative return for that. Ran tried to tell Barschel that, after all, what he was alleged to have done was not such a big deal outside the realm of politics, and so he'd be far better off letting it go and taking the money. Ran surely used the regular phrase the Mossad so likes to use, that money was no object.

Barschel was agitated. He insisted that Ran present him with the evidence that would clear his name or get lost. He wasn't interested in profiting from this affair, but he definitely was going to get even with whoever had framed him.

At that point, Ran realized that there was no way to sway the man. The operation had to move into the next phase, which was termination with extreme prejudice. Barschel was a threat to the safety of the Mossad personnel in the field. Thus, there was no need for approval from outside the Mossad for the elimination, as is the case with a political assassination, for which the prime minister must give written approval. Ran, however, wanted to get clearance from the head of the Mossad, who was kept closely informed and had come to Geneva that same morning. He was staying at the Des Bergues Hotel, just down the road from where Barschel was being handled. He was registered under the name of P. Marshon.

By the time the wine arrived in Barschel's room, it had already been spiked by a Kidon member. Some of the other team members were bringing bags of ice to their rooms in preparation for the final act. Ran told Barschel that he was only testing his resolve and that he realized he was dealing with an honest man, and therefore he would help him. Barschel was still aggravated and refused to deal with Ran unless he presented, right then and there, some proof that he in fact had a way to clear his name.

Ran made a call to the Mossad liaison, who was waiting in a safe house. He asked the liaison to contact his man in the BND and have him call Barschel in his room and tell him that things were going to work out just fine. The liaison, who was expecting this call and had previously talked with Ran regarding this option, had already called the BND man in advance and had him on standby, having told him that something important was going to take place.

Several minutes after Ran called the liaison, the BND man called Barschel's room and told him that things were going to be straightened out. Barschel, who thought he was getting a new lease on life, had a drink of the wine. Ran declined to do so, excusing himself with a story of a problematic stomach, but he did take some of the cheese he'd brought.

Ran knew that Barschel would be out cold in about an hour, and he wanted to get direct approval from the head of the Mossad to finish the job. He told Barschel that he was going to get some of the papers that would clear him and would be back in an hour.

Ran contacted the head of the Mossad and met him in his hotel room. He gave the chief the rundown on what had happened and said that in a few days, Barschel was to go before a committee formed to investigate the allegations of electoral misconduct. There was no way to stop Barschel from talking about what he knew in front of the committee. Ran could not guarantee that all the evidence pointing to Israel could be eliminated from the airfields in the short time that was left. The risk of exposure in such a case was far too great for the Mossad, and so the head of the Mossad agreed that the man had to be eliminated.

Ran called the couple on the fourth floor at Barschel's hotel and informed them that the operation was a go. They waited until sufficient time had passed for Barschel to be asleep from the sedative in the wine. After phoning to verify that he was not awake, they entered the room.

Barschel was on the floor, on the right-hand side of the bed. He'd apparently passed out and had fallen off the bed. The team put a plastic sheet on the bed and placed the unconscious man on top of it, legs facing the headboard to make the next steps easier. They place a rolled towel under his neck, positioning him as if he were about to get mouth-to-mouth resuscitation. At that point, five members of the team were in the room. Four were attending to the target, and one was filling the bath with cold water and ice, the noise of which was drowning out any noise the others might make. One man slowly pushed a long, well-oiled rubber tube down the sleeping man's throat, carefully so as not to choke him. While he did that, the others were holding the man down in case of a sudden convulsion. They had all done this before.

Once the pipe had reached the man's stomach, they attached a small funnel to the top of the pipe and started to drop a variety of pills into the tube, adding water from time to time to ensure that the pills reached his stomach.

After this stage was complete, they pulled down the man's pants and underwear. Two members of the team held up his legs as a third inserted a suppository of concentrated sedative and a fever-causing agent into the man's rectum. They pulled up his pants again and waited for the medication to work, putting a thermometer band on his forehead to observe his temperature.

Within an hour, he'd developed a high fever. They then placed him into the ice bath. The shock caused his body to jolt. The sudden change in temperature, together with the influence of the medication, brought about what looked like a heart attack. After a few minutes of observation, the team determined that he was, in fact, dead, and began to clean up the room behind them, leaving no evidence of what had taken place. They realized they'd made a mistake in not taking off Barschel's clothing before placing him in the bath, but it was too late to change that now. They also realized that the replacement wine bottle they'd brought with them was a Beaujolais, but not the correct brand, so they did not have a bottle to leave behind.

Things were getting tense. They'd spent several hours in the room, and some of them had left and returned several times.

After leaving the room and closing the door behind them, displaying the Do Not Disturb sign on the knob, they all went their separate ways, one couple checking out that night and the other doing so first thing the next morning. The other members of the team who weren't staying at the hotel left the city by car that same night, heading back to Belgium and the safety of the Mossad European headquarters. Ran was informed that the mission was completed, as was the head of the Mossad, to whom one of the team members delivered a Polaroid photo of the dead target.

"I still think this will make a great chapter for the book," I said.

"We'll see. For the time being, leave it out," said Ephraim. "You can use the story about the navy base in Sudan that was used to get the Ethiopian Jews out, in Operation Moses." I realized that there was no point in arguing, especially with Eli present.

We went on to prepare a list, and by the end of the day, it was done. There wasn't much I needed to write down at the time, because I knew most of the information myself. If there was any need later on for more information, Ephraim would supply it to me. He also insisted that he go over every page of the manuscript before I handed it in.

I brought up my greatest worry, that the Mossad would not respond at all to the book, leaving me hanging out to dry. Ephraim suggested that I include in the book some documents, such as the Danish intelligence report and a questionnaire that was prepared for a top Syrian agent regarding the Syrian military.

"There is no expert in this world," Ephraim said (and Uri nodded as he spoke), "who will doubt you once they see the questionnaire. You'd have to be from the Mossad to be able to know so many things to ask about."

I had to agree. We hashed over more subjects. It was important that we not include things in the book that might nurture anti-Semitism—at least, that was the way we saw it. We all agreed, for example, that the subject of testing medications on blacks in South Africa was too much and would strike too hard a blow against Israel, since the medical personnel who'd been sent to Africa would be associated with the state and not understood as being totally controlled by the Mossad. The same treatment was given to the direct links the Mossad had with the Kahane people, the Anti-Defamation League of the B'nai Brith, the AIPAC, and the UJA. The only subject that we decided needed airing was the Frames[2] and the youth camps called *Hets va-keshet* (meaning "bow and arrow") that the Mossad organizes to bring young Jewish kids to Israel for the summer. After filling the kids with a large dose of militant Zionism, the Mossad sends them back as the spies of the future.

They all agreed that I should include in the book all the names of case officers that I knew were burned. That meant people whose photos I saw in Egypt, in Jordan, and in the British embassy. Ephraim would make sure they weren't in the field when the book came out. Having their full names in the book would prevent them from working outside the country again, which was good for their own protection.

"So what do you think will be the book's biggest point?" asked Eli.

"If I had to choose one thing people will focus on, I'd say it will be the cooperation the Mossad gets all over the world from the Jewish community and the way it takes advantage of that trust." They all agreed with me. And we were all wrong.

I headed back home from the meeting and hid the list that I'd prepared at the meeting in a safe place where Bella wouldn't find it. She was still at the T-shirt store we'd opened on Bank Street in downtown Ottawa.

The following day, I scouted the bookstores and the library for names of local authors, searching for a man with the writing ability and the courage to join me in this effort to right wrongs. I knew find-

---

2. Frames: Jewish self-protection units set up by the Mossad all over the world.

ing him was not going to be an easy task. It had to be a man with a good reputation who had a nose for politics but who was not such an expert on the world of intelligence that he would try to make the book fit his idea of espionage. He had to live in the area, not be Jewish, and have the time and the interest to do it.

At a store several blocks from our place on Bank, I saw a book called *Friends in High Places* about the Canadian prime minister. The author, Claire Hoy, was a local reporter working in the parliamentary press gallery. I decided to call him and see what happened. He responded well, and we had a meeting at a small coffee shop on Bank Street. After I'd explained to him what I was proposing, he was all for it. I had a partner, and I was on my way to putting a real dent in the Mossad's armor. We were going to attack, from the outside, and put the Mossad in the only place in which it's vulnerable: in the spotlight.

Claire and I spent almost a month preparing the first chapter of the book and tightening the outline. Then we made our first approach to a publisher.

We had a meeting at the Toronto offices of the company that had published *Friends in High Places*. The publisher we spoke to turned us down. At the time, I was very nervous, since I realized the secret was starting to get out. There was no guarantee that the publisher who'd turned us down would not talk about what we'd told her in the meeting. All I know today is that if she did talk, then someone was asleep at Mossad headquarters, because they did nothing.

Claire continued with the writing while he tried to set us up with a new publisher. His work was cut out for him because he couldn't tell the publisher much, and he had to find one who would be willing to work in secret. The fact that we'd come out of the meeting with his first publisher in one piece was more a matter of luck than anything, as was the fact that I couldn't detect the Mossad anywhere in the vicinity. Nor did news of our unsuccessful meeting reach the ears of Ephraim or Uri, who by then were back in Mossad headquarters.

"We have a meeting with a man by the name of Nelson Doucet," Hoy said to me one day. "He's from a publishing house in Toronto called Stoddart, and he's a good man." By then, I'd come to know Claire and I trusted him, something I've never regretted. We met with Nelson at a restaurant in Ottawa called Hy's, and over a great steak (which I hardly got to eat because I was doing all the talking) and a bottle of good French wine, we closed a deal. Claire and I were going to be fifty-fifty partners as far as the authorship was concerned, and Stoddart was going to give us an eighty-thousand-dollar advance. Nelson believed the book would cause quite a stir. Stoddart had had experience with another spy book, called *Spycatcher*, which they had kept secret up to publication date, and then it was banned by the British. He was sure they'd be able to handle this one much the same way. "You don't suppose you'll be able to get the Israelis to ban your book, do you?" he asked as we were about to leave. I laughed. "I don't think so," I said. "After all, they have the British experience to learn from: the ban made the book a best-seller."

"I suppose you're right," Nelson said.

Once in the car, I wanted to jump up and down and shout for joy. Things were going great, and I was determined to move forward fast. I made a collect call from a pay phone to Ephraim, giving him the whole story. I was in the booth for almost an hour, leaving someone with a big phone bill.

Ephraim agreed with my assessment that the Mossad wouldn't try to stop the book, but he promised that he'd think of a way to at least make a loud bang, drawing attention to it. If this thing worked, we'd all achieve what we wanted.

CHAPTER 26

SATURDAY, JULY 2, 1988

Some time in the afternoon, the phone rang; Eli was on the line. He was calling from New York and wanted me to call him back in an hour. That was a prearranged message, and I knew that I should go to a clean phone and call him. I had the number, and he would accept the charges.

He was as unpleasant as usual, and I couldn't help imagining his square face with its thin crow's-feet wrinkles and steady squint, as though he were in the glaring sun even when he was seated in a semi-darkened movie theater. Before all this had happened, I knew him to be a pleasant man and quite a joker, but this whole anti-Mossad activity was troubling him. Even though he thought it was right, he would have preferred, as would probably every one of us, to be left alone and not know anything about it.

"Did you hear what happened in London?" he asked. He was referring to the Brits' having expelled just about all of the Mossad London station and their pointing to two of the three case officers loaned from the European headquarters in Brussels. The British had posted, in a very obtrusive fashion, police officers outside seven of the safe houses the Mossad was holding in London at the time. Even though they were unofficially pointing to only seven out of several hundred, the message was clear enough.

There was no way for the Mossad to know from that point on how many of its assets were compromised or whether any further meetings with *sayanim* would endanger them.

"Yes, I heard." I said. "How long before they have a new station in place?"

"That's none of your business," Eli replied.

"I don't like your attitude," I said. "It's only a matter of luck that

I'm here and you're there. It wouldn't take much to have our roles reversed, you know."

There was a short silence on the line. "I'm sorry if I sound like that. It's just that—"

"Just say your piece, and let's get this conversation over with."

He said that now that the London station was cleaned up, it was time, according to Ephraim, to hit the Paris station. He also said that the London station would have to work for the next few months from a new safe house and not from the embassy because they couldn't just send in a new batch of case officers all at once; they'd have to do it gradually. They believed they'd have the station back in operation by January 1989.

We talked over what was to be said to the French and how the contact should be made.

"I think that you should do this one," I said to Eli.

"What are you talking about?"

"You speak French, don't you?"

"Yes."

"I don't. I'll call Ephraim later and tell him what I think. I mean, what difference will it make? You talk to them."

"You're crazy," he said, but I could detect a tone of anxiety in his voice.

Later that day, I talked to Ephraim, who explained that if Eli was caught, it would mean an execution because he was in active service. It would be a much worse scenario than if I was caught. After all, I was already outside the organization. His explanation didn't hold water, but since I'd raised the matter only to irritate Eli, I let it drop. I did ask, though, not to have to talk to Eli again.

On Wednesday, July 6, I called the French embassy in Washington and managed to talk to the person in charge of security. Having done this several times before, I was becoming trained in the matter, and by the end of the week, I had a visitor from Washington. After several hours of conversation, he said he'd get back to me but wanted to know if I was willing to take a short trip to France.

I arrived in Paris on July 28 and was met at the airport by a very friendly Frenchman who reminded me of the French comedian Bourvil. After finding my luggage, the man had my passport stamped in a small office away from the crowd. Then he took me in his small Renault to Paris.

I lodged in a hotel by the name of Jardin de Eiffel, next to a local police station. The small but charming hotel was within walking distance of the Eiffel Tower.

For the next week, I was driven each morning from the hotel to what looked like an abandoned two-story office building outside the city, thirty minutes away. The building was attached to a small listening base somewhere north of Sarcelles—not far, I understood, from where Madame Pompidou has her country estate. The drive there was like a ride on a roller coaster. I grew up in Israel, where driving is a martial art, but this was crazy.

At the "farmhouse," I spent the day with the Bourvil look-alike and three other people. I knew they were from the French secret service, nicknamed "Le Pisson." They were extremely courteous and had apparently prepared a long list of questions in anticipation of my arrival. We'd break for lunch every day at the same time, walk over to the listening base, and have a great meal served to us in a small but elegant dining room. The commander of the base almost always joined us for lunch, and the opening of the wine bottles that someone different brought every day was a ceremony. Over the week, I developed a good relationship with one of the hosts in particular; he'd be my contact after I left. Since we both smoked more than the others, he earned the code name Cendrier.

First, we mapped out the departmental chart of the Mossad. There were many sections that they knew about and others they were curious about. They were mainly interested in the Komemiute[1] and Tsafririm departments.

Before long, they were versed in the structural tree of the organization and they could see the logic of the flowcharts, which must be very similar from one organization to another. They found it extremely hard to believe the lack of compartmentalization in the Mossad. But after a while, they realized that the quantity and the quality of the information I was giving them was indicative of a lack of compartmentalization, since I knew so much.

The second day was almost entirely spent viewing photographs of Mossad people. It was there that I learned that Mousa was stationed in Brussels. There were so many Mossad officers in their books that I felt naked. There was a photo of Oren Riff walking down a street in Paris with two other Mossad members. The three were totally unaware of the fact that they were under surveillance. I wondered who they were going to meet and how many agents and Jewish helpers they burned in that one visit to Paris. Then there were piles of photos taken

---

1. Komemiute: New code name for Metsada (department for clandestine operations).

from outside the Mossad building in Tel Aviv. There were sets of photos: One would show a man entering the Mossad headquarters on King Saul Boulevard in Tel Aviv, then there was a blow-up photo of his face, and next to it a passport photo of the man and his diplomatic papers.

They knew more Mossad people than I did. I remember when Cendrier said to me jokingly, "Look at all this." He was pointing at the list of diplomats from the Israeli embassy and comparing them with the photos and the personal documents. "Israel is one of the few countries where you find such a large number of older junior attachés. How stupid do they think we are? What do they think, that we're not watching?"

"They don't really care," I said, and that was a fact. They didn't. Sometimes it seemed as though the Mossad derived amusement from the surveillance that took place. I couldn't help asking, "If you know so much about them, how come you haven't done anything?"

"Because, as far as we know, the ones we know about don't do very much. Vidal, the head of the Mossad station, is hardly ever in the country, and the new man, Aaron B., only deals with the Jewish community. And we don't really want to stir things up with them."

All in all, they had over fifty of the Mossad field personnel pegged and located. They had them in other embassies as well, all across Europe. It was the cooperation between the Mossad and the Action Directe and between the Mossad and the fascist elements in France that they didn't know about. That, they found disturbing.

By the end of the week, I was ready to go, and it appeared they'd gotten from me all they were going to. I realized that I'd given them much less than I'd given the British, simply because, even before my arrival, the French had been more suspicious in dealing with the Mossad. I knew they weren't going to have a big showdown with the Mossad the way the British had, but that they'd clip the Mossad's wings in a much more subtle way.

On my last day there, I remembered I had to talk about the money they were to pay me for my help. They promised to do something about it, and the following day, at the airport, they gave me an envelope with three thousand American dollars. They also said that someone would be contacting me in a short while to see if I could do some odd jobs for them, and that he'd bring me the rest of what they felt they owed me. As Ephraim had instructed, after they'd given me the money, I immediately told them about the Mossad's involvement in the killing of a leader in the Pacific island of Vanuatu because of the Office's suspicion that he was trying to make contact with Qadhafi.

That was the official reason for their involvement; the real reason for the assassination was that particular leader's resistance to an Israeli arms dealer who wanted to use the island as a storage base for his arms sales to the region. The dealer was an ex-Mossad officer, and he had the contacts inside the organization to pull it off.

Back in Canada, I was visited several weeks later by a French contact man who invited me for a meeting in Montreal. First he handed me an envelope with seven thousand dollars, telling me they'd decided to pay me ten thousand for my little trip. If that wasn't enough, I could send a message with him back to Paris or call my friend Cendrier at the number they'd given me.

"No need for that," I said. "This will be enough for now. What is it you want me to do for you?" I knew the man hadn't come all this way just to deliver a package. He pulled out a sheet of paper and asked if I could act as a private investigator. After all, I had gotten what could be regarded as the best training in the world in gathering information.

"That depends on what it is you want me to investigate. If you want me to gather information that is available without breaking the law, I'll be more than happy to liberate you from as much money as I can. However, if you're talking about gathering political or military intelligence in North America, then forget it."

He said that he didn't know but would get back to me in a few days. And he did. This time, we met in Ottawa. He brought with him some photographs and a small file. First, he wanted me to see if I knew the man in the photographs. I recognized the man and said that we'd already identified him in Paris as Ran S., whom I knew the Jordanians and the Egyptians also had a photo of.

Ran had been seen meeting with a prominent leader in the Jewish community in Paris. Before approaching the man and telling him that they knew whom he was meeting with and that he should stop this activity, the French wanted to be sure that they had the right man and not just a lookalike. They were now making such approaches to many of the Jewish leaders whom the Mossad officers I'd identified were meeting with. They were also "turning" Arab and Palestinian agents whom they'd seen meeting with Mossad officers. I realized the French were going about it in a big way, and I knew I'd hit a home run in Paris.

In the file that the Frenchman had brought with him was what he called my next assignment. The French wanted me to see what information I could gather on some people who, they were worried, were out to destabilize their South Pacific colonies. The plan of these supposed "destabilizers" was to privatize a small country as a model for the world (in other words, create a small political system in which there is no government ownership and see if that model can be extrapolated to a wider setting). A subsidiary goal was to make money in various ways. The French were very sensitive about this and preferred that someone not explicitly connected with French intelligence try to find out more.

The first name on the list I was handed was Robert Pool, Jr. A prominent American, Pool was the leading advocate of privatization in the United States and was behind the privatization of the American aviation industry. He was the president of the Reason Foundation, located in Santa Monica, California.

The second name was that of Alfred Letcher, the president of Letcher Mint, a company originally located in Alaska but later situated in Lancaster, California.

Then there was a man called Harry Donald Schultz. He was living in the United States and, from time to time, in Monaco. Schultz's partner was named Riner Dienharts. The Frenchman said that all these names tied in somehow with a Canadian foundation in Vancouver, British Columbia, called the Phoenix Foundation.

He wouldn't expand on what they were looking for or what they suspected, but wanted to see what I could find out on my own. He said that if he told me what they knew (or, rather, thought they knew), then I might just follow in their footsteps and try to find the things I thought they wanted found. It was in the nature of the intelligence game, he said, for the information collector to try to please the customer.

I knew he was right, and yet, it made no difference to me whether he was or wasn't. All I wanted was to keep the link with the French open so that, if Ephraim or I needed it to nail the Mossad, it would be there.

Ephraim told me to do what the man wanted and see what I could collect for him. I decided to take a short trip to the States and check public databases to see what this was all about.

From reading press reports, I soon realized that this was a far more complex business than I cared to be a part of. Pool was a member, if not a leader, of the Libertarian party, which in itself was reason enough for me not to want to work on the case. From what I learned, I could hardly believe that there was no intelligence involvement already.

According to biographical information on Pool, he'd graduated from MIT in 1967, after which he'd worked at Sikorsky. In 1970, he moved to the General Research Corporation in Santa Barbara, and during his tenure there became head of the Reason Foundation, a privatization think tank.

I discovered that the foundation had supported a leader in the New Hebrides against a Communist yet popular leader named Father Walter Lenny. The Reason Foundation wanted to start a Libertarian party on the island. When that effort failed, they attempted to create a small country of their own on the Minerva reef, eight hundred miles from Fiji, naming it the Republic of Minerva. According to the records I found, the Letcher Mint from Lancaster, California, which also owned a copper mine in the Hebrides, had been selected to print the republic's coins. After the new citizens of Minerva were kicked off the reef by a patrol boat from Togo, the coins became what is known in the numismatic world as fantasy coins.

After this episode, Pool became an adviser to President Reagan on privatization. I also learned that the owner of the Letcher Mint, Alfred Letcher, had served with the U.S. Navy in the South Pacific in 1944. That was as far as I was willing to go. I returned to Canada and gave the French everything I'd managed to dig up. At a meeting in Ottawa, I told the man that I wouldn't be able to do any more for him in this matter. I was willing to help in any way possible to bring an end to Mossad activity in France, but I wouldn't work for them as a soldier of fortune on unrelated matters.

I notified Ephraim of what I'd told the Frenchman. I also asked him to try to get me some of the schedules I'd followed during my training at the academy, so that I could use them as notes for the book. He complied, and I went back to work on the book with Claire.

CHAPTER 27

Claire and I had gotten ourselves into something of a routine. After we established the correct chronology of the book, we met several times a week in my rented house in Nepean, a small city outside Ottawa. I'd tell Claire the details of the events that we'd designated for a particular chapter, and then, over numerous cups of coffee, he'd ask me an endless stream of questions. Several days later, he'd return with a typed chapter for me to go over, and at the same time, we'd talk about a new one. Then on the next visit, I'd show him the typed chapter with my remarks and corrections, and we'd discuss them. Ephraim would pass me his comments on the chapter and I'd either accept or reject them, depending on their validity. My main concern was that everything we were committing to paper be the truth and nothing but the truth.

It was a difficult task to tell the story of the Mossad as it really was, to show how flawed it was and how endangered anyone was who came into contact with it. Even in Claire's eyes, I could see the fascination the Mossad commanded. I knew I was in an uphill struggle, but at the same time, I knew the battle had to be fought.

Uri visited me several times and informed me that as far as the Mossad was concerned, I was occupied making T-shirts in Canada and that was all. They were extremely busy at the time preparing for what they called Operation Brush-Fire. This was an all-out LAP (Israeli psychological warfare) attack aimed at getting the United States involved militarily in the Middle East in general and the Gulf area in particular.

The Iran-Iraq war was over. It seemed that the Iranians had had enough and were happy to agree to end the war as the Iraqis wanted. The Mossad, for their part, pretended to the Americans that they wanted to topple Saddam Hussein, while at the same time passing on information to his Muchabarat from the Israeli embassy in Washington, warning him about various attempts on his life and on his regime. The Mossad regarded Saddam Hussein as their biggest asset in the area, since he was totally irrational as far as international politics was concerned, and was therefore all the more likely to make a stupid move that the Mossad could take advantage of.

What the Mossad really feared was that Iraq's gigantic army, which had survived the Iran-Iraq war and was being supplied by the West and financed by Saudi Arabia, would fall into the hands of a leader who might be more palatable to the West and still be a threat to Israel.

The first step was taken in November 1988, when the Mossad told the Israeli foreign office to stop all talks with the Iraqis regarding a peace front. At that time, secret negotiations were taking place between Israelis, Jordanians, and Iraqis under the auspices of the Egyptians and with the blessings of the French and the Americans. The Mossad manipulated it so that Iraq looked as if it were the only country unwilling to talk, thereby convincing the Americans that Iraq had a different agenda.

By January 1989, the Mossad LAP machine was busy portraying Saddam as a tyrant and a danger to the world. The Mossad activated every asset it had, in every place possible, from volunteer agents in Amnesty International to fully bought members of the U.S. Congress. Saddam had been killing his own people, the cry went; what could his enemies expect? The gruesome photos of dead Kurdish mothers clutching their dead babies after a gas attack by Saddam's army were real, and the acts were horrendous. But the Kurds were entangled in an all-out guerrilla war with the regime in Baghdad and had been supported for years by the Mossad, who sent arms and advisers to the mountain camps of the Barazany family; this attack by the Iraqis could hardly be called an attack on their own people. But, as Uri said to me, once the orchestra starts to play, all you can do is hum along.

The media was supplied with inside information and tips from reliable sources on how the crazed leader of Iraq killed people with his bare hands and used missiles to attack Iranian cities. What they neglected to tell the media was that most of the targeting for the missiles was done by the Mossad with the help of American satellites. The Mossad was grooming Saddam for a fall, but not his own. They wanted the Americans to do the work of destroying that gigantic army in the Iraqi desert so that Israel would not have to face it one day on its own border. That in itself was a noble cause for an Israeli, but to endanger the world with the possibility of global war and the deaths of thousands of Americans was sheer madness.

Toward the end of January, the British called and wanted to talk to me. They said it was urgent and asked if they could come the following day. I agreed. I decided that I'd take advantage of the meeting to convey the information about Saddam I'd gotten from Uri, and request that they pass it on to the Americans.

We met in the dining room of the Chateau Laurier Hotel in downtown Ottawa. "What can I do for you?" I asked the man, whom I'd met once before.

"I have only one question for you, and even though you might think it's off the wall, I was told to ask you."

"Go ahead."

"Do you believe or think or know if the Mossad may have had any involvement in what happened to Flight 103 over Lockerbie?"

I was dumbfounded. It took me several seconds to realize what the man had asked me. I responded almost automatically. "No way."

"Why?"

"No reason. Just no way, that's all. Up to this point, every time Israel or the Mossad has been responsible for the downing of a plane, it's been an accident, and related directly to the so-called security of the state, like the shooting down of the Libyan plane over the Sinai and the Italian plane (thought to carry uranium) in 1980, killing eighty-one people. There is no way that they'd do this."

"Are you speaking out of knowledge or are you guessing?"

"Wait right here." I said, leaving the table. "I'll make a phone call, and we'll talk after that."

I made a collect call from the lobby of the hotel, and after a few minutes got Ephraim on the line. "Did we have anything to do with Pan Am 103?"

"Why are you asking?"

"Just tell me. I have to know, because if we did, this will be the end of the Mossad."

"No," he answered without hesitating. I knew he was telling me the truth. He wouldn't pass up such an opportunity to taint the Mossad leadership.

"Thanks. I'll call you later."

I got back to the table and told the man what Ephraim had told me.

"So you're still connected?" the Brit said, smiling.

"Which is probably why I'm still alive," I said, smiling back. "Since we're here, there's something I think you should know about. It's called Operation Brush-Fire." I spent the next half-hour giving the man the rundown on what I knew, asking him to pass the information on to the Americans too. He made no promises but said that he would do his best. That was enough for me.

For several months after that, I was busy with the book; we were getting closer and closer to the end. I was getting more tense since I knew that the day was fast coming when I'd be hit by the spotlight and God knows what else.

SUNDAY, APRIL 1, 1990

I met with Uri in downtown Ottawa. We sat in my car in front of the Ottawa library for several hours. He had a new story for the book, and he wanted me to have all the information.

Uri is an extremely calm man, and he had never shown a sign of fear for as long as I could remember him. From the stories I heard about his military career, he was not one to whine. But now, sitting in my car, he was extremely nervous, staring back and forth all the time like an amateur cadet. He was reading from notes and then tearing them into small bits and thrusting them into his attaché case. I soon realized why he was so nervous. This was explosive material.

The previous August (1989) a contingent of the Matkal plus several naval commandos had headed up the Euphrates in a small boat purchased by a Mossad combatant from a local merchant. Their target was an explosives factory located in the city of Al-Iskandariah. The factory was one of five sites the Mossad had fingered as a possible chemical or nuclear facility. The others were farther north and harder to access, in Salman Pack Fallujah and Samarra. Jumbo[1] information the Mossad had received from American intelligence revealed that every Thursday, a small convoy of trucks came to the complex to be loaded with explosives that were then transferred to Karbala for the purpose of manufacturing cannon shells.

The objective was to take position near the base on Wednesday, August 23, and wait until the next day when the trucks would be loaded. At that point, several sharpshooters with special silenced rifles would fire one round each of an explosive bullet at a designated truck, causing it to explode. The plan was to fire at the trucks while they were in the process of loading so that there would be a carry-on explosion into the storage facility. The loading doors into the facility would

---

1. Jumbo: Personal information beyond official intelligence gathered by Mossad liaison officers from foreign intelligence officers using friendship as a vehicle.

be open at that point, and there would be several tiers of high explosives inside the bunker leading to the main storage area.

This operation was as close to a suicide mission as the Israeli military would ever come. The main escape route, which was back down-river, was secure as long as the Iraqi security apparatus believed that the explosion was an accident. Later, they might realize it was not, but by then the unit would be in the clear. The Israeli soldiers, who were all volunteers, were advised that there was no backup and, effectively, no possibility of rescue should they be caught.

The operation was quite successful, and the explosion generated the sort of publicity the Mossad was hoping for in attracting attention to Saddam's constant efforts at building a gigantic and powerful military arsenal. The Mossad shared its "findings" with the Western intelligence agencies and leaked the story of the explosion to the press, putting the number of casualties resulting from it in the hundreds.

Since this was a guarded facility, Western reporters had minimal access to it. However, at the beginning of September, the Iraqis were inviting Western media people to visit Iraq and see the rebuilding that had taken place after the war, and the Mossad saw an opportunity to conduct a damage assessment. A man calling himself Michel Rubiyer, saying he was working for the French newspaper *Le Figaro*, approached Farzad Bazoft, a thirty-one-year-old reporter freelancing for the British newspaper the *Observer*. Rubiyer was, in fact, Michel M., an Israeli with whom I'd trained. Michel, who'd once lived in France, had moved to Israel and joined the IDF, to be posted in SIG-INT[2] Unit 8200. Using his connections in the intelligence community, he was recruited to the Mossad and finally landed a job in the Paris station.

Michel told Farzad Bazoft that he would pay him handsomely and print his story if he'd join a group of journalists heading for Baghdad. The reason he gave for not going himself was that he'd been black-listed in Iraq. He stressed that he was after a story that would be very big. He pointed out that Bazoft could use the money and the break, especially with his criminal background. Michel told the stunned reporter that he knew of his arrest in 1981 for armed robbery in Northampton, England. Along with this implied threat, he promised Bazoft that he'd be able to publish the story in the *Observer* as well.

Michel wanted Bazoft to collect information regarding the explosion in Al-Iskandariah, ask questions about it, get sketches of the area,

---

2. SIGINT: Signal Intelligence.

and collect earth samples. He told the worried reporter that Saddam would not dare harm a reporter even if he was unhappy with him. The worst that Saddam would do was kick him out of the country, which would in itself make him famous.

"Why this particular reporter?" I asked.

"He was of Iranian background, which would make punishing him much easier for the Iraqis, and he wasn't a European whom they'd probably only hold and then kick out." In fact, Bazoft had been identified in a Mossad search that was triggered by his prying into another Mossad case in search of a story. Bazoft had attempted to gather information on an ex-Mossad asset by the name of Dr. Cyrus Hashemi, who was eliminated by Mossad in July 1986. Since Bazoft had already stumbled on too much information for his own good—or the Mossad's, for that matter—he was the perfect candidate for this job of snooping in forbidden areas.

Uri went on to tell of how Bazoft made his way to the location as he was asked, and, as might be expected, was arrested. Tragically, his British girlfriend, a nurse working in a Baghdad hospital, was arrested as well.

Within a few days of the arrest, a Mossad liaison in the United States called the Iraqi representative in Holland and said that Jerusalem was willing to make a deal for the release of their man who'd been captured. The liaison also said that the deal was only for the man, since Israel had nothing to do with the nurse. The Iraqi representative asked for time to contact Baghdad, and the liaison called again the following day, at which point he told the Iraqi representative it was all a big mistake and severed contact. Now the Iraqis had no doubt that they had a real spy on their hands, and they were going to see him hang. All the Mossad had to do was sit back and watch as Saddam proved to the world what a monster he really was.

On March 15, 1990, Farzad Bazoft, who'd been held in the Abu Ghraib prison some twenty kilometers west of Baghdad, met briefly with the British ambassador to Iraq. A few minutes after the meeting, he was hanged. His British girlfriend was sentenced to fifteen years in prison. His body was delivered to the British embassy in Baghdad, and the official spokesman noted that Prime Minister Margaret Thatcher "wanted him alive and we have just delivered his dead body to her."

The world was shocked, but the Mossad was not done yet. To fan the flames generated by this brutal hanging, a Mossad *sayan* in New York delivered a set of documents to ABC television with a story from a reliable Middle Eastern source telling of a plant Saddam had for the manufacturing of uranium. The information was convincing, and the photos and sketches were even more so. It was time to draw attention to Saddam's weapons of mass destruction.

Only three months before, on December 5, 1989, the Iraqis had launched the Al-Abid, a three-stage ballistic missile. The Iraqis claimed it was a satellite launcher that Gerald Bull, a Canadian scientist, was helping them develop. Israeli intelligence knew that the launch, although trumpeted as a great success, was in fact a total failure, and that the program would never reach its goals. But that secret was not shared with the media. On the contrary, the missile launch was exaggerated and blown out of proportion.

The message that Israeli intelligence sent out was this: Now all the pieces of the puzzle are fitting together. This maniac is developing a nuclear capability (remember the Israeli attack on the Iraqi reactor in 1981) and pursuing chemical warfare (as seen in his attacks on his own people, the Kurds). What's more, he despises the Western media, regarding them as Israeli spies. Quite soon, he's going to have the ability to launch a missile from anywhere in Iraq to anywhere he wants in the Middle East and beyond.

After the arrest of Bazoft, Gerald Bull, who was also working on the Iraqi big gun project called Babylon, was visited by Israeli friends from his past (the same ones who'd put him in contact with the South Africans regarding a mutual mobile long-range gun called the G-5 155mm, and the self-propelled G-6 155mm—both of which were originally built in Israel by Sultam[3]). The visitors, one of whom was David Biran, then Mossad's head of liaison, and the other, Ron Vintrobe, head of the Iraqi desk in Mossad headquarters, had come to deliver a warning.

They were both known to Bull as members of the Israeli intelligence community. But they were not from the field, so while their warning was very real, they themselves would not be in danger of exposure, since they were not operators engaging the enemy directly.

The Mossad psychological department had studied the position Bull was in and analyzed what was known about his character. It arrived at the conclusion that, even if threatened, he wouldn't pull out of the program, but instead would carry on his work with very little regard for his personal safety. Which is not to say the man would't worry. On the contrary, the department expected him to be terrified by the threats and feel high levels of stress.

Ultimately, Bull's continuing with his program would play right

---

3. Sultam: An Israeli weapons manufacturer.

into the Mossad's hands. Through the bullet-riddled body of Gerald Bull, the eyes of the world would be made to focus on his work: the Iraqi giant gun project called Babylon. The timing had to be right, though; Bull's well-publicized demise had to come right after an act of terror by the regime in Baghdad, an act that could not be mistaken for an accident or a provocation. The hanging of the *Observer* reporter on March 15 was such an act.

After the reporter's execution in Baghdad, a Kidon team arrived in Brussels and cased the apartment building where Bull lived. It was imperative that the job be done in a place where it would not be mistaken for a robbery or an accident. At the same time, an escape route was prepared for the team, and some old contacts with the right-wing element in the Belgian police were revived to make sure they were on duty at the time of Bull's elimination so that, if there was a need to call in a friendly police force, they'd be on call. They weren't told the reason for the so-called *alerte* but would learn later and keep silent.

Some members of the Kidon team had rented a vacant apartment next door to Bull's lodgings. The couple who'd rented it never actually moved in, but they did receive the keys to the main entrance to the complex. Eight days after the hanging of the reporter in Baghdad (while British intelligence was close to closing a sting operation in which the Iraqis would be caught attempting to smuggle some nuclear switches from the States, very similar to the switches Israel was caught smuggling only seven years earlier), a Mossad hit man was in the vacant apartment next to Gerald Bull's, waiting for a message from another member of the team who was outside watching the entrance. A third man was securing the staircase while two more were seated in two getaway cars waiting down the road.

When Bull reached the building at eight-thirty P.M., the man watching the entrance signaled the man in the empty apartment on the sixth floor to get ready: The target had entered the building. The shooter then left the apartment, leaving behind only an empty pack of cigarettes and a matchbox from a hotel in Brussels. He then hid in an alcove.

Almost immediately after the elevator door closed behind Bull, the shooter fired point blank at the man's back and head. The shooter then walked over to Bull, who'd dropped to the floor, and pulled out of his tote bag a handful of documents and other papers, which he placed in a paper shopping bag he had with him. He also collected all the casings from the floor and dropped the gun into the shopping bag.

Then he headed for the staircase, where his partner was waiting, and they left the building. As soon as he saw the two men come out, the watcher walked away and headed for one of the two cars. The two men entered the second car, and both cars drove away from the scene. They left the cars in an underground parking lot to be picked up the next day by a car *sayan* who'd rented the cars to them without registering the rental. They then drove to Amsterdam, where they boarded an El Al cargo plane back to Israel as part of its crew, leaving Europe the same way they'd come in.

In the following weeks, more and more discoveries were made regarding the big gun and other elements of the Saddam war machine. The Mossad had all but saturated the intelligence field with information regarding the evil intentions of Saddam the Terrible, banking on the fact that before long, he'd have enough rope to hang himself.

It was very clear what the Mossad's overall goal was. It wanted the West to do its bidding, just as the Americans had in Libya with the bombing of Qadhafi. After all, Israel didn't possess carriers and ample air power, and although it was capable of bombing a refugee camp in Tunis, that was not the same. The Mossad leaders knew that if they could make Saddam appear bad enough and a threat to the Gulf oil supply, of which he'd been the protector up to that point, then the United States and its allies would not let him get away with anything, but would take measures that would all but eliminate his army and his weapons potential, especially if they were led to believe that this might just be their last chance before he went nuclear.

I had all of it on paper and decided to call the Belgian police the following day and tell them all I knew. It was, after all, going to appear in my book in the near future. Uri was never as happy to leave a place as he was to leave Ottawa that day, and I was extremely anxious to work this chapter into the book with Claire.

By the next morning, I'd already called the Belgian police in Brussels and spent almost an hour on the phone repeating my story over and over again. I wouldn't give them my name or the source of my information, but I held back nothing else. I had no doubt as I hung up that they'd be able to substantiate my story and point the finger in the right direction.

The next day, Claire was to come and work with me on the new chapter. But I got a call from Ephraim: Kill the story Uri told you. I protested, but he wouldn't budge. He told me that I had to trust him on this one and that he'd explain it to me some other time. I didn't use it, and he never did explain it to me. Nor did the Belgian police ever solve the murder. However, what I found more disturbing than anything else was the lack of interest the Canadian government and press displayed in the murder of a fellow Canadian.

CHAPTER 28

By mid-March, Claire and I had just about finished the book. Ephraim had approved most of the things in it and had grudgingly accepted the rest.

Nelson Doucet, our sponsor at Stoddart Publishing, told us that he'd secured the services of an editor who was from outside the company but still sufficiently tied in to be reliable and discreet. Her name was Frances Hanna, and she was the wife of Bill Hanna, Stoddart's vice president for foreign rights.

She told us that she'd worked as an editor on another book that had dealt with the same subject matter called *Vengeance*, and was interested to know my opinion of it.

I replied that I'd read only the beginning of that book and found it so off the mark that I put it down. She seemed peeved at first, but as time passed and she got to know more about what really happens in the world of intelligence, I think she saw my point.

Once the editing of the book was complete, Bill Hanna made a trip to New York with the galley proofs in hand to give to Tom McCormick, president of St. Martin's Press. Tom was going to read the book overnight, and then I was to come to his office for a short meeting, after which he'd make up his mind whether to join in on this venture.

Bella and I drove to New York. By then, I was already very uncomfortable about security. There were so many people involved in the book by this time, and it was very possible that word had leaked back to the Mossad without the knowledge of Ephraim and the clique. Information could be kept within another clique just as secretively as we'd kept it within ours.

Bella and I registered at the Ritz. First thing in the morning, I left for my meeting with Bill, who was going to take me to meet Tom. Bella, meanwhile, had decided to go window-shopping.

I was extremely tense and found it very difficult to concentrate. I had a sense that I was being followed, yet I couldn't quite pin it down. I told myself it would make little difference if I was, since the fact that so many people were involved by now should function as a kind of shield.

The meeting with Tom was very pleasant. He asked some tough questions, but since there was really nothing to hide, they were fairly easy to deal with. Tom was very relaxed and created a good feeling with his biting sense of humor and his very low and deep voice. Bill had brought him the galleys wrapped in a cover sheet from another book, one by Pierre Elliott Trudeau—a precaution Bill thought necessary. I found the choice of camouflage rather amusing.

Almost two hours later, I left the meeting. Bill stayed behind to talk business. Although I had no definite answer, I had a good feeling as I headed back to the hotel.

We checked out and left town. I called Bill from a roadside restaurant, and he gave me the good news: St. Martin's was in. I informed Ephraim of the news once I got back to Ottawa, and he was ecstatic. "This will do it! I have no doubt that this will bring them down," he said.

I was not so sure. "They can say they don't know me. They can say it's all lies, as they have in the past."

"Not if I can help it, they won't. You're not Vanunu, and they know it. We'll just have to play it one day at a time."

"Do you know if any word has already reached them?"

"As far as I can tell, it hasn't. But you must be very careful and watch your back until the book comes out and you're shielded by the media."

"What you're telling me is that you have no idea if they know or not."

"That's about the size of it," he said, "but don't worry. If they were going to do something drastic, I'd hear about it for sure."

I had known very well what I was getting into the moment I'd decided to write the book. But his last statement did give me some peace of mind.

Sunday, September 2, 1990

"It's out of the bag," Ephraim said over the phone. "They have a disk of the book and are now printing a copy of it. From what I hear, things are not looking too good. It's now in the hands of the prime minister."

"The little bastard will tell them to have me killed," I said, and I wasn't laughing.

"I had someone give him a better idea, and I think he has taken the bait."

"Can you be more specific?"

"I would prefer not to, at the moment. But I want you to know that you'll have a visitor in the next few days."

"Anyone I know?"

"I'm not sure, but I think that it will be."

Nothing more was said. Claire and I made one more trip to Toronto. We had a meeting with representatives of St. Martin's Press, and we decided to postpone the publication of the book for a month, as they said they needed the time to come out with the book. At the same time, Stoddart's copies were coming off the press fast. They were stored in an empty warehouse adjacent to the publisher's building, and a special guard was placed on them. The tension was mounting; we were ready to go. I felt like someone about to jump from a very high cliff, and I sure hoped that there was a parachute in whatever I had strapped on my back.

Before we left Stoddart's, Jack Stoddart, owner and president of Stoddart Publishing, came to tell us that something very strange had happened. He'd just received an anonymous call from someone who said that Israel had hired the law firm of Goodman and Carr in Toronto to stop the publication of our book.

Jack was not sure whether this was for real or whether someone in the publishing house was pulling a prank. I had no doubt it was not a joke, but with nothing to go on besides this call, I could do very little.

We drove back to Ottawa. I knew we were not being followed.

At that point, Bella was aware of what was in the book although she hadn't read it. Some days earlier, we'd taken the girls to an Italian restaurant in Ottawa, and I'd given them a condensed explanation of what was going on. I explained to them why I was taking this step and braced them for the fury that might be ahead.

The evening following my return from Toronto, Bella and I went over to the Bayshore shopping mall. I needed a breather, and knowing the genie that was about to be let out of the bottle, I wanted to take advantage of the last few hours of anonymity I still had.

I spotted them when I made a call from the pay phone at the mall: a team of at least five people, following us at all times. I knew that this was it, and tonight was going to be the night. We left the mall and headed home. Several days previously, I'd stopped at the Nepean police station with a book jacket. I'd had a talk with the top cop at the station. I explained to him that I'd written a book about the Israeli secret service, the Mossad, and that the Mossad was going to be very unhappy about it. He promised to be vigilant; the police would respond to my call as fast as they could should there be a problem.

I didn't expect them to stand up to the Mossad, but still, their knowing who I was and that there might be a problem made me feel better. I'd also stopped at RCMP headquarters at 400 Cooper Street in Ottawa and spoken to a constable there. He told me that this sort of thing fell under the jurisdiction of CSIS, the Canadian secret service. They were located in the same building, so I went over to their offices and informed them as well.

At nine P.M., there was a knock on the door. I was standing in the small kitchen, getting ready to make a cup of coffee. Bella answered the door. Oren Riff and Aaron Sherf were standing there. (Oren was the personal assistant to the head of Mossad and my former cadet course commander. Aaron Sherf was head of the Tsafririm department in charge of monitoring and activating the world Jewish Diaspora, and my former academy commander.) Oren carried a shoulder bag, and Aaron was trying his best to put on a smile.

"We want to talk to you," Aaron said.

I picked up the phone and dialed 911, but before they could answer, I hung up. Something was preventing me from making such a drastic move yet.

Oren leaned his head slightly to one side and said, "We came to talk."

The phone rang; it was the police calling back to see what was going on. I told them everything was okay; if there was any problem, I'd call back. They accepted that. I walked over to the door. I could see that Bella was turning white; I thought she might faint at any moment. By the time I got to the door, she not only hadn't fainted but was giving our visitors a piece of her mind. No doubt the hysteria caused by their sudden appearance brought on this display of anger. She knew very well who they were, and their appearance on our doorstep made all her fears about the book become a reality.

"Can we come in?" Oren asked.

"No. I have nothing to talk to you about," I said.

"Please, let's be civilized," he said.

I couldn't help laughing at that. But then I considered my real situation, and it frightened me. Why hadn't I told the police there *was* a problem? I feared that while these two were at my door, the team that was planning to grab me and take me back to a stinking little hole in

Israel was taking position outside in the shadows. It was hard to believe that all they wanted was to talk.

"If you have anything to say to me, you do it here and now," I said. "You're not coming in. And I'd suggest for your own good that you be brief and then get the hell out of this area."

"We are at war," Aaron said, referring to the situation in the Gulf. Coming from one who was part of the mechanism that had brought that situation about, this was almost like someone who has killed his parents asking for mercy because he's an orphan.

"What is it that you want?" I was going to play along until I saw a window of opportunity. I wanted to move the problem as far as I could from my family. When she'd heard Hebrew being spoken, my daughter Leeorah had come down the stairs, thinking we had guests from Israel. But she ran back up as soon as she heard my angry tone.

"We want you to stop the book," Aaron said.

"I can't believe this from you," Oren said, putting in his two cents' worth. Aaron looked at him scornfully, as if to say, Don't anger the prey.

"It's not only my decision to make," I said, trying to act reasonable. "Besides, they've already printed the book and are ready to ship it."

"How many copies could there be for Canada?" Aaron said. "You have to stop this book."

"It's not that simple." I was stalling for time.

"You know money is no object," Oren said. "We'll cover all the expenses plus any projected profits—you know that."

"I have to talk to some people. I need time."

They glanced at each other. "Call me at the consulate in Toronto," Oren said. "I'll wait for your call there until tomorrow noon."

"Okay." I started to close the door. They turned and headed back to their red Chevrolet Cavalier. It had a Quebec license plate. They sat in the car for a few moments, and then they took off. I knew I didn't have much time to make my move. I was expecting the team to come through the door at any minute.

I could see fear in Bella's eyes. I knew she wasn't afraid for herself but for her dumb husband, who once again had gotten himself up the proverbial creek without a paddle. I put as much stuff as I might need into my attaché case and sat for a while, thinking about my next move. After a few minutes of analysis, I came to the conclusion that they wouldn't break in just yet. They'd wait and see if I had any protection that would spring into action after the bold visit I'd just received, in which case they wouldn't want to get caught in the middle.

I decided to leave on the stroke of midnight. I needed to go to a place where they had police around the clock, but a police station was not where I wanted to be. I had to get to the airport. It was open twenty-four hours a day, and police were on duty at all times. I could also make calls from there and try to get out of the city as fast as possible. I figured I'd be safer with my publisher. After all, he was my partner in all of this.

At twelve, I pulled out of my driveway and was immediately followed by a small gray car and a large gray windowless van. I made several evasive maneuvers and, having the advantage of knowing the area better than any newcomer, got away. I headed straight for the airport and the RCMP station there.

I spoke briefly with the constable at the airport, informing him that Mossad people had been on my tail in the city. He promised to inform the airport police to check on me every so often. There were no flights until the next morning, so it appeared I was going to spend the night at the airport.

I called Bella to tell her everything was okay, and then I called Claire Hoy to bring him into the loop. Nelson Doucet wasn't home, so I called Jack Stoddart. I expected him to take some action and maybe show some concern, but he didn't seem to realize the gravity of the situation. He merely said that he hoped all would be well and that he looked forward to seeing me the next morning in the office.

The flight took off at seven A.M. There were some problems landing in Toronto Island because of the fog. But we got there eventually, and after a wild cab ride, I arrived at Stoddart's offices.

There I had to wait for a while. Eventually, someone came to see me, and I explained what was happening. The Mossad was on our trail and was getting into position to take steps to stop us. I felt an obligation to Stoddart to give them a way out of this situation, and in a one-on-one talk with Jack Stoddart, I told him that if he wished to withdraw from this venture, he'd be handsomely reimbursed by the Mossad, whose representative Oren Riff was still waiting for my call at the consulate in Toronto.

Jack replied that publishing was not only a matter of money but also, for him, a matter of principle. He had no intention of backing down; the book was coming out, no matter what.

Angel Guerra, Stoddart's chief of publicity, had already convened a small group of reporters from the major papers and television stations. They'd been given a short summary of the book and were waiting for me in a conference room. Meanwhile, St. Martin's Press had been notified of the new developments and told to move forward as fast as they could. They had seventeen thousand copies of the book in their warehouse and decided to ship them out right then and there. The shipping was done via a system called blind shipping, in which a publisher ships books to the stores in the absence of specific orders. The stores are not obligated to take the books, but most do, and a widespread distribution is virtually guaranteed.

Bill Hanna, the rights VP, had also licensed the British rights to Bloomsbury, but St. Martin's, who would eventually supply them with books, had no extras to send them, having taken a wait-and-see attitude regarding sales volume.

I called Bella, who told me that Rina, one of her best friends, had called from Israel. Rina had told Bella that she, her husband Hezy, and several other friends of ours were going to be brought to Ottawa the following day to try to get me to stop the publication of the book. Bella told me that she tried to explain to Rina that such an effort would be futile and that it would be very unlikely that Rina would succeed where Bella herself had failed. Later, when Oren called looking for me, Bella told him to tell the people in Israel not to send all our friends on this stupid trip. Oren played dumb and said he had no idea what she was talking about. But she persisted, and he finally put an end to the matter.

Meanwhile, I was sitting at Stoddart Publishing, feeling extremely helpless. I could almost feel the presence of the Mossad team but could not communicate with Ephraim or any of the others. There were too many ears and eyes around.

Just before I headed for the news conference, a fax arrived from the offices of Goodman and Carr Barristers and Solicitors, sent by Joel Goldenberg on behalf of the state of Israel, telling Stoddart that they had obtained an order from a judge barring the distribution of the book and ordering me not to discuss the information in the book until things were clarified in court. I was muzzled, and for the first time in Canadian history, a foreign country had blocked publication of a book—all this before a single book had left the Canadian warehouse and before the lawyers and judge involved had even had a chance to see a copy, unless it was a stolen one. That my name was on the cover, and that it was a nonfiction book about the Mossad, was apparently enough to make it a danger to the state of Israel.

Before any legal steps could be taken in the States, St. Martin's Press had already shipped over twelve thousand copies to the stores in the U.S. Still, it wasn't long before Israel moved to try to block the book in the United States just as it had done in Canada.

Right from the outset, it was clear to the government of Israel that keeping the book permanently off the bookshelves in Canada and the United States was a futile act and that it couldn't possibly win. But they had other plans, ones that didn't involve the courts. It came out later in the Israeli press that the head of the Mossad had requested that some action be taken to give him additional time to stop me. He admitted to a special committee of the Israeli parliament, the Knesset, formed to investigate my case that he'd sent people to Canada to try to persuade me not to publish and that money was also offered, but that I'd refused. He then decided to take other action.

Later, after everything had calmed down, Ephraim told me what the chief's plans were. He wanted the legal process to prevent me from speaking and answering relevant questions for the first few days, which would give them time to grab me and take me back to Israel. The Mossad assumed that whatever public relations damage my kidnapping might cause would be negligible in comparison to the damage I'd cause if I were allowed to answer questions in the media. The possibility that the Mossad's personal conduct would be revealed bothered the Mossad chief more than the revelation of so-called state secrets in my book.

Ignoring me altogether was not an option as far as the head of the Mossad was concerned. This was in part due to Ephraim's saying in a Rashy[1] meeting that since I'd incorporated several documents in my book, its charges couldn't just be ignored, and that picking me up and bringing me back to Israel shouldn't be an impossible task. To bolster his argument that my claims would be taken seriously (even if the Mossad chose not to comment), Ephraim pointed out the questionnaire I had translated from Hebrew that showed a knowledge of the Syrian military that could not be obtained outside the Syrian army or the Mossad.

After those of us in Stoddart's offices had reviewed Goodman and Carr's fax, Sally Tindel, Angel's secretary, was sent back to the waiting reporters to request that they return the material they'd been given, including the book's summary, because it had just been learned that Israel had taken legal steps to block the book's publication.

To my surprise, the reporters returned the papers without a murmur. We held a short news conference in which I could not say much except that this was a book that I believed had to be published.

The Mossad made its move in the United States and managed to temporarily block further distribution of the book there. This was an

---

1. Rashy: Rashy Yehidot; a meeting of department heads

unprecedented move, and the reaction in the States was much more vocal and furious than the Canadian reaction. It's clear that Americans act much more aggressively when they sense that their freedom of speech is being restricted.

Within twenty-four hours, the ban was lifted in the States. By then, just about all of the seventeen thousand books that had been distributed there were sold out, and the stores were clamoring for more. Sales were breaking all records, but at the same time I was not allowed to speak about what was *in* the book. I was moving from one location to another in Toronto, planning my next move, forced to hold my cards very close to my chest. On the first day, the RCMP took me under their wing. They approached the job of protecting me with the vigor of people who mean business, and by day's end, they'd decided to take me back to Ottawa, where it would be much easier to protect my family and me, as they said, "in one package."

We drove back to Ottawa and stopped at the Nepean police station, where the two somewhat embarrassed RCMP constables told the duty officer that the RCMP brass had decided that it was the Nepean police's job to protect me and that they were leaving me in their hands.

I was told that the decision had been made during the night as we were driving to Ottawa. They didn't feel that the Mossad would dare take action in Canada, and therefore their continued presence was not needed.

There was really nothing I could do. The constable gave me his business card and told me that if I had any problem at all, I should feel free to call him at any time. That left my family and me, essentially, in the hands of the Nepean police force, which regards a string of shoplifting cases as a major crime wave. It was small comfort.

Bella was shocked to see me back, knowing full well what the score was and knowing that I was far more vulnerable in this setting. The next morning, we took evasive action. I got to the train station as the train was about to pull out, and was back in Toronto by that afternoon. Once there, I went straight to the Stoddart offices.

By then, the media blitz was at full intensity; I was either doing television interviews or giving over-the-phone radio interviews to places as far as Sydney, Australia, or as near as the Toronto Jewish press. However, I still couldn't talk about what was in the book, or about my personal experiences in the Mossad.

Then several Israeli newspeople showed up, acting both as reporters for their own papers and as commentators for the other media. One by the name of Ran Dagony, reporting for a daily newspaper in Israel called *Maariv*, published an extremely devastating interview with me that he claimed to have conducted in Toronto. The interview covered almost two full newspaper pages. The man only neglected to mention that we'd never met and that I'd never spoken to him.

The Canadian judge had barred all discussion of the book for a period of ten days. I knew that this was the interval of time that the Mossad had to try to stop me. From time to time, I caught them following me, and I would take steps to get away. Whenever I did, I thanked Mousa and Dov for the great training they'd given me.

Before the ten days were up, I realized it was time to get out of Toronto and go back home. I was running out of ways to leave the Stoddart offices without developing a pattern. I was also extremely frustrated. By then, I'd been on the ABC evening news with Peter Jennings, on NBC with Tom Brokaw, and on just about every major network, but because of the gag order, I could say almost nothing. There I was, like a dummy, in front of the whole world.

When I got back to Ottawa, I was met by a second wave of media that was with me from the moment the plane landed.

There were Israeli reporters and crews from the local media. What I found stranger than anything else was the fact that I was barred from talking about the contents of my book or even handling a copy, while Oded Ben-Ami, the representative of Israeli radio, was reading sections of it over the phone to his audience in Israel.

When I finally got to the house, I was surprised to receive a short message from my father, who'd heard about the book for the first time through the media. "Call me," the message said. "Whatever happens, I'm always your dad." I really needed that. We'd already established a relationship since I'd come to live in Canada. But this was something that I'd really hoped for. When I needed him most, he was there. I called him, and we took it from there, as if nothing had happened. I suppose I shouldn't have been surprised. After all, it was he who'd always maintained, even after the great frenzy of triumph that had swept the Jewish world after the Israeli victory in the Six-Day War in 1967, that Arabs should be treated with dignity and respect, that not all Arabs are bad and not every Israeli is automatically an angel. From that telephone call on, we were the best of friends.

Several days later, I managed to make contact with Ephraim. I learned that the Mossad was going to let me be for now. If any steps were to be taken against me, they would be in the disinformation department and not against my person. I still knew that this was a very unstable guarantee and that if I should leave Canada and venture even as far as the United States, things could change rather fast.

Accordingly, I decided to publicize *By Way of Deception* by doing radio shows across the United States and Canada via phone. I managed over two hundred shows in less than three months, and I also did a long string of television shows by satellite.

From Toronto, I appeared on *Good Morning America* with Charles Gibson, and found him to be as charming an interviewer as he was a host. It was quite a treat for me, since I'd watched him every morning from the day he'd debuted on the show.

Then there was the *Larry King Show*, by which time the gag order was lifted, where I received somewhat rougher treatment. To build some contentiousness into the hour, the show's producers had invited Amos Perelmuter, a professor from the American University in Washington, D.C., to join King and me. From the start, it was clear that Perelmuter was an enthusiastic supporter of the state of Israel, and that what he'd heard about my book—he admitted he hadn't read it— he didn't like.

There was never enough time on such shows to put Perelmuter and other "designated champions of Israel" on the spot. How did they know that everything I was saying was lies? *I* was the one who'd served in the Mossad, not they. Why was it that these loyal Americans were willing to accept any mud thrown at the CIA without even giving it a second thought, but insisted on defending to the hilt an intelligence agency of a foreign country that had been known to spy on the United States (as in the Pollard case) and hadn't refrained from attacking American interests (as in the case of the Lavon[2] affair in Egypt, among others)?

The first wave of fury the book caused was due to its revelation that the Mossad had advance knowledge of the notorious suicide bombing in Beirut (including the make and color of the car) but didn't pass on that information to American intelligence. In October 1983, two hundred and forty-one U.S. marines were killed when the car, rigged with explosives, rammed their barracks in Beirut. In many instances, this story from the book was taken out of context and told

---

2. Lavon affair: This affair took place in the 1950s and concerned Pinhas Lavon, then the Israeli minister of defense. Several Egyptian Jews were organized into a terrorist cell and sent to sabotage American targets in Egypt, the point being to try to sour the relationship between Israel and America. The plan failed, and the men were arrested. A lengthy and politically painful ordeal followed in Israel; it never became clear who gave the order for this disgraceful operation, but as minister of defense, Lavon was made ultimately responsible.

as if I'd said that the Mossad knew Americans were the target, which was not the case.

This and numerous other headline-making revelations helped propel the book to the number one spot on the *New York Times* best-seller list, where it stayed for nine weeks. *By Way of Deception* made the best-seller list in almost every one of the twenty-odd countries where it was published. It was published in some fifteen different languages (although it's still not available in Hebrew), and by the year's end had sold well over a million copies worldwide.

Had it not been for Bella's last-minute intervention, the names of all the field personnel would have been in the book. I had no problem with using the names, nor did Ephraim. We both knew that they were already burned, and by putting their names in, we might be saving them. But I was equally happy not to put them in.

Not that it saved me from being portrayed in the Israeli press as the devil incarnate. One Israeli reporter said in an editorial that someone should put a bullet in my head. Yet another said that I should be tied to a pole and all the people of Israel should come and spit on me. Few, if any, Israelis seemed to stop and say, "Maybe what he says has a grain of truth in it."

Because the book had been translated into so many languages, I'd met and answered questions from people around the world. Gratifyingly, at least as far as my credibility was concerned, as time passed, more and more things that were said in the book were proved to be true.

I'd moved to a bigger house and had started a new career. I was going to write a novel. I knew that writing fiction presented a whole new set of challenges, but I felt that my experiences provided great raw material from which a compelling story could be woven. Stoddart had decided to take a chance on me, and I was grateful.

Ephraim and I still spoke fairly frequently. He told me that the Israeli parliamentary commission investigating the "Ostrovsky affair" had come back with the conclusion that the only problem was that I'd been recruited in the first place. As for how things had changed inside the Mossad, there was barely any change at all. The one minor ripple my book caused was that several of the so-called moderates were blamed for recruiting me and kicked out.

Also, the fear that an oversight committee might be established caused various preventive measures to be taken. Ties were being strengthened with the settler movement in the Territories, and "spies" were being recruited in the Ministry of Defense and the military.

"I guess you still have a job to do," said Ephraim. "There are some elements around the new boss today who are far more dangerous than anyone you ever knew in your time."

"I can't do much now, with the kind of exposure I have."

"We'll see about that. For the time being, go with the flow. Just make sure you don't go under."

I took his warning seriously, knowing where it came from.

CHAPTER 29

The year 1991 did not turn out to be a good year for the Mossad, although at first it looked as though it would. There was a new boss on the throne, and to the joy of most of the opportunists, it was an insider. The Office had successfully managed to prevent the government from bringing in a general from the outside. And what's more, the Mossad had their man, Yitzhak Shamir, in the seat of power as prime minister. Israel's prime minister was a man who liked to be reminded of his Mossad past (even if within the Mossad it was never regarded as more than mediocre, with no lasting achievements).

This time, the insider had taken the top position in the Mossad in a natural succession, making it clear to all that from that day forth there was to be no more parachuting in of an outsider boss. A new layer of Teflon had just been added to the organization, which was always in the dirt but could not get dirty.

The new chief took office and made no changes in the organization, to the appreciation of his comrades-in-arms. What was happening, though, was an erosion of the link that had been maintained between the Mossad and the military by having a former general head up the intelligence agency. Once again, a leader was at the helm of the Mossad who didn't know the military or hold much respect for it. The new head regarded the military establishment as prima donna ballerinas, in constant need of nursing and incapable of making tough decisions without wearing iron underwear (as he used to put it while still head of operations during my term in the Mossad).

"The only way we could do something of any significance now," Ephraim said, "would be to target the Mossad one country at a time and try to make a difference that way."

"We've done that already. And what happened?"

"Look, I know of some activity taking place now in Norway. Why don't we use that country as a target and see what happens? What do we have to lose?"

"Did you ever consider taking over from the inside, now that all attempts to hit it from the outside have failed?"

"I always consider that. If there was a chance of my taking the scepter, trust me, I would. But they have secured it for God knows how long. As long as Shamir is in office, we don't have a chance to do anything. He hates the whole world, and what better way to get his revenge than to use the Mossad? He hates Bush for humiliating him in Washington and holding him by the short hairs regarding the loan guarantees. He hates the British." He paused. "Well, he always hated the British. He doesn't trust the French, and we know what he thinks of the Arabs and everybody else."

"So what now?"

"I have a friend in Norway who knows a reporter for a newspaper called the *Oftenposten*. I can have my friend suggest that the reporter call you and see if there might be a story there for him regarding the Mossad."

"Is there a story there?"

"Sure there is."

We pored over the details of this story and found several references to it in the Danish documents that I had. All I had to do now was wait for a call and take it from there. We'd placed little hope in this escapade, but it was better than doing nothing. And even though I was in the middle of writing my novel, I knew there were more important things to be done.

I felt that if there was a change in government in Israel, there'd be a chance for some peace negotiations. So I had in some ways changed my goals. From that point on, it wasn't just the Mossad I was after. I was also looking for ways to embarrass the government. For me, 1991 was going to be a very good year.

Within a few days, I received a call from a reporter in Norway calling himself Mr. Stangheler. He said he was working for a Norwegian paper, the *Oftenposten*, and wanted to ask me a few questions. Then followed the usual niceties; he buttered me up to assure my cooperation, telling me that he enjoyed my book and that he was hoping I would write another, etc., etc. He eventually got to the point. He wanted to know if I knew of any Mossad activities in Norway.

I explained to him that I had no dealings with the Norwegian desk but that I could offer him a kind of projection from the activities of the Mossad in Denmark, which I had detailed quite extensively in the book. I also said that there was no doubt in my mind that the Mossad was in fact as active in Norway as it was in Denmark, and that if he wanted to put the time in and investigate, I'd be more than happy to assist by directing him and helping him assess whatever information he might find. I also offered to sketch for him what I believed was going on in Norway. All he'd have to do was color in the outlines with facts derived from investigation.

The man was extremely pleased, and I knew I was about to hand the Mossad another painful punch on the nose—that is, if it didn't get smart on me and pull out of whatever it was doing in Norway at the time. But as usual, the Mossad just went on doing what it did best, which was to abuse the friendship of a good ally and, when the time came, leave it holding the proverbial baby.

I told my new friend that the Mossad could be expected to have a close relationship with the local intelligence, mainly dealing at the intermediate level. He could find the links by obtaining the names of people from the police and intelligence communities who'd gone on various seminars to Israel. The second avenue I suggested was taking a closer look at Palestinian refugees who were seeking asylum in Norway. Just as in Denmark, and as I'd described in my book, the Mossad would offer the local intelligence agency a service that, in its words, would guarantee security and the weeding out of potential terrorists from the waves of incoming refugees.

The Mossad would offer to send experts to Norway, who, upon arrival, would receive Norwegian identity cards from the Norwegian secret service. These experts would interrogate the asylum seekers in a language they understood (meaning both Arabic and brute force). The Israelis would then translate the conversations and hand the Palestinians over to the Norwegians. This process would prevent the country from being infiltrated by troublemakers, and in a more general way, keep Norway out of the bloody Middle East game.

I also told him that there was no doubt in my mind that the police and intelligence service were sure they were doing the right thing. For the sake of protecting the safety of their Mossad friends, they'd have to keep it all secret from the politicians, who weren't to be trusted in matters of security.

Stangheler was on his way to cracking the biggest intelligence scandal in Norwegian history, and he knew it. The communication between us was sporadic, and he would call me at strange hours, seeking advice. We started to work together on the story in January 1991; he was ready to publish in August and went to press at the beginning of September. The expected fury of the Norwegian population was there, as were the lame explanations by the Secret Service. I was correct on just about all counts, and even though I received little credit for what had taken place, I knew there was egg on the Mossad face, and that was a real treat for me.

The story had exposed what could only be described as the Mossad's intimate relations with the Norwegian secret service and police. The Norwegian secret service had provided Mossad personnel with Norwegian papers and brought them into the interrogation room to interrogate Palestinians who were seeking asylum in Norway.

The Mossad officers interrogated the Palestinians in Arabic, although most of the Palestinians were fluent in English, as were the Norwegian police. However, none of the Norwegian police spoke Arabic, and therefore they had no idea what was being said. The Mossad officers threatened the Palestinians with deportation if they wouldn't cooperate with Israel—all this in the presence of Norwegian police, or in some cases without that presence, in which cases the interrogations took on a much more violent aspect.

As a result of the story, the Norwegian minister of justice, Kari Gjesteby, called for a full investigation of the matter. This was of course to appease the citizenry—some of whom saw the whole affair as Israel's second violation of the sanctity of Norway (the first "violation" occurred in Lillehammer in 1974 and involved the Mossad's killing of a Moroccan waiter whom they'd mistaken for Ali Hassan Salameh[1]).

The evening before the article's publication in *Oftenposten*, Stangheler had phoned me at a late hour from Norway. He sounded very strange. He was laughing and crying alternately and was asking me to forgive him and to realize he didn't really mean it. Then he hung up, and I grew very worried. I thought that perhaps someone had gotten to him just before publication and that he was in danger. Since I didn't know anybody in Oslo and could not reach Ephraim to see what could be done, I called Frank Esman, a reporter from the Danish broadcasting corporation who was posted in New York. I summarized the situation, and he in turn called some people he knew in Norway, who then called me back and also contacted the police in the vicinity of Stangheler's residence. Several nerve-racking hours later, I learned that the police had visited Stangheler's house and found him drunk out

---

1. Ali Hassan Salameh: Also known as the Red Prince, said to be the planner of the Munich Olympics massacre. He was later assassinated by the Mossad in Beirut.

of his wits. As it turned out, he'd called me in the midst of a post-investigation blowout celebration, and I'd simply misinterpreted his exuberance.

As it was, Stangheler had a right to feel pleased. The council for Norwegian organizations for asylum seekers, known as NOAS, filed a lawsuit against the secret service for willfully violating the Norwegian penal code sections 325 and 121. Within days of the exposé, the chief of the secret service (Overvaakintjeneste), Svein Urdel, handed in his resignation.

Although the Norwegian political establishment attempted to portray the whole affair as a simple misunderstanding, Ephraim told me that, in fact, the Norwegians made it very clear through hidden channels that they wouldn't tolerate any Mossad activity in Norway. To prove it, they pulled back their liaison man from Tel Aviv and requested that Mossad liaison not visit Oslo until further notice. This was a hard blow to the Mossad.

What happened in Norway came on the heels of several other slaps in the face that I'm proud to have participated in. What my book couldn't do (convince Israelis of the Mossad's fallibility), has, in fact, been accomplished by the fallout from these accumulated bunglings. Although the Mossad is still regarded as a god, it's a lesser god than before.

While Stangheler was doing his investigation, Eli, with whom I wanted to have nothing more to do, came to visit me in Canada and told me that he was planning to leave the Mossad, since the task of blending in with the rest of the organization was becoming unbearable. More than half the new recruits, he said, were from the Messianic religious sect. If I thought that the prevailing attitude in the Mossad had been bad when I was there, I couldn't imagine what it was like now, Eli said. Half the Mossad members were now living in settlements in the occupied West Bank. That in itself was enough for me to realize how far right-wing the organization had become. He wanted to know if I had a channel of communication to the American security services.

I had none, except for the occasional phone call that Ephraim had me make to pass on some information. As things were now, I thought it would be too late, since anyone I might contact now would surely think I was looking for material for a new book. Besides, no intelligence agency has any real sympathy for a whistle blower, since one never knows whom he'll blow the whistle on next.

I did, however, have a circle of friends I'd managed to create who were involved on a volunteer basis in trying to help the plight of the

Palestinian people. Some of them might have connections. But I'd have to have a very good reason to pull such strings, and the people involved would have to know exactly what it was all about.

Eli said he'd pass that information to Ephraim, who'd sent him on this trip so that he could take advantage of the free travel to set up something for himself in the United States. He had family there and could get a green card with no problem.

"I guess the last one will have to turn the lights out in the Ben-Gurion airport," I said, bringing up an old joke that used to be told in Israel during the depression prior to the Six-Day War, which had of course changed everything around. We both laughed for a long time, letting off steam for not being able to make a difference.

It was then, in talking to Eli, that I realized I'd gone much farther down the road than he had. Eli, and Uri too, for that matter, still believed in the Zionist dream. They were more like the people I knew in Israel, my old friends and family. Even though they participated in what would be regarded by most Israelis as extremism, they were doing it out of the belief they had in an idea, the Zionist idea.

I had already realized for some time that I no longer shared that ideology, that for me the state of Israel was no longer the fulfillment of an ancient dream. For me, it was more a nightmare of prejudice, wallowing in racism and waving the white and blue flag as a banner of oppression. I wanted no part of it. What I was doing now was showing the carriers of the banner their vulnerability, so that they would stop and reappraise their own purpose. Maybe then they could join the family of nations on an equal footing.

"They are planning something in Cyprus," Eli said, and handed me a small piece of paper. It looked like a page torn out of a small notebook.

"What is this?"

"That's a phone number in Cyprus; it's the police. You are to make a call to them and tell them that someone is breaking into this office building."

"What is it?"

"I have no idea, and I really don't care. Ephraim said that you should make the call the day after tomorrow. Make sure you do it at five-thirty Cyprus time."

"Is that all you know?"

"I know that a Yarid team will be there and that they will be doing something they shouldn't be doing."

"That's good enough for me," I said.

Eli didn't stay long. He was somewhat ashamed that he was leaving the Mossad and the country, and I sensed the discomfort he felt around me. I couldn't explain it, but I could feel it too, so I made no attempt to have him stick around, although there were a million questions I would have loved to ask him.

TUESDAY, APRIL 23, 1991

I made the call at the appointed hour and, after spending almost twenty minutes on the phone, succeeded in making it clear to the officer in charge of the police station that I thought an entry into the office building had been made by some people who shouldn't be there.

The man was not especially impressed, but after checking to see what was at that address and realizing that the Iranian embassy occupied the top three floors of the building, he decided he'd better send someone to check things out. As it turned out, the Yarid team, which consisted of six members, four men and two women, was not expecting any trouble. They had registered in two different hotels on the island to avoid drawing attention to themselves, a couple in each of the hotels, pretending to be tourists. Two of the men had taken possession of an apartment in a building adjacent to where a listening station was to be set up. They had already set up all the equipment, ready to receive the incoming information from the bugs the installers were supposed to position.

One of the couples was to enter the building and put the bugs on the telephone lines, while the other couple was supposed to stay outside and watch, so that if there was a problem, they could warn the installers. However, they were extremely lax. After all, they were members of the great Mossad. What could go wrong?

Everything could.

The couple outside was not comfortable on the street with no place to melt away into, so they decided to enter the building and give their friends inside a helping hand. This way they could finish the job faster and get on with the fun part of the operation—having a good time and charging it to the Mossad.

In fact, there was not much they could do, since only one of the installers was a so-called expert; only he could do the actual work. Everybody else just stood around making him nervous.

He was in the process of separating the wires according to a blueprint they'd brought with them and trying to identify the Iranian embassy's lines when the policeman walked in. The four were huddled around the open telephone wire box with the tapping devices in their hands, handing them to the expert as he found the proper wires.

The policeman was as surprised at what he'd encountered as the team was. "What are you doing here?" he asked, first in Greek and then, when no answer was forthcoming, in English.

The four dropped what they were holding in their hands and turned to face the cop. They exchanged glances, not knowing quite what to do.

Ran Sofe,[2] the commander of the team, was the first to speak. A thirty-three-year-old veteran of Yarid, he was supposed to have stayed outside with Amit Litvin, who was dressed in a provocative way to draw attention to herself in case there was a need to detain someone (a trick that might have worked had they done their job right), while David Dabi and Anna Dolgin were inside installing the bugs. "We're looking for a washroom," said Ran. "You know, a toilet. The girls just can't hold it, you know."

The others nodded their heads, like a group of children caught with their hands in the cookie jar, trying to sell a lame story even they didn't believe.

The policeman wasn't buying. He hauled them all into the police station in downtown Nicosia.

WEDNESDAY, APRIL 24

The four were brought in front of a judge, who remanded them in custody for eight days on suspicion of wiretapping.

It wasn't long before the scandal hit the news wires and all hell broke loose. The Mossad pulled every string they had on the small island to close the story, and fast.

THURSDAY, MAY 9

There followed several days of intense bargaining and fending off curious reporters. Eventually, the Cypriot authorities released the four, after they'd entered a guilty plea for unlawfully entering private property to commit a felony. They were fined the equivalent of about eight hundred U.S. dollars and were released into the hands of the Israeli representative.

---

2. Ran Sofe, David Dabi, Anna Dolgin, and Amit Litvin were the names they gave to the police, and under those names they were indicted, fined, and released.

By the end of the day, the four were back in Israel, still hiding their faces and refusing to talk to reporters.

Almost a week after the event, I was contacted by a reporter from the Israeli newspaper *Yediot Aharonot,* who asked me if I could elaborate on what had happened in Cyprus. He called me because I was the only known Mossad ex-member who was willing to talk to the media. And there was no doubt that I was in fact an ex-Mossad officer, unlike many who'd come forth in the past, claiming to be from the Mossad to get attention but having no idea what the Mossad was all about.

I gave the reporter the story he wanted. I told him what had taken place, one step at a time. I made it clear to him that this was only an educated guess by me. He went on to write an eight-hundred-word article that was stopped by the military censor. The newspaper wanted to take the case to court but was advised not to by friends in the security apparatus. The paper complied, not wanting to risk losing its share of "inside information," which maintains its ability to "inform" its readers.

It seemed that, in this somewhat insignificant intervention, we'd managed to puncture the Mossad armor, causing a small stream of criticism of the organization on the operational level to start dampening the soil around it. It was still far from being the torrent that would be necessary to sweep the Mossad off its feet, but every little bit helped.

CHAPTER 30

WEDNESDAY, OCTOBER 30, 1991, MADRID

Air Force One was about to touch down, followed by the second twin Air Force One. The two jumbo jets (which are identical in all but the call numbers inscribed on their fuselages; one carries the president and the second brings along the rest of the entourage and is used as a backup in case of emergency) were en route to deliver the president of the United States and a large media contingent to the Madrid peace talks that were about to start between Israel and all its Arab neighbors, including Syria and the Palestinians, who were part of the Jordanian delegation.

In the months leading up to this theatrical occasion, the American president had truly believed he'd be able to bring about a change in the hardheaded attitudes that had prevailed in the region for decades. In an effort to bring the right-wing government of Yitzhak Shamir to the negotiating table in what was to be an international peace conference, the president had applied the kind of pressure that an American president rarely has been brave enough to apply. Against the wishes of an angry Jewish community, George Herbert Bush had put a freeze on all loan guarantees to Israel, which were to come to a total of ten billion dollars over the next five years. This freeze was not intended to punish Israel for the construction of settlements in the occupied West Bank and the Gaza Strip (regarded by the United States as illegal,) but to force the cash-strapped Likud government to the negotiating table.

Upon making that decision, the president was instantly placed on the blacklist of every Jewish organization in the United States, and regarded as the greatest enemy of the state of Israel. In Israel, posters depicting the president with a pharaoh's headgear and the inscription "We have overcome the pharaohs, we will overcome Bush" were pasted across the country. Shamir called the president's action "Am-Bush."

Israeli messengers in all the communities across the United States immediately went into high gear, launching attacks against the president. They fed the media an endless stream of criticism, while trying at the same time to make it clear to Vice President Dan Quayle that he was still their sweetheart and that what the president was doing in no way affected their opinion of him.

This love affair with a vice president was not a new thing; it had been almost standard procedure ever since the creation of the state of Israel. Any time a president was not on the best of terms with Israel, the Jewish organizations were instructed to cozy up to the vice president. That was the case with Dwight Eisenhower, whom Israel regarded as the worst president in history (although, ironically, the vice president they regarded as a friend, namely Richard Nixon, himself became an enemy once he was president). It was what lay behind the strong support Israel and the Jewish community gave to Lyndon Johnson, who almost doubled aid to Israel in his first year as president, after John Kennedy had come down hard on the Israeli nuclear program, believing it was a first and dangerous step in the proliferation of nuclear weapons in the region.

That strategy was behind their hatred for Nixon and their admiration for Gerald Ford. And then there was Jimmy Carter, whose whole administration was regarded as a big mistake as far as Israel was concerned, a mistake that had cost Israel the whole of the Sinai in return for a lukewarm peace with Egypt.

And now there was this peace process, put forth by the country club idiot. The right-wingers' silent cry was to somehow stop the process, which they believed would lead to a compromise that would force Israel to return more land. Refusing to believe that such a compromise would ever be made, settlers in the Occupied Territories had launched a new wave of construction, with the unrelenting help of Ariel Sharon, the minister of housing.

A certain right-wing clique in the Mossad regarded the situation as a life-or-death crisis and decided to take matters into their own hands, to solve the problem once and for all. They believed that Shamir would have ordered what they were about to do if he hadn't been gagged by politics. Like many others before them, in countless countries and administrations, they were going to do what the leadership really wanted but couldn't ask for, while at the same time leaving the leadership out of the loop—they were going to become Israeli versions of Colonel Oliver North, only on a much more lethal level.

To this clique, it was clear what they must do. There was no doubt that Bush would be out of his element on October 30 when he arrived in Madrid to open the peace talks. This was going to be the most protected event of the year, with so many potential enemies meeting in one place. On top of that, there were all those who were against the talks: the Palestinian extremists and the Iranians and the Libyans, not to mention the decimated Iraqis with their endless calls for revenge for the Gulf War.

The Spanish government had mobilized more than ten thousand police and civil guards. In addition, the American Secret Service, the Soviet KGB, and all the security services of all the countries involved would be on hand.

The Madrid Royal Palace would be the safest place on the planet at the time, unless you had the security plans and could find a flaw in them. That was exactly what the Mossad planned to do. It was clear from the start that the assassination would be blamed on the Palestinians—perhaps ending once and for all their irritating resistance and making them the people most hated by all Americans.

Three Palestinian extremists were taken by a Kidon unit from their hiding place in Beirut and relocated incommunicado in a special detention location in the Negev desert. The three were Beijdun Salameh, Mohammed Hussein, and Hussein Shahin.

At the same time, various threats, some real and some not, were made against the president. The Mossad clique added its share, in order to more precisely define the threat as if it were coming from a group affiliated with none other than Abu Nidal. They knew that name carried with it a certain guarantee of getting attention and keeping it. So if something were to happen, the media would be quick to react and say, "We knew about it, and don't forget where you saw it first."

Several days before the event, it was leaked to the Spanish police that the three terrorists were on their way to Madrid and that they were probably planning some extravagant action. Since the Mossad had all the security arrangements in hand, it would not be a problem for this particular clique to bring the "killers" as close as they might want to the president and then stage a killing. In the ensuing confusion, the Mossad people would kill the "perpetrators," scoring yet another victory for the Mossad. They'd be very sorry that they hadn't been able to save the president, but protecting him was not their job to begin with. With all the security forces involved and the assassins dead, it would be very difficult to discover where the security breach had been, except that several of the countries involved in the conference, such as Syria, were regarded as countries that assisted terrorists. With that in mind, it would be a foregone conclusion where the breach was.

As far as this Mossad clique was concerned, it was a win-win situation.

Ephraim called me on Tuesday, October 1. I could sense from the tone of his voice that he was extremely stressed. "They're out to kill Bush," he said. At first, I didn't understand what he was talking about. I thought he meant that they were going to ruin the president. I'd already heard of several books that were in the making on the man, and there was a smear campaign regarding his alleged involvement in the Iran-Contra affair (which I knew personally to be fake).

"What's new about that? They've been out to get him for a long time."

"I mean really kill, as in assassinate."

"What are you talking about? You can't be serious. They would never dare do something like that."

"Don't go naive on me now," he said. "They're going to do it during the Madrid peace talks."

"Why don't you call the CIA and tell them? I mean, this isn't just some little operation you don't want to be involved in."

"I'll call whoever I have in the European intelligence services. I don't have friends in the American, not people I can trust, anyway."

"So what do you want me to do?"

"We are going to do what we can at our end. But nothing we will do will become public. I want you to make this thing public. If they know that the Americans know about it, there is a good chance they will not go ahead."

I knew that what he said was correct. If I could draw attention to it and make it public, that would do more to stop them than all the intelligence agencies put together. The trick would be to make it public without coming on like some lunatic with yet another conspiracy theory. I would have to say something in a relatively small forum and hope it would get out. If that didn't work, I'd contact some reporters I knew and give them the lowdown.

As it happened, I was invited to be a speaker at a luncheon held at the Parliament buildings in Ottawa for a group called the Middle East Discussion Group. It's a loosely formed think tank supported by the National Council on Canadian-Arab Relations, headed by a former Liberal MP named Ian Watson. The aim of this group is to inform members of Parliament and the diplomatic community on issues that might not be freely accessed by the media and to promote dialog on the Middle East.

The luncheon was attended by some twenty members of the think tank and a few MPs. I made a short presentation in which I explained the goals of the Mossad and the danger it presented to any peace initiative in the region. I also said that in my opinion, as things stood, the only chance the Middle East had for peace would be the cutting off of financial aid to Israel by the United States. I emphasized that a large chunk of this aid finds its way to the West Bank and the settlements, which were probably the biggest stumbling block to the peace initiative. Then I opened the floor to questions.

I was asked what the Mossad would do to stop the process that was now taking place. I said that from sources I had, and based on my knowledge of the Mossad, I would not be at all surprised if there was a plot right at this moment to kill the president of the United States and to throw the blame on some extreme Palestinian group.

Later, I learned that one of the people at the luncheon had called an ex-congressman from California, Pete McCloskey. The substance of what I'd said was conveyed to him, and since McCloskey was an old and close friend of the president's, the caller felt that he might want to take some action.

On October 15, McCloskey called me and introduced himself. He said that he'd heard from a friend what I'd said about the president and wanted to know if in my opinion there was a real threat, or was this only a metaphor of some kind, to make a point? I made it clear to him that there was no metaphor involved and that I was dead serious regarding the threat to the president. I also said that I believed that exposing this threat might be enough to eliminate it, since to carry it out would then become too risky.

He said he could come to Ottawa within a few days and asked me if I'd be willing to meet with him. I saw no reason why not, and we made an appointment for October 19, which was a weekend.

I met Pete at the Westin Hotel, and we walked over to a small coffee shop where we sat for several hours. He asked me questions from every possible angle, trying to understand what I was talking about. I could see that he was looking for information he could present that would make the threat realistic. There was no way I could tell him that I'd gotten the information straight from the horse's mouth, but I had to let him know that I was not completely disconnected from the Mossad. That in itself was a risk; it was the first time I'd allowed this to come out. I felt compelled, however, by the stakes involved.

The next day, Sunday, October 20, McCloskey was in Washington to participate in the meetings of the Commission on National and Community Services. He stayed at the Hotel Phoenix Park, from which he called the Secret Service at the White House. He was referred to Special Agent Allan Dillon at the Secret Service offices, 1050 Connecticut Avenue, N.W., Washington, D.C.

Pete faxed Dillon a copy of the memo he'd written after our meeting in Ottawa. The same day, he met with a former White House aide from the Ford era, named Don Penny, who gave him the spin on me. I was not at all surprised when McCloskey told me later what Penny had told him: that he'd heard about me from Senator Sam Nunn and other sources in the CIA who said that I was a traitor to Israel and totally unreliable. And that if McCloskey associated with me, he'd be putting a target on his own back. As it turned out, Pete later spoke to Nunn, but the senator could not recall talking about me. Meanwhile, a well-known Washington columnist, Rowland Evans, told Pete that he'd asked his sources in the CIA about me several months earlier, and they'd told him that I was "for real."

McCloskey had an interview on October 22 with agent Terry Gallagher from the State Department Diplomatic Protection and then, the same day, a meeting with Dillon from the Secret Service. On October 24, the Secret Service asked to speak to me. They placed a formal request via the American embassy in Ottawa through CSIS (the Canadian security service), and I met with a member of the Secret Service in the presence of a member of CSIS.

I told the man what I thought was going to take place, only omitting that I'd obtained the information from an active member of the Mossad. I did make it clear to him that I had a connection, which I mainly used to learn about impending personal danger.

The information leaked to the media, and in a syndicated column, Jack Anderson presented the whole story. So did Jane Hunter in her newsletter, which is a must for any Washingtonian specializing in the Middle East.

I was confident that by now the president was no longer in imminent danger, although the less time he spent in Madrid, the better. But the decision to eliminate him would not be withdrawn; it would only be postponed. I had pointed out to the Secret Service agent that the president was extremely vulnerable aboard Air Force One, both to attack by a surface-to-air missile and to a piece of explosive luggage that could be carried aboard by an unsuspecting reporter who didn't realize that a segment of his recording or photographic equipment had been switched for a deadly device.

the two final days of the tour. Knowing the history of the Mossad in Belgium and the corruption of the Belgian police force, I knew I was walking into a snake pit. But Ephraim's promise was all the shield I needed. On the last day in Belgium, I was scheduled to appear as a guest on a television show in Brussels. All was fine until the show was over and my security team and I headed for the car that was supposed to be waiting to take us back to the hotel in Antwerp. The car wasn't there, and neither was the driver. There seemed to be some confusion regarding what had happened to him. Then an alternative car was suggested by someone from the station. This didn't smell right to me or my team, and since the television station wasn't far from the Brussels international airport, we decided to move fast. We ordered taxis and split into groups. Our Belgian publisher drove one of the team and me to the hotel, and the others took two cabs. We left the place in three different directions and even sent an empty cab off somewhere else.

All I wanted to do was get out of that city and get Ephraim on the line. If something was going on, I was sure he'd know about it and instruct me on what to do. It was after midnight when I made the call.

"Hello." I heard Ephraim's sleepy voice.

"Ephraim?"

"Yes, who is that?"

"It's me." I said, somewhat relieved that he wasn't alarmed.

"Me who?"

"Victor. Wake up, man."

"I'm awake." I could hear a sudden tension in his voice. "Victor who?"

"What is this? I'm not in the mood for games, Ephraim."

"Is this Victor Ostrovsky?" He sounded genuinely surprised.

"What are you playing at?"

"How are you? Where are you?"

"You know where I am."

"What are you talking about?"

"Ephraim, I'm warning you. Don't play games with me, I'm not in the mood."

"Don't you ever threaten me." I could clearly hear the menace in his voice. "Don't make the same mistake Spiro did. Am I making myself clear, my boy?"

"You son of a bitch." I said and hung up. I was deeper in it than I cared to think. Ian Spiro was a *sayan* who'd worked with the Mossad for many years. He was a very helpful contact to have, since he dealt on numerous occasions with various Lebanese factions. He was a British citizen living in the United States. His contact with the Iranians and the Shi'ites in Lebanon made him a lot of money over the years. But he'd taken one cut too many.

The Mossad had given him several million dollars to pay off some Lebanese family who could in turn bring about the release of captured Israeli airman, Ron Arad. As a result of Spiro's involvement with the Iran-Contra affair, the Lebanese were not willing to deal with him anymore. But he held on to the money. When the Kidon team came to his house November 7, 1992, to get the money back, something went wrong, and his wife and three children were killed. He was taken to the desert, where the team forced him to reveal where he'd stashed the money, after he first tried to claim he'd given it to the Lebanese. He was then fed some poison that he happened to have with him. The poison was a substance used to check the purity of gold he'd been interested in mining.

At that point, I had no doubt that my time was starting to run out. Early in the morning, we all got into a cab and headed back to Holland. Crossing the Dutch border was a great relief, but I knew I wasn't out of the woods until I was back on Canadian soil. I made one last call from the hotel to Uri, but for some reason, I was cut off.

During the flight, I finally realized what had happened. I was going to take some steps to verify it, but I was pretty sure I knew. There had been a power struggle in the Mossad for the top job. By now, it was safe to say that Ephraim and his clique were probably the only ranking officers in the Mossad not to have screwed up. That being the case, Ephraim was more than likely the man to be tapped to run things, unless a new man was brought in from the outside. And, in all likelihood, it would only be a matter of time before he and the clique came gunning for me.

I was the weak link *and* the most vulnerable one. So it seemed that what I had to do was clear. I had to put everything else aside and write this story for everyone to see.

Now it's done, and it's out of my hands. You be the judge.

NOTES

CHAPTER 1

"Belgium Probes Terrorist Links with NATO-wide Resistance Group," Reuters, November 9, 1990.

Michael Binyon, "Head of Belgian Detective Force Arrested," *Times,* April 26, 1990.

Raf Casert, "Belgium Orders Investigation into Secret Anti-Communist Group," Associated Press, November 9, 1990.

Dan Izenberg, "Apparent Blunder: Israel Jets Intercept, Release Libyan Plane," Associated Press, February 4, 1986.

Stephan Ketele, "Subs for Aalst Dateline on Sked Alert Issued in Supermarket Massacre," United Press International, November 10, 1985.

James M. Markham, "Terrorists Put Benign Belgium Under Mental Siege," *New York Times,* February 6, 1986.

Judith Miller, "Belgium Is Shaken by Bombs and 'Crazy Killers,'" *New York Times,* November 24, 1985.

David Nordell, "Israeli Leaders Have No Apologies for Grounding Plane," Associated Press, February 5, 1986.

David Usborne, "Belgium Throws the Book at Its Bungling State Security Service," *Independent,* May 8, 1990.

"When Mossad Shoots Itself in the Foot," *Manchester Guardian Weekly,* February 16, 1986.

Andrew Whitley, "Israel Forces Down Libyan Jet," *Financial Times,* February 5, 1986.

CHAPTER 2

Brenda C. Coleman, "Company Accuses Israel of Stealing Trade Secrets," Associated Press, August 19, 1986.

"Loral Wins Contract for Joint Service Image Processing System," *PR Newswire*, September 22, 1987.

Edward T. Pound and David Rogers, "How Israel Spends $1.8 Billion a Year at Its Purchasing Mission in New York," *Wall Street Journal*, January 20, 1992.

Edward T. Pound and David Rogers, "Inquiring Eyes: An Israeli Contract with a U.S. Company Leads to Espionage—Arbiters Say Israel Stole Data, and It Wasn't First Time the Ally Spied in America," *Wall Street Journal*, January 17, 1992.

Edward T. Pound and David Rogers, "Politics and Policy: Roles of Ex-Pentagon Officials at Jewish Group Show Clout of Cold-Warrior, Pro-Israel Network," *Wall Street Journal*, January 22, 1992.

Chapter 4

"Danish Officials Confirm Illegal Mossad Activities," *Washington Times*, October 10, 1990.

Thalif Deen, "Mossad Sells Arms to Tamil Tigers," *Sri Lanka Sunday Observer*, September 30, 1990.

"Denmark: Mossad Is Working in Our Territory Against the Law," *Yediot Aharonot*, September 22, 1990.

Peter Eisner, "Judge in Noriega Trial Stops Questions on CIA, Mossad," *Newsday*, September 25, 1991.

Embassy of the Democratic Socialist Republic of Sri Lanka, Washington, D.C., press release, September 20, 1990.

Julian M. Isherwood, "Danish Parliament Investigates Israel's Mossad," United Press International, October 10, 1990.

Yohanan Lahav, "The Mossad Assisted Tamils in Sri Lanka: As Told by Indian Minister of Finance Subramanis Swami," *Yediot Aharonot*, December 14, 1990.

"Mossad Behind Bugging of Danish Parliament's Ombudsman, Paper Says," Agence France Presse, December 2, 1993.

Ygal Rom, "Danish Government Enquiry into Mossad's Bugging of Professor Sud Gameltvapt, from the Danish Paper Extrablatt," *Yediot Aharonot*, December 3, 1993.

"With Noriega, the End of Harari," *Latin American Weekly Report*, January 18, 1990.

Chapter 8

"Around the World; Police in Paris Sees Link Among Political Slayings," *New York Times*, April 10, 1982.

Ian Black and Benny Morris, *Israel's Secret Wars: The Untold History of Israeli Intelligence,* London: Hamish Hamilton, 1991, pp. 426–427.

Kathleen Brady, "A Paris Court Stands Firm; Life in Prison for a Terrorist," *Time,* March 9, 1987.

Karin Laub, "Shamir Denies He Decided to Fire Mossad Chief," Associated Press, January 12, 1989.

Stanley Meisler, "France Will Put Arab on Trial in 2 Assassinations," *Los Angeles Times,* January 29, 1987.

Steven Strasser, Milan J. Kubic, James Pringle, Julian Nundy, and Ray Wilkinson, "A Terrible Swift Sword," *Newsweek,* June 21, 1982.

Robert Suro, "Unmasking a Terror Group: Typical Pattern of Travel, Havens and Killings," *New York Times,* April 13, 1986.

John Vinocur, "American Diplomat Shot in Strasbourg; C.I.A. Link Denied," *New York Times,* March 27, 1984.

Ehud Ya'ari, "Behind the Terror," *Atlantic,* June 1987.

CHAPTER 11

Michael Arndt, "More Mainstream Jews Drawn to Kahane's Side," *Chicago Tribune,* April 20, 1986.

Leonard Buder, "Prison for Ex-J.D.L. Chief in Bombing," *New York Times,* October 27, 1987.

Allyn Fisher, "American Immigrant Doctor Blamed for Hebron Massacre with Israel-Unrest," Associated Press, February 25, 1994.

CHAPTER 12

"Five in Bermuda Ordered Deported in Iran Arms Sale Plot," Reuters North European Service, May 16, 1986.

Thomas L. Friedman, "How Israel's Economy Got Hooked on Selling Arms Abroad," *New York Times,* December 7, 1986.

Thomas L. Friedman, "Israel Denies Smuggling Cluster Bomb Technology," *New York Times,* July 10, 1986.

CHAPTER 14

"Arms Fraud Probe Said Widened to Two Israeli Firms," Reuters, July 11, 1988.

Kim I. Mills, "Two Israelis Charged in Ongoing Probe of U.S. Defense Industry," Associated Press, April 29, 1993.

James Rowley, "Paisley, Former Assistant Secretary, Pleads Guilty," Associated Press, June 14, 1991.

CHAPTER 15

Jacob Erez, "A High-Ranking Officer in the Office of the Prime Minister Was a KGB Agent," *Maariv Israeli Daily,* September 3, 1993.

"Suspect Held over Disco Blast That Sparked US Raid on Libya," *The Independent,* July 28, 1990.

Bob Woodward, "Protecting Reagan: CIA Built Case Against Qadhafi U.S. Interception of Messages Led to Raid on Libya," *Chicago Tribune,* September 28, 1987.

CHAPTER 19

"British Say Israelis Faked Passports; Mossad Accused of Using Forgeries in Attacks on Foes," *Los Angeles Times,* March 16, 1987.

Simon O'Dwyer-Russell, "Israel Halts Secrets Trade with MI6 After Expulsions," *Sunday Telegraph,* August 21, 1988.

Simon O'Dwyer-Russell, "Israel Link in Blowpipe Scandal," *Daily Telegraph,* May 16, 1989.

Simon O'Dwyer-Russell and Christopher Elliott, "Israeli Intelligence Cell Pulled Out of Britain," *Sunday Telegraph,* July 24, 1988.

Menachem Shalev, "Best of British . . . " *Jerusalem Post,* January 17, 1989.

"Syria Says British and Israeli Secret Services Cooperate," Reuters, June 25, 1988.

John Weeks, "End of MI6-Mossad Rift Vital to Terrorist Hunt," *Daily Telegraph,* December 30, 1988.

CHAPTER 21

G. Keenan, "Worsening Relations with Israel Inevitable," *Vancouver Sun,* March 26, 1992.

"Shamir Insists Israel Not Involved in Pollard Affair," Reuters, March 23, 1987.

Michael J. Sniffen, "Appeals Court Upholds Guilty Plea and Sentence for Spy," Associated Press, March 20, 1992.

"U.S.A.: Israel, Inman and Pollard," *Intelligence Newsletter,* February 10, 1994.

CHAPTER 22

Graeme Kennedy, "Pacific Express Expands Air Freight Fleet," *National Business Review,* December 4, 1992.

Graeme Kennedy, "Pacific Express Finds Demand for Dirty Work," *National Business Review,* April 30, 1993.

"Swiss/Soviet Metro Freight Carrier Topples," *Flight,* July 17, 1991.

CHAPTER 23

Chaim Bermant, "Israel's Not-So-Secret Weapon: Chaim Bermant on the Sub-plots of the Vanunu Affair," *Sunday Telegraph,* July 19, 1992.

"British Newspaper Says Israel Among World's Nuclear Powers," Reuters, October 4, 1986.

Peter Hounam, David Leppard, and Nick Rufford, "Author Hoaxed over Maxwell Mossad Link," *Sunday Times,* November 17, 1991.

George Jones and Philip Johnson, "Book Links Maxwell to Mossad," *Daily Telegraph,* October 23, 1991.

Alastair McCall, "New Charges in Vanunu Affair," *Daily Telegraph,* November 13, 1991.

R. Barry O'Brien, "Conman Link Admitted by Hersh," *Daily Telegraph,* November 18, 1991.

Daniel Schifrin, "Traitor or Patriot?: Mordechai Vanunu Is in Jail for Exposing Israel's Alleged Nuclear Secrets. But His Brother, Meir, Calls Him a Hero," *Baltimore Jewish Times,* August 13, 1993.

Sam Seibert, Ronald Henkoff, and Barbara Rosen, "A Right to Disobedience? Israel Tries Vanunu," *Newsweek,* September 17, 1987.

"U.K. Cuts Syria Ties over El Al Bomb Plot: Jordanian Suspect Is Convicted," *Facts on File World News Digest,* October 31, 1986.

CHAPTER 25

Ron Csillag, "Profile: Benjamin Netanyahu; Israel's Ambassador to the U.N. and the Opening of the War Crimes Archives," *Lifestyles,* vol. 15, no. 92, 1988.

David Gow, "Mr Clean Under Fire over New Dirty Tricks Revelations," *Guardian,* May 1, 1993.

"Iran Pulls Envoy After Alleged Gas Deal," *St. Petersburg Times,* June 28, 1989.

"New Theories About Death of West German Politician," *Reuter Library Report,* August 3, 1988.

"Scandal-Hit West German Politician Was Murdered, Brother Says," *Reuter Library Report,* October 12, 1987.

"Second Autopsy Ordered on Body of West German Politician," Reuters, October 23, 1987.

Anna Tomforde, "SPD Win Schleswig-Holstein," *Manchester Guardian Weekly*, May 15, 1988.

CHAPTER 26

"Vanuatu: South Pacific News Coverage Upsets Leaders," *National Business Review*, July 7, 1989.

CHAPTER 27

David Connett, Tim Kelsey, and Julian Nundy, "Inside Story: Who Was This Man Who Was Hanged as a Spy?" *Independent*, March 18, 1990.

Anton Ferreira, "Iraqi Chemical Threat Seen as Response to Fears over Israel," *Reuter Library Report*, April 10, 1990.

"How Britain Armed Saddam," *Observer*, November 15, 1992.

Petre Huck, "Iraq: Saddam's Superguns," *Australian Financial Review*, March 27, 1992.

"Iraq: Evidence Was Faked to Smear Bazoft," *Observer*, June 10, 1990.

Michael Kneissler, "So Killte Ich Saddam Hussein," *Wiener*, February 2, 1991.

David Leppard, "Ex-Police Chief Reveals Bazoft Talks at Yard," *Sunday Times*, March 18, 1990.

Finlay Marshall, "Bazoft Cleared of Spying, Says Observer," *Press Association Newsfile*, March 17, 1990.

Charles Miller, "Murder Link Theory in Arms Find," *Press Association Newsfile*, April 12, 1990.

Richard Norton-Taylor, "Director Tells How He Foiled Supergun Plot," *Guardian*, July 1, 1993.

Steve Weizman, "Slain Weapons Expert Helped Israel Improve Big Guns," *Reuter Library Report*, April 13, 1990.

CHAPTER 28

Mike Anderson, "Deception and Controversy," *Metro*, vol. 3, issue 9, November 1990.

Gagy Baron, "Israel Turned to a Canadian Court Because Mossad Wanted to Buy Time: Ostrovsky Refused a Financial Offer in Return for Not Publishing. A High Source 'The Book Would Have Gained Prominence Anyway,'" *Yediot Aharanot*, September 19, 1990.

Ian Black, "Agency Chiefs Mop Up After Mossad Book," *Manchester Guardian Weekly*, September 23, 1990.

Joshua Brilliant, "Ex-Mossadnik Said to Be 'Greedy, Ambitious,'" *Jerusalem Post,* September 11, 1990.

Antonio Carlucci, "Il Mossad è nudo," *Panorama,* October 14, 1990.

Bertrand Desjardins, "UN Ex-Agent se Met a Table et Dévoile des Secrets," *Le Journal de Montréal,* January 26, 1991.

"Détruire la Bombe de Saddam!" *Paris Match,* November 8, 1990.

"Les États-Unis sont-ils manipulés par Israël?" *Le Journal de Montréal,* January 26, 1991.

Robert Fife, "Israeli Spying Detailed," *Ottawa Sun,* May 15, 1992.

Ken Gross and J. D. Podolsky, "As Israel Tries to Smother His Book, a Former Mossad Spy Spills Some Dark Secrets of That Shadowy Service," *People,* October 1, 1990.

Angel Guerra, "Publisher Did Not Claim Writer's Life Threatened," *Toronto Star,* October 3, 1990.

"How Israel Blew Up Saddam Bomb," *Sunday Times,* September 16, 1990.

Jane Hunter, "Steven Emerson: A Journalist Who Knows How to Take a Leak," *Extra!,* October/November 1992.

"Inside the Mossad," *Newsweek,* September 24, 1990.

"Israel Rejects Charge of Kidnapping Shiite Cleric," Agence France Presse, April 8, 1992.

Mark Kennedy, "Spy Inquiries Touched Off by Allegations," *Ottawa Citizen,* February 5, 1992.

Jamie Lamb, "A Mystery Story," *Vancouver Sun,* November 17, 1990.

"Lebanon—April 8—Israel Denies Sadr Kidnapping," *APS Diplomatic Recorder,* April 11, 1992.

"Mossad Background," *APS Diplomat Strategic Balance in the Middle East,* September 7, 1992.

"Mossad's Dirty Laundry," *Antigo (Wisc.) Journal,* October 31, 1990.

Dan Raviv, "One Angry Spy," *Toronto Star,* October 6, 1990.

"Tony Brown's Comments," *Washington (D.C.) Informer,* October 3, 1990.

Batsheva Tsur, "Navy Saved Ethiopian Jews in '80s," *Jerusalem Post,* March 18, 1994.

"Victor Ostrovsky and Mossad," *El Aharam,* April 9, 1992.

Art Winslow, "Mossad's Cover Story," *Nation,* October 22, 1990.

Chapter 29

Irwin Block, "Rights Groups Want Release of Palestinian," *Gazette* (Montreal), November 19, 1991.

"Canada Deports Former PLO Colonel to Algeria," *Reuter Library Report*, February 26, 1992.

"Intelligence Chief Resigns After Scandal," Associated Press, October 11, 1991.

"Israel—Oct. 11—Mossad Scandal in Norway," *APS Diplomatic Recorder*, October 12, 1991.

Miriam Jordan, "Arrest of Four Israelis in Cyprus Puts Mossad in Spotlight," *Reuter Library Report*, April 25, 1991.

Katherine McElroy, "Cyprus: Israelis Fined for Attempting to Bug Iranian Embassy," *Guardian*, May 10, 1991.

"Mossad Said to Offer Cash in Return for PLO Killing—Paper," *Reuter Library Report*, April 24, 1992.

"Norway: Asylum Organization Files Action Against Secret Service," Inter Press Service, November 8, 1991.

"Norway Lets Palestinians Stay After Israeli Interrogation Row," *Reuter Library Report*, January 17, 1992.

"Norway: Mossad Agents Allowed to Interrogate Palestinians," Inter Press Service, September 27, 1991.

"Norway Police Lets Mossad Question Palestinian Asylum Seekers," *Reuter Library Report*, September 18, 1991.

"Norwegian Intelligence Service Confirms Mossad Cooperation," Agence France Presse, September 18, 1991.

CHAPTER 30

Jack Anderson, "Israel's Shamir Has No Great Love for Bush," *Northwest Arkansas Times*, November 7, 1991.

Paul Bedard, "Security Keen for Bush's Jets; Terrorist Bombing Threatened," *Washington Times*, November 10, 1991.

"Bush Flying to Maine Saturday to Inspect Damage to His Compound," United Press International, October 31, 1991.

Christopher Dickey, Margaret Garrard Warner, and Theodore Stanger, "What If the Talks Aren't All Talk?" *Newsweek*, November 4, 1991.

John Dirlik, "Canada-Israel Committee Calls Bush 'Idiot,' Baker 'Pompous Jackass,'" *Washington Report on the Middle East*, n.d.

Maxim Ghilan, "Madrid," *Israel & Palestine Political Report*, no. 167, November 15, 1991.

"Glittering Start to Madrid Talks; Arab-Israeli Peace Talks Regional Focus," *Middle East Business Weekly*, November 8, 1991.

"Reuter Middle East Highlights 1830 GMT OCT 30," *Reuter Library Report*, October 30, 1991.

Ira Rifkin, "Shamir's G.A. Speech Fuels Peace Debate," *Baltimore Jewish Times,* November 29, 1991.

"Security Alert on Air Force One," United Press International, November 6, 1991.

"Shamir to Walk Out of Peace Talks for Heaven's Sake," *Reuter Library Report,* October 31, 1991.

"Spain Ousts Israeli Demonstrations After Shamir Hotel Row," *Reuter Library Report,* October 31, 1991.

"Spanish Police on Alert for Three Terrorists," United Press International, October 29, 1991.

Margaret Garrard Warner and Christopher Dickey, "Behind the Insults," *Newsweek,* November 11, 1991.

"World News Summary; Wednesday, Oct 30 (since 0300 GMT)," Agence France Presse, October 30, 1991.

Chapter 31

Peter Bale, "UK MPs Urge Probe over Alleged Maxwell/Israel Ties," Reuters, October 22, 1991.

Richard Beeston, "Israel Buries Maxwell with Full Honours," *Times,* November 11, 1991.

Jimmy Burns, "The Big Lie—Inside Maxwell's Empire: Questions Raised by Maxwell's Last Hours," *Financial Times,* June 19, 1992.

"Claims About Mirror-Israeli Links to Be Probed If Justified," Xinhua General Overseas News Service, October 22, 1991.

"Flamboyant Life and Times of Robert Maxwell," *Guardian Weekly,* November 17, 1991.

"Former KGB Boss Makes Life Easier for New Friends in Prison," *Reuter Library Report,* October 31, 1991.

Natalia Gevorkyan, "Was Maxwell a KGB Agent?" *Moscow News,* December 18, 1991.

Joshua Hammer, Daniel Pedersen, and Rod Norland, "A Tycoon's Final Days," *Newsweek,* November 18, 1991.

Richard Homan, "Israel Threatens Beirut; U.S. Urges Cease-Fire," *Washington Post,* June 11, 1982.

Lin Jenkins, "Maxwell 'Lived for Four Hours in Sea Before Heart Attack,'" *Times,* November 13, 1991.

"The Making of a Billionaire," *Newsweek,* November 18, 1991.

"Maxwell Buried in Israel; Was He Murdered? Publisher Robert Maxwell," *Editor & Publisher,* November 16, 1991.

"Maxwell Relayed Israeli Proposals to Soviets, Paper Says," Associated Press, December 19, 1991.